The Challenge of Globalization for Germany's Social Democracy

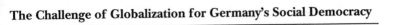

INTERNATIONAL POLITICAL CURRENTS
A Friedrich-Ebert-Stiftung Series

General Editor: Dieter Dettke

The Challenge of Globalization for Germany's Social Democracy

A Policy Agenda for the Twenty-First Century

Edited by

Dieter Dettke

Berghahn Books
NEW YORK • OXFORD

Published in 1998 by

Berghahn Books
Editorial offices:
55 John Street, 3rd Floor, New York, NY 10038 USA
3, NewTec Place, Magdalen Road, Oxford, OX4 1RE, UK

Library of Congress Cataloging-in-Publication Data
The challenge of globalization for Germany's social democracy : a
    policy agenda for the 21st century / edited by Dieter Dettke.
        p.   cm. – (International political currents ; v. 4)
    Includes index.
    ISBN 1-57181-180-X (alk. paper)
    1. Germany–Economic policy–1990– 2. Germany–Politics and
government–1990– 3. Germany–Social policy. I. Dettke, Dieter,
1941–   . II. Series: International political currents : vol. 4.
HC286.8.C46   1998
338.943'009'049–dc21   98-47227
                                                                   CIP

British Library Cataloguing in Publication Data
A CIP catalogue record for this book is available from
the British Library.

Printed in the United States on acid-free paper

Contents

Foreword

Dieter Dettke

Globalization is a powerful agent of change. It affects great and small powers, nations and regions, economic systems, the individual, groups and society at large. And, inevitably, there are winners and losers. Even rather successful and advanced economies in Europe and Asia had to go through painful adjustment processes and they continue to do so. Three highly interrelated factors in particular contributed to an economy that is now globalized more than ever before:

- Technological progress
- Economic reform in the 1980s
- The collapse of communism

The technological breakthroughs in the computer and information industries clearly drove both economic reform in the West during the early and mid-1980s, led by the United States and Great Britain, as well as by the implosion of the Soviet Empire and the capitulation of central economic planning to the forces of markets and democracy.

As a result, Germany had to simultaneously face the dual challenge of unification and globalization. And unification—because it happened as a serendipity and not as a result of deliberate Western policies and strategies—turned the attention of political and economic leaders away from meeting the challenge of globalization head on, at least temporarily. Focusing on national unity and concentrating on domestic markets, the larger task of competing in a globalized economy clearly became a second priority. For this, Germany had to pay the price of long-term high unemployment and pent-up economic reform in a unified Germany and a more integrated Europe, with a single market and even more importantly, with a single currency.

Today, at the threshold of the twenty-first century, "Modell Deutschland" badly needs a complete overhaul. Radical modernization is necessary in many respects—in its corporate culture and behavior, as well as in its social services and institutions. But reform is a complex undertaking that cannot succeed as a one-dimensional process, pushing only for lower wages, reduced social services, and decreased retirement incomes. Social and economic justice must remain high on any political agenda, because social erosion—not to speak of political instability—is infinitely more costly in the long run. In addition, Germany is not a poor country and it would be foolish to start a race to the bottom. A comprehensive, multidimensional approach is necessary in order to keep Modell Deutschland fit for the future.

This volume of the Friedrich-Ebert-Stiftung series "International Political Currents" presents a collection of essays, written in 1997 and early 1998, which—taken together—amount to an outline of a liberal economic reform program for Germany. It is a comprehensive reform program for Modell Deutschland and its economic, social, and financial policies as well as foreign policy, education, research, and the environment. Corporate governance in Germany needs change and will change if this volume's prescriptions from leading politicians, scholars, and labor-market specialists find their way into the realm of public policy.

Acknowledgments

This volume could not have been published without the support of the staff of the Washington Office of the Friedrich Ebert Foundation. Helen Pataki helped on a regular basis to move the book project forward. Initial research was conducted by Dr. Heike Grimm and Jan Martin Witte. Most of the necessary translations were done by Dr. Jeremiah Riemer. Christine Connelly and David Edminster also contributed to the translation of some of the essays originally written in German.

I am particularly grateful to Heidi Whitesell who used her great editing skills for a final inspection of the manuscript, valuable linguistic improvements of the texts, and for the index. Finally, but also most importantly, I would like to thank Kerstin Jäckel for her tireless efforts to produce the final version of the manuscript. Her help in the last phase of this book project is much appreciated.

List of Illustrations

Figures

Table

Introduction: Globalization and International Cooperation—Social Democratic Policy in the Age of Globalization

Oskar Lafontaine

Globalization and International Cooperation

In recent years the world economy has changed rapidly, becoming much more international, which many see as a new quality. This change is known as globalization. Notable elements of globalization can be detected in concrete developments. Take, for example, the European Union. Following its enlargement to fifteen countries consisting of a total of 370 million people, it has become the largest domestic market in the world. The fall of the Iron Curtain has made a gradual eastward enlargement of the European Union possible. In addition, as Russian reforms progress, this large country will also be further integrated into the world market.

Former developing countries and threshold countries are increasingly turning into high-performance competitors. On the model of the single European market, new regional trade blocs have emerged worldwide. This is illustrated by the North American Free Trade Agreement (NAFTA) between the United States, Canada, and Mexico. Moreover, the removal of international trade barriers within the framework of the World Trade Organization (WTO) and the development of a global financial market have added new and important incentives to international economic interaction.

Due to the globalization of the economy, the mobility of goods and services, as well as the amount of capital and technological skill, have increased considerably. Modernized production systems and information technologies have spread across the world. Today there is a trained workforce available in many different countries. The international division of labor includes the prospect of increased prosperity and the opportunity for every nation to receive a fair share of the rewards that come from economic and technological progress. One must ask, however, what political conclusions should be drawn from the globalization of markets.

In a market economy—even a globalized one—prosperity, technological progress, growth, and employment are not only ensured by the government, but by the market, in other words, by competing companies. Social Democrats support competition between private companies, especially with regard to innovation and performance. Therefore, on the domestic and international levels, everything possible should be done to guarantee functioning competition.

Traditional economic policy associated with names like Margaret Thatcher, Ronald Reagan, and Helmut Kohl regards international competition as not only between companies but also as competition about business locations (*Standortwettbewerb*). In this form of competition, countries attempt to attract and maintain investment from abroad to increase or maintain domestic employment.

From an economic point of view, there is nothing wrong with competition for the most innovative research environment or the best public infrastructure because it enhances prosperity and raises the standard of living. However, this form of competition becomes problematic when it turns into a devaluation race—in reality often a race to the bottom. Real wages, corporate taxes, and social standards decrease, and environmental protection is neglected reprehensibly. A disastrous deterioration of social structures results that can only lead to undesirable economic circumstances, not mutual benefits. Thus from both an economic and political point of view, this downward race is a mistake because it contorts and impedes healthy international competition between companies. Moreover, it obstructs the optimal allocation of resources and undermines the economic, social, and ecological foundations of our society.

Ultimately, this policy suffers from a strange contradiction: while the economy becomes increasingly globalized economically, politically the result is a return to traditional nationalistic thinking. In other words, politics react to the globalization of markets with a renationalization of policy. A downward race between countries, is, however, by no means an inevitable consequence of globalization. It is the result of a misconstrued policy and can be corrected.

The conservative discourse on the issue of the most attractive location for business (*Standort*) is, in itself, a policy driven by self-interest. It uses the public's fear of joblessness and the possible loss of social status as an instrument to shape a system of distribution that actually works to the disadvantage of the majority of the population. This proves the conservative policy to be purely ideological and not in the best interest of mainstream society.

The challenge of globalization cannot be met successfully by the current downward race. Yet neither the denationalization of policy nor protectionism provide the answer. To avoid the further erosion of our economic, social, and cultural foundations, we must rethink current economic policy. We need to find a new political answer for the globalization, which must be international cooperation. This is not just wishful, utopian thinking. For just a few years ago, the single European market also seemed to be an unattainable vision. Today it is a reality. The international marketplace needs a regulatory foundation. Principles that apply to a national economy should also hold true for the international economic system.

The political foundation of the European Union is an economy based on social and ecological responsibility. This market economy could operate as a useful model for a regulatory framework of the new global economy. With this guide, the most favorable conditions could be created for competition between companies based on performance and ideas, while simultaneously ensuring fair trade for the benefit of all.

In addition, because the flow of international trade and investments—the core area of globalization—concentrates on the "big three," that is on the European countries, the United States, and Japan, the required preconditions for cooperation already exist. Globalization is not beyond our political sphere of influence. We must use our political power to improve international cooperation. In particular, we need to focus on seven tasks for economic policy:

1. The stabilization of exchange rates
2. An interest-rate policy promoting stability and growth
3. A budget policy encouraging employment and providing economic incentives
4. The harmonization of tax policy
5. The development of a common technology policy
6. The establishment of an international social charter
7. An international initiative to prevent global destruction of the environment

Stabilization of Exchange Rates

There is no question that the high volatility of exchange rates is a burden for the international division of labor and causes a substantial loss of prosperity. We must therefore do everything in our power to stabilize exchange rates, which will require, on the one hand, improved cooperation between the governments and central banks of Europe, Japan, and the United States. On the other hand, this requires the fulfillment of the European Monetary Union.

Social Democrats clearly support a single European currency. A stable European currency will stimulate growth and employment. Only on the basis of a stable European currency will we be able to make full use of the advantages of the domestic European market. While observing the stability criteria, everything must be done to ensure that we keep the date now set for the start of monetary union in Europe, 1 January 1999. The European Monetary Union proves that the kind of international cooperation I have in mind is already off to a solid start. As an equal partner with the dollar and the yen, a strong single European currency will provide the opportunity to develop a new and stable global monetary system. It is a great opportunity for all.

An Interest-Rate Policy Promoting Growth and Stability

Low real interest rates are a fundamental precondition for increased investment and higher employment. With close cooperation between American, Japanese, and European central banks, all opportunities must be seized to reduce real interest rates.

A Budget Policy Encouraging Employment and Providing Economic Incentives

In most countries a growing public debt has become a rather heavy burden. As a result, rising interest payments on deficits alone have, in many countries, reduced the possibility of launching new domestic political programs. A credible consolidation policy is needed in order to ensure a reduction of interest rates, which, in turn, would stimulate growth and counter corporate and public fears of tax increases. All efforts must be made to reduce structural government deficits. In addition, an economic policy commensurate with the economic pace is also necessary: what should be avoided at all costs is an increased pro-cycle stagnation of growth. It is particularly important to encourage investment and innovation as a precondition for new and dynamic growth. This should be the aim of efforts to restructure budget policies.

Harmonization of Tax Policies

The beginnings of improved international cooperation in the field of tax policy already exist. The most relevant and forward-looking proposals have been made by the European Union. For instance, in April 1996, the EU conducted an impressive analysis of the disastrous consequences caused by the international scramble to offer corporate tax reductions. The result of this policy was, of course, that the tax burden and the weight of nonwage labor costs shifted to the workforce. This, in turn, led to a decrease in mass purchasing power, which caused a decline in domestic demand, higher unemployment, and increased national debts. The aim of the European Commission is to reduce the social and economic disadvantages caused by the race toward international tax reductions. Consequently, it favors a tax union. With regard to corporate taxes, the taxation of capital, and environmental taxes, the European Commission proposes an EU-wide implementation of an effective minimum tax rate.

This is the definitively correct approach. These minimum tax rates must also be structured to provide a "safety net"—requiring companies to contribute adequately to the financing of public services. The European Commission realizes that a harmonization of European taxes is not the sole solution to the problems caused by globalization. It therefore demands a coordinated course of action from fellow member countries in the Organization for Economic Cooperation and Development (OECD).

Common Policy on Technology

New technologies create growth, markets, and employment, and they facilitate structural change. But the necessary research and development costs often exceed the capabilities of individual countries. A good example for this is the aerospace industry. Individual countries' technological capabilities for research facilities and companies need to be pooled. Through international cooperation, the development of new technologies will be pushed forward, eventually leading to an increase in the prosperity of participating nations.

International Social Charter

A functioning social state is one of the elementary preconditions for the success of a modern economy. To improve economic performance, all necessary measures should be implemented to avoid social dumping and exploitation. We must demand the observance of fundamental human rights and elementary worker-safety regulations. Therefore, we support the US government's initiative at the Social Summit, which includes freedom of association, the right to organize and bargain collectively, the prohibition of forced labor, the elimination of exploitative child labor, and the requirement of nondiscrimination at the workplace. Within the European Union, the Social Union must be implemented. Like the Monetary Union, a Social Union is necessary to complete the European Single Market.

International Initiative to Prevent Global Destruction of the Environment

Environmental dumping is both economically shortsighted and morally unjustifiable. Every country has a responsibility to future generations to ensure the conservation of the natural environment. Global dangers to the environment can best be combated through global efforts. Therefore, it is only logical to demand an international initiative that would seek to combat the global destruction of the environment.

Industrialized countries should jointly implement an ecological tax reform. This would require a restructuring of the tax and duty system along environmental lines. It would not translate, however, into an increase in taxes or duties. The lowering of the tax burden on the workforce will lead to higher employment. And higher taxation on energy sources, which threaten the environment, will encourage the market to move toward innovative energy-saving technologies and environmental protection.

Ecological tax reform is a program designed to create new and safe jobs. It would be a serious policy failure if the environmental protection through economic measures were not pushed forward internationally. International cooperation cannot serve as a replacement of national economic policy. The task of putting one's house in order cannot be taken over by a supranational organization. This is the duty of each individual country.

We need a comprehensive modernization of the economy, government, and society. The policy aim and focus of structural change, however, must be directed particularly at the creation of new and safe jobs. The key concepts for such a successful policy are: innovation and qualification, research and development, education and science. National policy will fail if it does not simultaneously acknowledge that current economic policy must incorporate a global dimension. Simultaneous national efforts and international coordination are necessary to achieve our goals.

If we want to seize the new and great opportunities that globalization has to offer, we must rethink our economic policy. We need improved international cooperation in order to overcome the disastrous downward race between countries. A social democratic concept of modernization, social justice, and international cooperation is the only promising policy for the future.

Part I

GERMANY AND EUROPE
IN A GLOBAL ECONOMY

1. German Economic Policy from a European and Global Perspective

Gerhard Schröder

There is a new quality to the international division of labor embodied by the concept of globalization, which has not only led to more intense competition in globalized markets for goods and services but has also subjected labor markets to unprecedented international competition. Using national policies to protect these markets has become largely impossible. International approaches are effective to a degree, but they are frequently undone by nationalistic practices, such as the exploitation of comparative cost advantages by up-and-coming and reformed industrial states.

In order to hold their own in global competition—and thereby remain competitive and secure a share of prosperity for the broad masses of working people—the only open path is comprehensive economic and social modernization. This kind of modernization will be explored here pertaining to three broad themes. An analysis of the German economy will be followed by thoughts on how social and economic policy ought to develop. Finally, I will sketch some concrete alternatives for Germany in the immediate future.

Germany's Strengths As a Business Location

It has become almost fashionable to speak unusually negatively about Germany as a place to conduct business, even—if not especially—among public opinion leaders. In international discussions, this phenomenon has been diagnosed as the "German disease." The suspicion arises that this debate has relatively little to do with realities in Germany, but much to do with competition.

Therefore I would like to start my analysis by pointing out some unmistakable strengths Germany has as a business location, including four in particular:

1. For seven years now, Germany has been transferring DM 150 billion in net payments from the West to the East. This is not a symptom of our economy's weakness, but rather a symptom of strength. I maintain that few economies in the world could do this successfully, and none is required to do so. If reunification occurred in Korea, for example, they would now understand the impact on their international markets and competitiveness. I say this with all due respect for the transferal of money, which I regard as essential. Undoubtedly it puts an enormous strain on the German economy, but we are shouldering it.

2. While transferring money, Germany has still managed to register (measured over the last three years) a foreign trade surplus of approximately DM 100 billion annually. The danger remains that the German share of a growing world export market may recede. Nevertheless, this foreign trade surplus is not a symptom of our economy's weakness, but a sign of strength. Once this is clear, in the interest of social cohesion, it becomes obligatory to take occasional pride in the achievements being performed, not by just a few, but by millions.

3. Even though the strength of the Deutsche mark has recently receded slightly, it remains strong. Again, this is not a symptom of the German economy's weakness but one of strength. Still, over the last three years, the strong Deutsche mark has occasionally made things difficult for our exports.

4. Finally, vocational training, techno-scientific brainpower, and skilled labor in Germany are at a level equal to any in the world. This advantage cannot be emphasized strongly enough, especially in times of such tough international competition to attract investors.

Germany's Difficulties As a Business Location

Any description of Germany's strengths as a business location should not avoid discussing the problems. In Germany the pace of innovation—the time required to transform a development or discovery into a product or process—lags by any international, including

European, comparison. The first and foremost reason for this is that Germany's economic elite have not paid close enough attention to the importance of rapid innovation. It is not the fault of assembly-line workers or white-collar professionals but rather a failure of top managers.

To better innovation in our economic and research system for international competition, we need a more decisive technology policy and closer cooperation between business and science. This would improve the chance of rejuvenating the indubitable strengths of German researchers and companies. Increasing the pace of innovation would also mean acknowledging how politics—and I certainly say this in a spirit of self-criticism—has often established the wrong framework. In Germany we have carried bureaucratization too far.

I will illustrate this by the example of environmental policy: in the past, the state set and controlled standards in the environmental field, if necessary with the help of disciplinary law. But anyone who has looked closely at the history of environmental protection and its improvement will see that the limits of administrating environmental protection have been reached. Neither municipalities nor state governments are in a position to maintain the necessary bureaucracies, nor does this make economic sense. Therefore, governmental action in this area must increasingly shift toward formulating demands while leaving it up to market forces to achieve them. A debureaucratization of this policy field is possible without implying less material protection for the environment.

An additional problem our country has as a business location regards the insufficient use of investment capital, usually referred to with the byword "flexibilization." Keeping in mind what has already been achieved, we still need progress in this respect. Here in Germany we are already on the right track. To allow for a better use of major investment capital, among other things, work should be more optimally organized; this means negotiating the length of time machines run and changes in the workweek. These negotiations have to take place within the framework of broad collective bargaining agreements that keep open the possibility of showing greater sensitivity to the needs of specific firms and regions than has occurred in the past.

It also worries me that Germany does not have a well-developed service culture. This has less to do with shop-closing times than with how services are evaluated on a societal scale. In contrast to comparable countries, in Germany those working in production are ranked differently from those in services, regardless of the specific field;

this is true even more for the so-called (and frequently disparaged) private sector. If we do not succeed in developing (where needed) a service culture corresponding to, say, America's, then we will not create enough jobs.

The Need for Productivity Gains

We have already made gains in productivity, and we will need them in the future. It is a delusion to assume we can do without productivity gains. No one can promise high wages, (which I believe to be absolutely justified) while simultaneously criticizing the development of productivity. In high-wage countries productivity development is absolutely necessary to remain competitive. Yet this means a need for fewer people to provide more goods and (increasingly) services, which results in structural unemployment in the affected sectors.

This can be mitigated by employing two strategies: on the one hand by developing a genuine and efficient service culture that includes private services; on the other hand, by consciously developing what I would label higher value production. Whenever the wage-cost share exceeds 25 percent, problems arise. When we in Germany succeed in developing higher value-added production, we shall indeed be well placed to retain it. We have, then, only two possible responses to our shortcoming: developing services (industry-based as well as private) and higher value-added production in Germany.

The Divergent Organization between the Commercial Economy and Governmental Bureaucracy

There is an excessive difference between the way the commercial economy works and the way the state is organized. In the last century businesses were organized hierarchically, and it was very similar with the state. The two entities understood each other since they were organized along similar lines: this has now completely changed. Successful businesses today are organized laterally in teams. In the state, by contrast, everything has stayed the same. The resulting friction is producing enormous losses.

In addition, there is a significant divergence in productivity between the commercial economy and the state, something we can simply not afford any longer. No one can pay for it, regardless of the level of government. Therefore, both sectors need to be restructured; we have to remove the productivity gap. This means that those involved in state service have to adapt to fewer people wanting (and needing) to produce more services. Those unable to comprehend this will encounter implacable budgetary obstacles.

We have to make a serious effort to implement team thinking and remove hierarchies—to shift decision making toward lower levels. This approach, found today in business, would be fruitful for government as well. It will take some time for this change to take effect, but it will work. We are currently on the right track. Independent of the party in power, controlling and budgeting are now part of state bureaucracies' vocabulary.

Even more important than such organizational changes is the process of completely changing our thinking. Public service has become accustomed to regarding people engaged in economic activity (as in ordinary citizens) as "subject to power." This is a classical concept learned in law school that has to change. Governmental administrative employees need to comprehend that these citizens are, above all else, our customers. We are service providers and therefore servants, not masters. Implementing this new attitude will require fortitude. If we cannot bring ourselves to summon up the strength, we will fail. And we will have failed because the losses caused by the friction between government and business will increase rather than decrease to an extent we quite literally cannot afford.

Old-fashioned thinking in public service, too many burdensome regulations, an insufficient pace of innovation—these are indeed weaknesses in, or part of, the downside to Germany as a business location. And we appreciate those who, like the trade unions, have recently contributed a respectable measure of flexibility to the commercial sector.

Societal Development

What direction should our society's development take as it moves into the new millennium? We are acquainted with two possibilities for politically organizing and managing developed industrial societies, one being the Southeast Asian model. No one can dispute that highly efficient industrial societies have developed there, creating serious competitors for Europe, including Germany. These industrial societies function organizationally by denying the working masses (with state assistance) a just share of the acquired wealth; capital accumulates among a few private actors and is used to spur development at home and to occupy strategic ground abroad so the country can remain competitive with America, Europe, and other developed industrial states. In other words, these are societies based on deferral, and they accept that the working masses must make sacrifices. Human rights are not considered important, nor is an equitable distribution of acquired wealth.

In Germany, as elsewhere in Western Europe, industrial societies developed differently. After World War II the working masses received their fair share of acquired wealth and also retained a voice, due to codetermination and other forms of institutional security. The "sharing society" will probably be the successful means of organizing and politically leading a society in the next millennium. Such an assertion requires justification, especially in a microeconomic context.

The question is what actually makes a business more or less successful. Ultimately, it is the capacity to interest people in the firm's success and to inspire their commitment to the business's welfare. People tied to the life of the firm are the most important resource we have. If there is too large a gap between the need and effort to motivate people and what a society is willing to concede, the result will be disastrous. The concept of a sharing society is undeniably superior and necessary.

Society is changing dramatically. The financing of unification and globalization are not evil illusions but a reality affecting the country's economic foundation. It is absurd to assume that a society could continue to function if dramatic changes in one portion of society occur without the societal superstructure keeping pace. This requires a willingness to realize changes in the social superstructure, more rapidly than in the past. Rapid economic changes need to be followed by rapid societal restructuring.

The political debate for the immediate future should thus focus not on the necessity of changes, for they are necessary. Rather the question should regard the principles used to effect change. In part, sharing means making an effort to interest societal groups collectively in change and keeping the need for consensus alive. The sharing society does not, therefore, mean preserving the status quo but allowing for change to occur by consensus, which means occasionally opposing interest groups or infringing on one's own interests. The Netherlands, in this respect, is an example worth emulating.

What Must Be Done

Politics must be definitively reoriented toward workers. Only when politics is oriented toward the millions of people who create societal values, when their interests are considered central, can the strength and power to do something for social minorities be made possible. Workers must understand that being sick does not mean being better off than when working. Yet repairing a washing machine should not cause undue economic strain on a household budget. This is the reason (my reason, at any rate) we suggested preserving sick pay at 100 percent. Those people who while not exactly living close to poverty nevertheless subsist from paycheck to paycheck and maintain rather modest savings need a sense of security. Especially when the need for societal change is so crucial, people need to know they will not run into difficulty.

To effect change, two basic conditions must be strictly upheld. First, we need a policy embracing the idea of having and retaining a voice in society; second, we must recognize that refusing dialogue in a society like ours not only causes political disruption, but also economic difficulty. I would therefore like to end with a plea that sharing be placed at the center of political debate, that social consensus be sought whenever possible, and that we equip ourselves thus to pass the test of global competition.

2. German and European Responses to Globalization

Ernst Schwanhold and Reinhard Pfender

Preface

Historical statistics (admittedly, not entirely accurate) show that as late as the mid-eighteenth century, today's developing countries (especially China and India) were responsible for nearly 75 percent of commercial production in the known world at that time. The great British Empire was the unrivaled economic power of the nineteenth century. The present century is to a large extent dominated by the United States as the number one political and economic power. Yet the prospect remains that in the twenty-first century, Europe as well as East Asia—especially China—can catch up if they make consistent and energetic progress. Surely this demonstrates that the world was and remains in motion. Material prosperity is not God-given but must be continuously renewed through hard work. This calls for, above all, economic initiative, innovation, and the establishment of a political framework through sound judgment and vision.

The globalization of the world economy today is a fact. Ignoring this development would prove fatal and reveal serious negligence on the part of Germany as well as Europe. Globalization must be analyzed thoughtfully and accompanied by politically reasoned responses. This essay is a contribution to that undertaking and as such is primarily about the economics of globalization and not about its implications for foreign, security, or social policy.

Point of Departure: Areas, Effects, and Challenges of Globalization

Essential areas of economic globalization, or growing global economic interdependence, include international trade, global direct investment, international capital transactions, the international migration of labor and associated wage-cost competition regarding potential business sites, the loss of borders concerning environmental problems and associated production conditions, and international competition within a variety of economic sectors. The following current data better illustrate these phenomena.

- Organization for Economic Cooperation and Development (OECD) figures show the volume of world trade growing about twice as fast as production worldwide. From barely $2 trillion in 1980, global imports and exports rose to around $5 trillion by 1995. The dynamic growth of trade in services—caused by modern developments in information technology and telecommunication—plays a special role here. Consider some important shifts from a regional standpoint: the OECD countries experienced a decline in their share of world trade from 73.2 percent in 1990 to 71.3 percent in 1995. Market winners in the 1980s were the East Asia Tigers—Hong Kong, Singapore, South Korea, and Taiwan; winners in the first part of the 1990s were both Asian and Latin American countries—China, Indonesia, the Philippines, Argentina, Brazil, and Chile.
- In recent years direct investments across borders grew even more intensively than global imports and exports. While worldwide direct investments in the mid-1980s accounted for just around $77 billion annually, their volume was already three times as high by 1994, and jumped again to around $315 billion by 1995. As with international trade, there was a simultaneous, gradual shift in emphasis since the beginning of the 1980s. To be sure, now as then, Western industrial countries dominate, both as source and target countries for foreign investment; however, the developing, emerging, and transforming (former communist) countries have gained markedly in importance, especially as target regions, but to a lesser extent also as points of origin for internationally mobile investment capital. For example, the People's Republic of China (according to annual inflows) developed into the third-largest recipient country for foreign direct investment; the

second-largest recipient was the United States, and the greatest the European Union, which attracted over a third of all direct investment in 1995. Since the fall of the Iron Curtain, countries in Central and Eastern Europe, including successor states of the former Soviet Union, have also seen their share of cross-border investments grow from an almost negligible amount to a respectable showing of close to 4 percent.

- International financial markets have developed explosively. Worldwide liberalization of international capital transfer has led to rapid growth in worldwide financial transactions—often, however, without having a foothold in the real economy. Daily currency trading grew from $60 billion worldwide in the 1980s to around $1.2 trillion in 1995; the daily volume in derivative instruments—traded both inside and outside stock exchanges—is estimated at $1.45 trillion for 1995. Issues on international securities markets reached historic heights in 1995 with net sales at $313 billion.

- Globalization of the economy may be perhaps even more clearly illustrated by the aggregated total data for the most decisive players, namely businesses and employees: around 40,000 multinational enterprises, along with 250,000 affiliated companies abroad and over 70 million employees, invest and produce across national borders today.

- Unfortunately globalization also means the internationalization of problems, such as environmental dangers, drugs, crime, bribery, and tax evasion.

Paving the way for globalization is technical progress, created by improved transportation methods and modern information and communication technologies. The improvement of transportation, however, is subsidized irresponsibly through the sacrifice of the environment. Also important is how recent decades have seen national boundaries (in the form of tariff barriers, for example) being torn down, and both factor and product markets liberalized.

From an economic perspective, globalization has brought incontestable welfare gains to Europe through an enhanced international division of labor (for example, from trade and investment). Yet globalization has also exposed and intensified weaknesses in growth, investment, and innovation in Europe and has led to exceedingly high unemployment rates. And it is precisely on these challenges that the German and European political responses must focus over the coming years.

Economic Policy Responses to Globalization

As shown above, the economy and businesses have already availed themselves of the opportunity and freedom to globalize. So it becomes equally important for politics to have the chance to Europeanize and globalize if government is going to regain any capacity for action. It is therefore vital—at the German, European, and international levels—to develop and implement comprehensively political responses that can remove the major disadvantages of globalization for Europe (the foremost being unemployment). Simultaneously, however, these responses must offer a future-oriented framework for efficiently utilizing the advantages and opportunities of globalization, to which the national economies of Germany and Europe (dependent as they are on foreign trade) have become accustomed. The following are some of our concrete economic policy recommendations.

The National Level

Germany, along with other member states of the European Union, must provide coordinated responses to the challenges of globalization, each country at its respective national level. These responses must improve the capacity for growth, innovation, and competition and must effectively combat unemployment as well. With this kind of fortification, globalization's opportunities can be fully utilized by the EU. Below are our recommendations for appropriate political responses from European economies at the national level; these are especially applicable to Germany but must also be seized upon (in appropriately modified form) by the other EU member countries.

Persistent, coordinated, and consistently growth-oriented and employment-oriented fiscal, economic, and monetary policies seeking dynamic economic growth Regarding fiscal policy, a central concept should be tax relief for lower and middle incomes as well as business tax reduction for reinvested profits. Financing must essentially take place by removing unjustified tax subsidies and loopholes, which should also simplify the tax code. In addition, we need a harmonization of tax policy in the EU to create new and equal opportunities for competition, for example, by introducing a minimum tax on business and capital yields. On the expenditure side, there must be a shift toward making more money available for investments, especially for education, including universities, transportation infrastructure, and economically weak regions (such as the Eastern

German states); public contracts should be awarded with priority given to firms providing vocational training.

An initial, practical economic policy task is to reduce significantly expensive fringe benefits and provide (especially medium-sized) businesses relief from high labor costs. This can be financed through a moderate, ecologically useful increase in consumption taxes. In addition, all opportunities must be exhausted for reducing labor costs through greater efficiency, reduction of overtime, and greater work flexibility. Fast approval for investments is indispensable for achieving enhanced growth. New markets in the area of renewable energy and energy-saving services, telecommunication, biotechnology, and genetic technology must be fully utilized for additional jobs. For economically weak regions like the Eastern German states, it is important to focus on promotional measures and target infrastructure programs.

The main goal of monetary policy is indisputably to secure low inflation rates. However, wherever there is leeway for stabilization measures, a responsible monetary policy must also take business cycle and labor-market policies into account. In the interest of economic recovery, this means not increasing interest rates but—when possible—using available leeway in monetary policy to reduce interest rates.

Strengthening medium-sized business The above suggestions for a dynamic economic policy would strengthen domestic cyclical forces and innovation. This is the topsoil on which medium-sized businesses flourish as the major sources of jobs and training opportunities.

Medium-sized businesses also need special attention in the form of coherent, distinct promotion. Start-up assistance must be increased and consolidated. We need new ways to mobilize venture capital for medium-sized business, for example, tax breaks to make liability capital available. Germany also needs a nationwide venture capital fund to facilitate direct shares, one that is capable of serving as a fund for refinancing corresponding measures undertaken by individual states. In addition, capital resource programs need to be extended. We also need national, medium-sized business agencies to consolidate the numerous programs promoting mid-sized firms, providing a central operation for advising and promoting medium-sized business. Last but not least, we must see to it that globalization and technical innovation increase the opportunities for creating regional networks of medium-sized business. Such a networking process has many advantages that we need to support.

Politics for innovation A broad offensive for innovations in new products, processes, and structures is necessary. Businesses, just like governments, must increase their research expenditures. Research in fields close to the market need to be promoted, and research personnel in small and medium-sized businesses should be subsidized.

Knowledge transfer from research facilities to enterprises must be improved. This means the gap between (basic) research and bringing products to market must be closed. New technologies must be more readily accepted and more promptly implemented. Here we need clear and effective public models. Business and labor market policy must strengthen advanced and continuous training; top-level technologies require top-level research and world-class institutes.

Strengthening social democracy The dismantling of employee rights and social welfare threatens societal coherence and must be stopped. It has badly damaged social peace and the willingness for collective bargaining, both of which are fundamental advantages to Germany as a business site. This dismantling is also wearing down the equanimity of trade unions when it comes to growth and employment policies.

The one-sided cutbacks in sick pay must be retroactively reversed, and protection against firing restored. Social services need to be readjusted rather than simply and unjustly dismantled. To reduce the high rate of sick time claimed we need to create new forms of work, motivate the staff, and reach agreement with employee representatives on incentives. Health costs should be contained through a more efficient use of medication and more competition in health care.

Modern administration and efficient government German administration at all levels must be modernized and the ability to provide services for citizens and companies improved. Bureaucratic procedures must be accelerated, deadlines for decisions shortened, appeal time consolidated, and responsibilities assigned clearly. Civil service law should be reformed according to performance criteria, and its application restricted to sovereign affairs of state. When government is assigned tasks that can be completed more efficiently and at a lower cost by private business or public-law nonprofit organizations, the delivery of these public services should be correspondingly restructured.

Simultaneously, the state's sovereign responsibilities should be strengthened. Security, law, and order in the economy must be implemented more effectively. This includes combating illicit work, illegal employment, and environmental offenses, as well as tax evasion, corruption, and economic espionage.

Conclusion Germany needs new thinking in its economic policy. There must be a political change of course. Sights must be set on an economic policy of constancy, reliability, and sound judgment, and the policy should be capable of restoring economic optimism and dynamism.

The European Level

Coordinating economic policy The Amsterdam EU summit—in spite of the German government's resistance—invited economics and finance ministers to give advice about coordinating economic policy among the member countries and strengthening the EU's employment policy perspective. Crucial to this is EU-wide coordination of the above-mentioned macropolicies that are organized at the national level—especially fiscal, economic, and monetary policies. These need to focus consistently on strengthening growth, employment, and innovation.

On the one hand, the approaching European Monetary Union (EMU) is creating a foundation and appropriate framework for macropolicy coordination. On the other hand, the EMU demands the very same: the European Central Bank can only achieve lasting stability by close cooperation in economic and fiscal policy. Moreover, the EMU is itself a response to globalization, contributing to the stabilization of international exchange rates whose fluctuations endanger the international division of labor and cause enormous welfare losses. In addition, the expansion of the EU, together with the introduction of a common European currency, will secure new markets and open up further growth potential.

Especially important for the EU-wide coordination of national macropolicies are:

- An interest rate policy aimed at growth: the European central bank(s) must—in close cooperation with their American and Japanese partners—use every available opportunity to fashion real interest rates that are cyclically and employment-oriented.
- A harmonization of tax policy: together with the European Commission, we call for tax harmonization within the EU, and for the entire OECD, introducing effective minimum taxes on business and capital yields.

European Union measures Supplementary to the employment-oriented economic policy measures at the national level, which are to be coordinated throughout the EU, the European Commission has its own approach to economic policy; this needs to be aggressively oriented toward growth, innovation, and employment. Central to this offensive should be measures in structural policy, technology policy, trans-European networks, infrastructure, medium-sized business policy, as well as labor-market and vocational training policy.

- On structural policy, for structural assistance to successfully promote employment and innovation, it is necessary to concentrate especially on the development and marketing of new technologies and products, on new fields for employment (especially by strengthening employee training and individual initiative), as well as on structural change within firms and the prevention of unemployment.
- On technology policy, we need EU expenditures for technology policy to be raised as well as a concentration on priority areas like the environment, energy savings, transportation systems, and telecommunication.
- On trans-European networks, what matters is the prompt implementation of the central projects regarding transportation, energy, and telecommunications envisioned by the growth- and employment-oriented 1993 Delors White Book. Especially urgent are outstanding investments in the transportation sector. A trans-European track system can make a vital contribution in an environmentally friendly way to employment and to Europe as a business location. The necessary funds, supplemented by the European Investment Bank (EIB) and EU budget, are to be essentially provided by private financing.
- As for infrastructure, following the mandate of the European Council at Amsterdam, the EIB should expand job-creating investments, especially in the fields of early education, health, the environment, and urban development.
- On medium-sized business policy, the prompt development of an EIB strategy, including the European Investment Fund, is necessary especially to make risk capital available to innovative firms and to support future technology projects for small- and medium-sized businesses.
- On labor-market policy, to supplement the commitments already undertaken by member states, model projects, regular

exchanges of different countries' experiences, and evaluation of programs at the Community level should be promoted.

- As for vocational training, new job descriptions and vocational training concepts must be developed, especially in the field of communication services. In order to achieve this, overly complicated regulatory systems should be simplified and European regulations harmonized.

The International Level

At the international level, especially by working together with North America and Eastern Asia, Germany and the European Commission must promptly and decisively develop agreements on currency stabilization as well as on standards for labor, the environment, investments, and competition. This has market-opening potential and creates conditions for fair competition and jobs, diverting wage, social, and environmental dumping.

Without these tactics, the public would, in part, be adversely affected by globalization and no longer willing to support the principle of world trade based on the division of labor. This could impact the resulting creation of wealth and might even threaten world trade over time. Yet, international guidelines cannot be so stringent or highly idealized so as to impede Third World approval. It would be more reasonable to seek international agreement on a framework for basic or minimum standards regarding labor, the environment, investments, and competition. In detail, we can imagine the following:

- More effective agreements, especially at the Global Seven (G7) and International Monetary Fund (IMF) level, on stabilizing exchange rates. The necessity of this was demonstrated by the fairly recent currency and stock market crisis emanating from Asia. The development of a system for protective currency stabilization would help secure calculable exchange relations and an international recovery of trade, investment, and employment. Exchange rates and real economy fundamentals must be brought back into harmony with each other.

  In this context, there should be a serious re-examination of Nobel Prize winner James Tobin's suggestion to assess a (slight) tax on international capital transfers for the purpose of dampening speculative fluctuations. The practical difficulty here is that a Tobin tax can only reach its goal if all major financial centers worldwide willingly subject themselves to it. However, fiscal policy would stand to gain as much as trade policy: even if only one-tenth of international currency transactions was affected by such a tax, it would bring a total return of some $700 billion into government treasuries.

- For international labor and social welfare standards, it is essentially a matter of getting globally binding commitments to basic labor standards that already exist under the aegis of the International Labor Organization (ILO). These mostly apply directly to so-called basic rights of labor and social policy, such as the prohibition of forced labor, the prohibition of child labor, the freedom of trade unions to organize, and the right to strike. A second stage, however, should seek agreements on minimum wages, which (depending on the situation) can be staggered geographically according to the original levels. Here we can fall back on the good preparatory work done by the ILO and also on the part of the OECD and the World Trade Organization (WTO). Characteristically, policy in France and the US especially has already moved in this direction.

- With international environmental standards, the guiding aim of the environmental conference at Rio de Janeiro in 1992—a "sustainable" environment—offers a point of departure and an opportunity for intensive international cooperation in the environmental field. It creates the same system of coordinates for all countries worldwide. This would, however, initially make production more expensive in the old industrial countries, with their heavier climate burden, before increasingly affecting competitors in the Southern Hemisphere.

  In a parallel effort to this, the OECD has already worked up international policy recommendations that consider environmental points of view within international economic and trade treaties. Yet, instead of allowing these policy recommendations to be formally passed by the OECD's ministerial council so that they might take effect, the recommendations were put on the back burner by shifting the discussion to the purely trade-oriented WTO (with its worldwide diversification of interests).

- On international investment agreements, it is most essential that the complicated and confusing network of bilateral treaties to protect and promote investments, which covers the globe like a spider web, be replaced by an international investment agreement. The development of a Multilateral Agreement of Investment (MAI), which defines transparent and internationally standardized rights and obligations for investors and recipient countries, puts us fundamentally on the right path; we must promptly take steps to rejoin. It is especially important to keep in mind the above-mentioned international labor and environmental norms, which could otherwise be undermined by the MAI.

- On international competition policy, the establishment of an "international competition order" is indispensable, above all for export-dependent countries like Germany. Increasingly, international barriers to market access are no longer to be found at a particular country's border; instead, they are overwhelmingly manifested today through behavior that impedes competition within domestic economies. An example is Japan's *keiretsu* system, a vertical cartel between producers and the firms responsible for storage and delivery; foreign producers can barely penetrate this system with their own goods. Meaningful first steps toward an international competition order could consist of cooperation among national antitrust authorities and mergers of these institutions under regional covers, such as at the EU level. Fundamentally, it is a question of eradicating arbitrariness and securing growth and jobs through fair competition.

As an afterword on national foreign economic policy, we note that increasing globalization and integration of the world economy makes intensified international cooperation necessary and also possible. But even if good progress is going to be made here, it must be accompanied by foreign economic policy measures at a national level. For Germany, it is both important and indispensable to have a cohesive foreign economic policy. This should reflect cooperation and coordination among the relevant institutions, a higher measure of consolidation among interests in the international economy, and more transparency within the existing machinery promoting foreign economic policy, especially for medium-sized firms. Additionally, we call for the foundation of an "Investment Company for Germany" (*Investmentgesellschaft Deutschland*), which can display the advantages our country offers as a business location, procure foreign direct investment for Germany, and provide foreign investors with a one-stop agency where they can obtain assistance from a single source.

3. Balancing Positive and Negative Integration: The Regulatory Options for Europe

Fritz W. Scharpf

Integration and the Loss of Problem-Solving Capacity

During the golden years from the 1950s to the mid-1970s, the industrial nations of Western Europe had the chance to develop specifically national versions of the capitalist welfare state—and their choices were in fact remarkably different (Esping-Andersen 1990). In spite of the considerable differences between the "social-democratic," "corporatist," or "liberal" versions, however, all were remarkably successful in maintaining full employment and promoting economic growth, while also controlling, in different ways and to different degrees, the destructive tendencies of unfettered capitalism in the interest of specific social, cultural, and/or ecological values (Scharpf 1991a; Merkel 1993). It was not fully realized at the time, however, how much the success of market-correcting policies did in fact depend on the capacity of the territorial state to control its economic boundaries. Once this capacity is lost, countries are forced into a competition for locational advantage, which has all the characteristics of a Prisoner's Dilemma game (Sinn 1994). It reduces the freedom of national governments and unions to raise the regulatory and wage costs of national firms above the

Reprinted with permission of the author from a policy paper of the Robert Schuman Centre of the European University Institute, Florence. References for this chapter begin on page 54.

level prevailing in competing locations. Moreover, if nothing else changes, the "competition of regulatory systems" that is generally welcomed by neoliberal economists (Streit and Mussler 1995) and politicians may well turn into a downward spiral of competitive deregulation and tax cuts in which all competing countries will find themselves reduced to a level of protection that is in fact lower than that preferred by any of them.

While *economic* competition has increased globally, the member states of the European Union also find themselves subjected to a wider range of *legal* constraints that are more effectively enforced than is true under the worldwide regime of the General Agreement on Tariffs and Trade (GATT) and the WTO. These requirements of "negative integration" are derived from the commitment, contained in the original treaties and reinforced by the Single European Act, to the free movement of goods, services, capital, and workers, and to undistorted competition throughout the European Community. In the abstract, the basic commitment to create a "common market" was certainly shared by the governments that were parties to the treaties and by the national parliaments that ratified these agreements. What may not have been clearly envisaged were the doctrines of direct effect and supremacy of European law that were established early on through decisions of the European Court of Justice. Once these doctrines were accepted, the European Commission and the Court of Justice had the opportunity to continuously expand the scope of negative integration without involving the Council of Ministers. As a consequence, national policy makers now find themselves severely constrained in the choice of policy instruments as they try to cope with rising levels of mass unemployment and other manifestations of a deepening crisis of the European welfare state.

At the same time, there is now a deep skepticism regarding the original hopes, in particular on the part of unions and the parties associated with them, that regulatory capacities lost at the national level can be re-established through "positive integration" at the European level. While the Commission and the Court advanced negative integration, as it were, behind the back of political processes, measures of positive integration have always required the explicit agreement of national governments in the Council of Ministers. As long as the Luxembourg Compromise still applied, the price of unanimity was an extremely cumbersome decision process. The Single European Act of 1986 was supposed to change this, for harmonization decisions "which have as their object the establishment and functioning of the internal market" (Art. 100A), by returning to qualified-majority voting in the Council. However, rules have been adjusted in such a way that the opposition of even small groups of countries united by common interests can rarely be overruled.[1] In any case, the veto remains available as a last resort even to individual countries, and the unanimity rule still continues to apply to a wide range of Council decisions. Thus, the need for consensus remains very high for measures of positive integration, and when national interests are in serious conflict, Europe is unable to act at all.

Such conflicts are likely to arise from differences among member states in the levels of economic development—and hence differences in the average productivity of firms and in the consumers' ability to pay. Conflicts will also arise from differences in institutional structures, and hence differences in the cost of adjustment if one of the other national models is chosen for uniform European solutions. In addition, there are also ideological differences among governments, regarding either the division between the market and state functions, or the division between national and European policy responsibilities. In short, agreement is difficult to reach, and disagreement and hence policy blockage quite likely arise when positive integration is attempted (Scharpf 1996).

As a result, national problem-solving capacities are reduced by the dual constraints of more intense economic competition and by the legal force of negative integration, while European action is constrained and often blocked by conflicts of interests under decision rules imposing very high consensus requirements. There is a real danger, therefore, that in the face of rising levels of crisis the manifest helplessness of governments at the national and at the European level will undermine the legitimacy of democratic government as it did in some countries in the Great Depression of the 1930s.

European Support for National Solutions?

There is thus every reason to search for options at both levels that could increase problem-solving effectiveness even under conditions of international competition and high consensus requirements. This paper will focus on the latter possibility. I am convinced, however,

1. Conversely, of course, even large majorities cannot have their way. It is important to realize, in other words, that the qualified majority and unanimity rules have extremely asymmetric consequences—favoring inaction and reducing the chances of success of policy initiatives departing from the status quo.

that the main burden must be carried by national governments, which, even though constrained by the legal prohibitions of negative integration in Europe and by the economic pressures of regulatory and tax competition in the integrated market, are by no means helpless. As I have shown elsewhere, *national* solutions do exist in the critical fields of employment, social policy, and taxation that are more durable under the challenges of economic integration and systems competition than is true of present policy patterns (Scharpf 1997). It is also true, however, that many of these solutions would require far-reaching and deep-cutting policy changes and institutional reforms on a scale that can only be compared to those brought about by the Conservative government in Britain.

But eighteen years of single-party rule are hard to imagine in other European countries—in many of which, moreover, multiparty government coalitions, federalism, corporatism, judicial review, and central-bank independence create many more "veto points" in the political process than is true in Britain (Tsebelis 1995). Hence, even if national solutions are available in principle, it is unlikely that they could be speedily adopted and implemented everywhere.

In any case, high and rising levels of mass unemployment, tightening fiscal constraints, the growing pressure of political dissatisfaction and, in some countries, political radicalization, are not generally conducive to the longer-term perspective required by institutional reforms of a fundamental nature. Moreover, even if national policy makers were not incapacitated by internal conflicts and the myopia of crisis politics, they would still be struggling, as it were, with one arm tied behind their backs by the legal constraints of European competition policy and regulatory competition against other member states—both of which tend to create enormous comparative advantage in domestic politics for political parties and interests favoring the dismantling, rather than the reconstruction, of welfare state institutions. Thus, if it is considered important that the social achievements of the postwar decades should be defended under the conditions of globalized markets and European economic integration, then there is reason to search for solutions at the European level that can facilitate and support national efforts, and that can be adopted even under decision rules requiring near-unanimous agreement.

The Treaty of Amsterdam has done little to increase the general capacity for "positive integration" and effective European problem solving in the face of unresolved conflicts of interest or of ideology among member governments. The president of the Commission, it is true, will be strengthened by having a voice in the appointment of commissioners, and the European Parliament is strengthened by a considerable expansion of the items on which it has an effective veto under the co-decision procedure. But no agreement has been achieved with regard to voting rules in the Council of Ministers—instead, even countries like Germany and France, which in the past have promoted majoritarian decision rules, now seem to be more concerned about the risk of being outvoted in an enlarged Community.

Nevertheless, the Amsterdam Summit produced some compromises that represent moves in the right direction—forward on employment policy and backward (or more cautiously forward) on negative integration. After considering the possible implications of these agreements, I will then turn to European options not discussed, or not accepted, at Amsterdam—which, however, should be sufficiently compatible with the interests of national governments to make further consideration worthwhile.

Coordinated National Action on Employment?

The Amsterdam agreements on employment have generally been criticized as compromises on the level of the lowest common denominator, or as exercises in symbolic politics (Wolter and Hasse 1997). They may in fact turn out to be just that, and they have certainly disappointed those among their promoters who had hoped for a commitment to Keynesian full employment policies, pursued through Community programs initiating large-scale infrastructure investments. But what was agreed upon, may, in fact, have more positive implications than a return to the deficit-spending philosophy of the 1970s could have had.

A "New Title on Employment" will now be included in the Treaty of the European Communities. Its Article 1 commits the member states to "work toward developing a coordinated strategy for employment"; Article 2 defines "promoting employment as a matter of common concern"; and Article 4 requires each member state to provide the Council and the Commission with an "annual report on the principal measures taken to implement its employment policy"—on the basis of which the Council may "make recommendations to Member States." Moreover, the Council will establish an "Employment Committee" that is to "monitor the employment situation and employment policies" in the member states and to formulate opinions in preparation of Council proceedings. Taken together, these provisions hold three important promises.

First, by declaring national employment policies a matter of common concern for all member states, and by creating the organizational and procedural conditions for monitoring and evaluation, the Amsterdam Treaty may, for the first time, provide some safeguards against the temptation of all countries to protect domestic jobs through "beggar-thy-neighbor" policies, competitive deregulation, and tax cuts. In the past, certainly, European governments have observed and responded to each others' moves: at the same time that Britain deregulated labor markets, the Netherlands extended the limits on temporary employment, and Germany eliminated employment security in firms with ten or fewer employees. Similarly, just when France chose to reduce employers' contributions to social insurance, Germany and Sweden cut sick pay, and Germany is now lowering pension levels and requiring patients to bear part of their health care expenses in order to reduce nonwage labor costs. If others then respond again, all players in the European competitiveness game may find themselves at lower levels of social protection without having improved their relative position. While I am not suggesting that all of these competitive stratagems should have been prevented, it nevertheless could have been very useful to have them examined internationally.

Second, the commitment to compare and evaluate national policies with a view to share information about "best practices," and to promote "innovative approaches" (Article 5) creates conditions that are conducive to the joint discussion of the structures and causes of employment problems, and to the joint exploration of employment policy options at the national level. Since these discussions in the reconstituted "Employment Committee" of the Council will be more detached from immediate political pressures and acute crises than is true of national politics, there is a hope that innovative solutions to common problems could be worked out—solutions that would not have been found in the rough-and-tumble of competitive party politics dominating national policy processes. Given an active role for the Commission, and opportunities for "deliberative" interactions in a permanent committee of senior civil servants, there is at least a chance that an understanding of the causes of the "European employment gap" and of potentially effective employment strategies could emerge that would go beyond the ubiquitous recipes of the OECD Jobs Study (1994) for labor market deregulation, public-sector retrenchment, and the reduction of social benefits.

Last, but by no means least, the explicit postulation of an employment goal, coequal with the fundamental commitment to the four freedoms of the internal market, may have beneficial effects against the dominance of neoliberal interpretations of what European integration is about in the practice of the Commission and in the decisions of the European Court of Justice. At any rate, it will now be harder to argue that, as a matter of positive law, the Community should be strictly limited to achieving, and protecting, the "four freedoms" and undistorted market competition (Mestmäcker 1987; 1994). In this regard, it may also help that the Treaty now incorporates the full set of fundamental rights guaranteed by the 1950 European Convention for the Protection of Human Rights and Fundamental Freedoms as well as a more explicit commitment to "a high level of protection and improvement of the quality of the environment." What is to be hoped for, in other words, is a reconsideration of the legal scope of negative integration in the light of social and political goals other than the maximization of market competition.

Limits on Negative Integration

As a matter of fact, Amsterdam has taken some very explicit steps in that direction, and there have also been Council directives and decisions of the European Court of Justice which have had the effect of limiting the reach of negative integration in order to protect national solutions that could otherwise be challenged as violating the prohibition of nontariff barriers to trade, as interfering with the free movement of services, or as competition-distorting state aids or regulations.

Amsterdam Agreement

At the Amsterdam Summit itself, some sort of agreement was reached on three issues arising from the extension of European competition law into service areas "affected with a public interest." The first, and potentially most far-reaching, will include a new Article 7d in the Treaty whose delicately diplomatic formulations are worth being quoted in full:

> Without prejudice to Articles 77, 90 and 92, and given the place occupied by services of general economic interest in the shared values of the Union as well as their role in promoting social and territorial cohesion,

the Community and the Member States, each within their respective powers and within the scope of application of this Treaty, shall take care that such services operate on the basis of principles and conditions which enable them to fulfill their missions.

On its face, this clause, which had long been promoted by public-service associations (Villeneuve 1997) and the French government, seems to lack any operative content—which may be due to political disagreement among member governments over the legitimate scope of a *service-public* exemption from European competition law. But even if the Council had been of one mind, it would have been difficult to constrain the scope of negative integration in a general way. Since the Commission and the Court had extended that scope in a case-by-case process of individual decisions, each of which was accepted and implemented as the law of the land by the governments immediately affected, the Council could neither enact a wholesale reversal of past decisions nor could it formulate a clear-cut rule that would satisfy, for an unknown variety of future cases, the equally legitimate interests in reducing economic protectionism and in protecting the substantive "missions" of various *service-public* institutions. Since the relative importance of these potentially conflicting concerns must be determined with a view to the specific circumstances of concrete cases, the Council could only signal to the Commission, the Court,[2] and the legal profession that—in light of the "shared values of the Union"—more weight ought to be given to the purposes served by public service missions. Whether that signal will be respected or ignored is largely beyond the Council's control.[3]

The Amsterdam Summit sent a similar signal with its "Protocol to the TEC" regarding public service broadcasting which, rather than amending the text of the Treaty, reminds Commission and Court that "the system of public broadcasting in the Member States is

2. That the message is indeed intended for the Court is also made clear by a "Declaration to the Final Act" which stipulates that "provisions of Article 7d on public services shall be implemented with full respect for the jurisprudence of the Court of Justice, inter alia as regards the principles of *equality of treatment, quality and continuity of such services*"—principles, that is, which the Court itself had on occasion accepted as justification for *limiting* the reach of European competition law.

3. There is, of course, the possibility that national governments might influence the Commission by twisting the arms of "their" commissioners and the members of their cabinets (Schmidt 1997). But that option was always considered highly inappropriate (Ross 1995), and it will become less effective, now that the President of the Commission must agree to the appointment (and reappointment!) of individual commissioners.

directly related to the democratic, social and cultural needs of each society," and then goes on to formulate "interpretative provisions" according to which the Treaty does not rule out the funding of public service broadcasting. Again, however, the assertion is qualified by the proviso "that such funding does not affect trading conditions and competition in the Community to an extent, which would be contrary to the common interest...."

The same is true in the third instance of the "Declaration to the Final Act" in which the Intergovernmental Conference notes that "the Community's existing competition rules" are not violated by the existence of, and the facilities granted to, public credit institutions in Germany—an assertion which once more is followed by the qualification that such "facilities may not adversely affect the conditions of competition to an extent beyond that required" by the infrastructure functions of these institutions. In other words, the Commission and the Court will retain their role in balancing competing principles in specific cases, but they have now been alerted to the importance of some of the countervailing values to be considered. That effect should not be underestimated—but it is far removed from a reassertion of direct "intergovernmental" control over the functions delegated to the Commission and the Court of Justice. In the field of negative integration, these "agents" will continue to play their "supranational" roles (Garrett 1995; Mattli and Slaughter 1995), but they will do so in the context of a political discourse with governments and the Council over the proper performance of that role.

Council Directives

In areas where hard and fast rules can be defined, it is of course possible to limit the impact of negative integration more directly through the adoption of Council directives—provided that the Commission is willing to take the initiative, and that the directive is not blocked by conflicts of interest among member governments within the Council itself. An example is the "posted workers directive" (96/71/EC) adopted in December 1996 after many years of negotiations. It deals with the paradoxical problem of labor mobility that could only arise after the single-market program had also effectuated the guarantees of free movement for services. Whereas the free movement of workers had previously given rise to numerous directives and court decisions to assure that foreign workers would receive the wages and social rights available to national workers (Ireland 1995; Tsoukalis 1997, ch. 6), the new freedom of the cross-border service provision was now to be realized under the ground rules of "mutual recognition"—meaning that service firms could operate anywhere in the Community under the regulations of their home country. The logical implication was that firms (and even individual workers operating as independent contractors) could provide services abroad while applying the wage rates and social insurance rules of their country of origin—conditions that were particularly attractive to firms located in Portugal, Britain, and Ireland, and that had particularly damaging effects on the construction industries in high-wage countries such as Germany, France, or Austria.

The solution finally arrived at was a Council directive that, essentially, allows countries of destination to require all firms operating on their territory to pay at least the minimum wages generally applicable at the place of work. The directive has the effect of suspending some of the legal consequences of service liberalization—provided that the country affected is interested in, and domestically capable of,[4] taking advantage of that option. In that sense, its logic is similar to that of the "safeguard clause" in Art. XIX of the GATT that allows countries to defend themselves against sectional crises caused by free trade—an option that is not generally available to the member states of the European Community.

Court and Commission

Finally, a number of cases have shown that either the Commission or the European Court of Justice are beginning to limit the reach of negative integration and of European competition law, especially in the service-public areas. In fact, the Amsterdam "Declaration" on the status of German public banks merely took note of "the Commission's opinion to the effect that the Community's existing competition rules allow services of general economic interest provided by public credit institutions existing in Germany." In other words, the Commission itself had refused to intervene against the distortion of competition that allegedly follows from the fact

---

4. The solution is unproblematic in countries with statutory minimum wages, but creates new difficulties in countries like Germany, where collective-bargaining agreements are customarily, but without legal obligation, applied even by firms that do not belong to an employers' association.

that the operation of these public banks is secured by assets of the local and regional governments that own and use them for industrial policy purposes.

Similarly, the Amsterdam "Protocol" on public service broadcasting was adopted at a time when the Commission had not yet taken action against publicly financed networks that were also allowed to compete with their private counterparts for advertising revenue. In both instances, therefore, the Commission itself had proceeded with caution, rather than extending competition rules to their logical conclusion. In that sense, the Amsterdam declarations and protocols were not doing much more than expressing approval and political support for the existing practice of self-restraint.

Since the Commission remains a political actor, even if its accountability is weakly institutionalized, it is perhaps to be expected that it will hesitate to apply the syllogisms of competition law regardless of the political salience of countervailing concerns. But to the great surprise of the legal profession (Reich 1994), the Court itself also seems to have done just that in the famous Keck decision[5] that refused to intervene, on the basis of the *Cassis* doctrine, against national rules regulating the marketing of products, rather than product quality. Similarly, after foreign carriers had gained the right of free *cabotage* through the liberalization of road haulage, the Court quite unexpectedly allowed the continuation of compulsory national tariffs, provided that they applied to foreign and domestic firms alike.[6]

Finally, and most importantly in the present context, the Court also accepted the possibility that the granting of monopoly rights to the postal service and to regional suppliers of electricity (with the consequence of excluding competitors from commercially profitable services) might be acceptable if justified by a need to cross-subsidize unprofitable services in rural areas.[7] In other words, the Court itself had begun to strike a balance between the goals of competition law and the purposes served by national service-public

5. Joined Cases 267/91 and 268/91, *Keck and Mithouard* (1993).

6. Case 185/91, *Bundesanstalt für den Güterverkehr and Reiff* (1993). Ironically, the German Bundestag, anticipating a negative ruling of the ECJ, had unanimously repealed the legislation before the case was decided (Héritier 1997).

7. See, Case 320/91P, *Procureur du Roi and Paul Courbeau* (1993) with regard to the Belgian postal monopoly, and Case 393/92, *Gemeente Almelo v. Energiebedijf Ijsselmij NV* (1994) with regard to the exclusive-supplier contracts of a Dutch electricity network. Both cases had come to the Court on a preliminary-opinion procedure, and both were remanded for additional factual clarification.

arrangements (Gerber 1994), well before the Amsterdam Summit explicitly requested it to do just that.

There is reason to think, therefore, that with the completion of the internal-market program and its extension into core areas of existing (and highly diverse) service-public solutions of nation-states, political sensitivity to the risks associated with the single-minded maximization of free market competition has increased, not only among member governments but also in the Commission. At the same time, the European Court of Justice has also begun to develop conceptual instruments that allow it to consider the relative weight that should be accorded, in light of the specific circumstances of the individual case, to the competing concerns of undistorted competition on the one hand, and the distributive, cultural, or political goals allegedly served by, say, postal monopolies, subsidized theaters, or public television on the other hand.

It is true that the Court's "balancing test" has not yet produced explicit criteria that would provide clear guidelines to lower-court judges (Hancher 1995) or national policy makers, or the Commission, for that matter (Maduro 1997). For the time being, however, that may be just as well. The "creative ambiguity" created by the Court's dicta and the Amsterdam resolutions is likely to sensitize the zealots of undistorted competition in DG IV and elsewhere to the opportunity costs of their pursuit of legal syllogisms. At the same time, however, the ambiguity of the new rules may still appear sufficiently threatening to the protectionist proclivities of national policy makers to encourage the search for solutions that will achieve national purposes without doing so at the expense of their neighbors. In other words, what one might hope for are approximations of what I described in an earlier article as the bipolar criteria of "community and autonomy" autonomy' (Scharpf 1994; see also, Joerges 1996; Joerges and Neyer 1997).

Under present conditions, it is suggested, European integration can only proceed under rules of "federal comity," where European policy of negative as well as positive integration must respect the need for autonomous solutions at the national level that reflect idiosyncratic preferences, perceptions, policy traditions, and institutions. At the same time, however, national actors must respect the fact that they are members of a community of nation-states that must take each others' interests and the commitment to a common venture into account when arriving at their autonomous solutions. If these complementary commitments are translated into law, the appropriate instrument can only be a balancing test whose specific implications must unfold through the case-law logic of inductive generalization from one well-considered precedent to another (Holmes 1881).

My conclusion is, therefore, that the dangers arising from the direct (legal) effect of negative integration on national problem-solving capacities are now better understood and less likely to get out of hand than could have been expected a few years ago. That, however, does not reduce the indirect (economic) effect of increased transnational mobility and competition on the regulatory and taxing capacities of the nation-state. Elsewhere (Scharpf 1997) I have discussed national policy options that might be more resistant to the economic pressures of regulatory competition than existing solutions. But these will only go so far, and the interest in positive European integration remains alive among those groups and political parties that in the past have benefited from state intervention in the capitalist economy.

In the remaining sections, I will therefore discuss strategies that might increase the European contribution to problem solving in ways that are less likely to founder on conflicts of interest or ideology among national governments in the Council. Among these, "package deals" and "side payments" in the form of EC structural and "cohesion" funds have in the past played a considerable role in obtaining the agreement of governments that would otherwise oppose certain measures (Haas 1980; Kapteyn 1991). Under the present fiscal constraints of the EU and its member states, however, these opportunities appear to be more limited, and they will be even less available under the likely conditions of Eastern enlargement. I will not discuss them further here. Instead, I will explore the potential of varieties of "differentiated integration" for facilitating European action in policy areas of high problem-solving salience and divergent national interests.

Differentiated Integration

At least since Willy Brandt's suggestion of a two-tier or two-speed Community was taken up in the Tindemans Report (1975), the idea that positive integration could be advanced by some form of differentiation among the member states has been on the agenda of the European Community. But the notion of what criterion should be decisive for assignment to the metaphoric upper or lower echelon, to the vanguard or the rearguard, or to the core and the periphery of

European integration was always oscillating between an emphasis on the political willingness of countries to renounce national sovereignty and to commit themselves to closer integration on the one hand, and an emphasis on the economic *capacity* of countries to cope with more intense competition or to meet more demanding standards of performance, on the other (Grabitz 1984; Giering 1997).

Since these conflicting perspectives were never resolved one way or another, the notion of differentiated integration retained its connotation of second-class citizenship, even after "opting out" from common European commitments had achieved a degree of respectability from the British and Danish precedents. At any rate, the results of the Intergovernmental Conference leading up to the Amsterdam Summit, which had "closer cooperation" and "flexibility" as one of the major items on its agenda, turned out to be very disappointing. With regard to matters within the domain of the European Community (as distinguished from the second and third "pillars" of the European Union), closer cooperation among members states is now possible within the institutions, procedures, and mechanisms of the Treaty, but its potential range is closely circumscribed by the requirements that cooperation

- must always include at least a majority of member states, and that any other member state may later join on application to the Commission;
- that it must be authorized by a qualified majority in the Council, and even then can be vetoed by a single government;
- that it must not affect Community policies, actions or programs;
- and that it must not constitute a restriction of trade or distortion of competition between member states.

If these conditions are to be respected, closer cooperation will not provide new opportunities for positive integration in policy areas where European solutions are presently blocked by fundamental conflicts among member governments. There are three types of such conflicts that may involve either:

1. ideological disagreement over the proper role of the state vis-à-vis the economy, and the proper role of the European Union vis-à-vis the nation-state; or
2. fundamental conflicts of economic self-interest arising from very large differences in the level of economic development as well as from structural differences in the ability to profit from unrestrained competition; and

3. disagreement over the content of common European policies arising from fundamental differences in existing institutional structures and policy patterns at the national level.

In the past, these conflicts have impeded or blocked European solutions in a number of critical policy areas where national solutions are impeded or blocked by negative integration and the economic pressures of regulatory competition. These policy areas include

- environmental process regulations that significantly increase the cost of production of products that are exposed to international competition;
- industrial-relations regulations that are perceived as interfering with managerial prerogatives or as reducing the flexibility of labor markets;
- social-policy regulations that are perceived as raising the cost of production or increasing the reservation wages of workers; and
- the taxation of mobile factors of production, of capital incomes, and of the incomes of internationally mobile professionals.

It is not obvious that any of these issues could be dealt with more effectively under the rules and procedures of closer cooperation and flexibility as they were adopted at Amsterdam. In the sections following below, I will instead discuss a number of strategic approaches that could allow progress to be achieved on these conflict-prone issues even within the present institutional structures and procedures of the Community. I will begin with the possibility of adopting nonuniform standards for environmental process regulations.

Regulations at Two Levels?

Highly industrialized countries are generally affected by higher levels of environmental pollution (and contribute more to global pollution) than less-developed countries. At the same time, the higher productivity of their firms and their consumers' or taxpayers' greater ability to pay allow the advanced countries to adopt stringent emission standards. However, if these same standards were applied in less developed countries, they would either destroy the competitiveness of their firms or overtax consumers and taxpayers. As a consequence, agreement on regulations at high levels of protection is difficult or impossible to obtain, and the European record in the field of environmental process regulations is spotty at best (Golub 1996a; 1996b; 1997).

But why should it matter if countries with more serious pollution problems and a preference for more stringent regulations remain free to adopt the standards that are appropriate to their conditions? Since their higher costs are compensated by higher productivity, the threat of competition from less productive economies with lower levels of pollution control should not, in principle, deter them from doing so. What matters very much, however, is the regulatory competition among countries producing at roughly the same level of productivity. Even if the result is not a "race to the bottom," the loss of international competitiveness has become a practically unbeatable "killer argument" against all proposals to *raise* the level of environmental process regulations, or of "green" taxes, by unilateral action at the national level.

The impasse might be avoided, however, by a specific variant of the idea of a "two-tier Europe," which would allow the adoption of European regulations defining different levels of protection, rather than a single, uniform emission standard for all member states. As far as I know, this possibility has not been specifically considered in the Intergovernmental Conference. Nevertheless, its underlying logic is by no means alien to the universe of European policy options which, typically in negotiations over the entry of new members, include a considerable variety of techniques for softening or postponing the impact of the full *acquis communautaire* on countries that would face specific difficulties in adjusting.[8] Moreover, articles authorizing Community action may include specific "safeguard clauses" allowing temporary exemptions for states that are not yet ready to shoulder the full load. A specific example is provided by Art. 130s, V TEC, which allows for temporary derogation and/or financial support from the cohesion funds if environmental policy measures should involve "costs deemed disproportionate for the public authorities of a member state."

However, all of these techniques maintain a pretense of universality, and they are narrowly constrained by the need to show that the differences allowed are temporary. As a consequence, countries that could not economically afford high levels of protection must try either to block European action or to soften the impact of European regulations in the process of implementation. The price of imposing uniform rules on nonuniform economic constellations is then paid in terms of nonuniform patterns of implementation that are very difficult to control. And if not controlled, these are likely

---

8. Overviews of such solutions are provided by Nicoll (1984), Langeheine and Weinstock (1984), and, most comprehensively, Ehlermann (1984).

to erode the willingness to enforce, or to obey, European rules in other countries as well. This could be changed by an explicit and general acknowledgment of the differences in the state of economic development and average productivity among the member states of the Community, and of the fact that these also imply differences in the ability to absorb the cost of regulations affecting production processes.

Once that premise is accepted, the solution seems obvious: in order to facilitate the adoption of higher standards, and to eliminate the temptations of competitive deregulation,[9] there is a need for the harmonization of process-related regulations at the European level —but not necessarily for a single, uniform standard. Instead, there could be two standards, offering different levels of protection at different levels of cost.[10] Countries above a specified level of economic development could then adopt the high standards corresponding to their own needs and preferences. At the same time, less developed countries could also establish common standards at lower levels of protection and cost[11] that would still immunize them against the dangers of ruinous competition within that group.

If that possibility did exist, one could expect that agreement on two-level standards would be more easily obtained than agreement on uniform European regulations, which would have to be applied equally by all member states. As a consequence, European environmental policy could assume a more active role than seems presently possible. Conversely, if the Eastern enlargement of the Union is taken into view at all, progress in European regulations of production processes would come to a stand-still unless differentiated standards allow the less developed countries to survive economically.

9. It is remarkable that negative integration in the European Community includes elaborate rules to prevent distortions of competition arising from subsidies, preferential public procurement, and other forms of "affirmative action" favoring national producers—but none against the practices of competitive deregulation and competitive tax reductions.

10. If environmental policy were to rely less on technical standards for emissions and more on "green taxes" on energy inputs or emissions, it would be plausible to use a sliding scale rather than two distinct levels of regulation. Thus it has been proposed that the revenue to be raised by an EC-wide environmental tax might be defined as a percentage of GDP in order to avoid disproportionate burdens on the less developed member states (von Weizsäcker 1989).

11. It is true that the Commission's move (at British insistence) from emissions standards to immissions-oriented air quality standards (Héritier et al. 1996) also reduces the regulatory cost of less polluted (i.e., less industrialized or less windward) countries. However, wide-ranging or global pollution problems cannot be controlled through measures oriented at local immissions.

A Floor under Welfare Spending?

Conceivably, the logic of differentiation may also help to overcome, or at least reduce, some of the difficulties created by regulatory competition in the social policy field. The harmonization of European welfare states is extremely difficult as a consequence of the structural and institutional heterogeneity of existing national solutions. Under these conditions, any attempt at European harmonization would require fundamental structural and institutional changes in most of the existing national systems, and we should expect fierce conflicts over which of the institutional models should be adopted at the European level. In the countries that lose out in this battle, it would be necessary to dismantle, or to fundamentally reorganize, large and powerful organizations from which hundreds of thousands of employees derive their livelihood and on whose services and transfer payments large parts of the electorate have come to depend. In short, the political difficulties of harmonizing the institutional structures of mature welfare states would be so overwhelming that it is perfectly obvious why nobody, neither governments nor opposition parties, neither employers associations nor trade unions, are presently demanding that the harmonization of social policy be put high on the European agenda. But does that also rule out a positive European role in the reorganization of existing welfare systems, which is presently on all national agendas?

There are indeed options for a reorganization of European welfare states that could reduce mass unemployment and maintain aspirations for distributive justice even under conditions of an internationalized economy. These include, for example, the reorganization of rules covering the sheltered sectors of European economies to price low and unskilled labor into work, and the adoption of a negative income tax to offset the consequent loss of income by such workers. But these solutions are difficult to design and to adopt (Scharpf 1997). Under the pressures of regulatory competition and acute fiscal crises, chances are that the changes, which are in fact adopted, will amount to nothing more than a piecemeal dismantling of existing social benefits. As all countries are now competing to attract or retain investment capital and producing firms, all are trying to reduce the regulatory and tax burdens on capital and firms (S. Sinn 1993; H.-W. Sinn 1994), and all are then tempted to reduce the claims of those groups—the young, the sick, the unemployed, and the old—that most depend on public services and welfare transfers.

But in the light of what was said immediately above, how could European decisions make a difference here? If there is any reason for optimism at all, it arises from the observation that, regardless of how much they differ in the patterns of social spending and in their welfare-state institutions, the member states of the European Union are remarkably alike in their revealed preferences for *total social spending* (measured as a share of GDP). By and large, the richer member states (measured by GDP per capita) have proportionately larger public social expenditures than less rich countries. This is by no means a trivial observation, since it does not hold true for the total set of industrialized OECD countries, for which there is practically no correlation between wealth and welfare spending (see Figure 3.1).

The correlation is much stronger, however, if analysis is restricted to the present members of EU 15, and it becomes very high if the analysis (based on the latest available 1994 and 1993 OECD data) is limited to the member states of EU 12 (thus eliminating the upper outliers Sweden and Finland which, at that time, were facing very special problems; Figure 3.2). By and large, the richer European countries commit proportionately larger shares of their GDP to welfare expenditures than do poorer countries. Thus, if we leave aside Sweden and Finland, past patterns of overall social spending are almost completely explained by differences in the ability to pay.

Figure 3.1 Wealth and Social Spending in OECD Countries

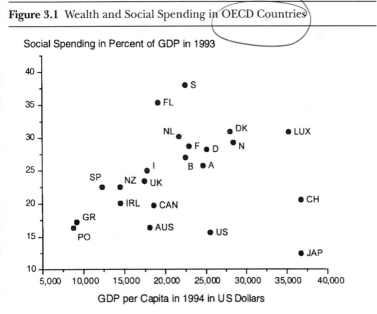

Figure 3.2 Wealth and Social Spending in EU 12 Member States

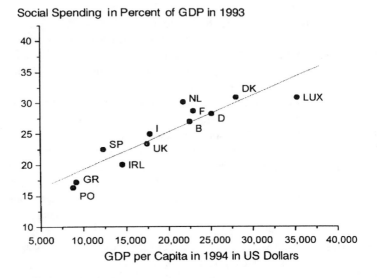

Social Spending in Percent of GDP in 1993

GDP per Capita in 1994 in US Dollars

These figures suggest the existence of a latent consensus among the member states of the Union according to which, regardless of structural and institutional differences, the welfare state should increase in relative importance as countries become more affluent. Beyond that, the figures also suggest the possibility that the latent consensus might be transformed into an explicit agreement among European governments. All countries would then avoid welfare cutbacks that would push their total welfare expenditures below a lower threshold which might be defined at, or slightly below, a line connecting the locations of Portugal and Luxembourg, i.e., the lower outliers in Figure 3.2.

If such a rule were in force now, in other words, it would limit the extent to which countries could reduce overall expenditures on social transfers and services, but it would leave them free to pursue whatever structural or institutional reforms they consider necessary above that purely quantitative threshold.[12] Such an agreement would eliminate the danger (or the promise) of "competitive welfare

12. Two technical problems would require attention, however. First, since welfare spending is highly sensitive to changes in the level of unemployment, reductions of expenditure that are caused by an increase in employment should probably not be counted in defining violations of the threshold agreement. The second is that the

dismantling" from the mutual perceptions of European countries, and hence from the range of options that could be considered in debates over welfare reforms at the national level; and it could thus help to liberate national policy choices from the tyranny of regulatory competition.[13]

Coordinated Institutional Reforms?

By itself, however, agreement on a lower threshold of welfare spending would be merely a holding operation that could buy time for the inevitable structural transformation of European welfare states. These transformations will have to be performed at the national level, but they could benefit in various ways from coordination at the European level. These benefits are, perhaps, more obvious for social-policy transfers and services provided by the state than they are for industrial relations at the level of the firm and the industry. In fact, however, they are important in either sector of the European welfare state.

Social Policy

Even if welfare state reforms must be adopted at the national level, it is important for the future of social policy in Europe that the present institutional heterogeneity among national social-policy systems be reduced. But if institutional heterogeneity presently precludes social-policy coordination, is there any reason to think that it would not also rule out convergent institutional reforms? That would indeed be likely if convergence were to be attempted as a one-step process. The institutional status quo positions seem too far

---

definition of what is to be included in the definition of "Total Social Expenditure" would require much more careful attention than was required for purposes of the OECD study on which the diagrams above are based (OECD 1996)—this will be particularly important at the borderline between what is defined as "public expenditure," "mandatory private expenditure" required by statute or by collective-bargaining agreement, and "voluntary private expenditure." But since the agreement, as well as the data base on which it depends, will be the product of intergovernmental negotiations that cannot succeed unless governments are interested in stipulating effective constraints, they can also make sure that the criteria by which they are willing to be judged fit the specific conditions of the countries involved.

13. Conceivably, a similar approach, oriented toward the share of GDP contributed to public revenue by taxes on income from capital, could also help to overcome the long-standing blockage of European tax harmonization (Rasch 1996).

apart to make negotiated agreement on common solutions a practical proposition. But it might nevertheless be possible to proceed in two steps. At the first stage, one might attempt to reach agreement "in principle" on the future contours of European welfare systems that would be able to assure high levels of employment together with social protection against the risks of involuntary unemployment, sickness, and poverty, under conditions of demographic change, changing family structures, changing employment patterns, and intensified economic competition.

In fact, as contributions to the OECD High-Level Conference "Beyond 2000: The New Social Policy Agenda" have shown, these contours are already visible. Proposals from quite diverse quarters seem to converge on a combination of employment-intensive forms of tax-financed basic income support with health insurance systems and (funded) pension schemes that will be financed through individual contributions, part of which will be mandated by law, and subsidized for low income groups (Bovenberg and van der Linden 1997; Esping-Andersen 1997; Haveman 1997). In fact, proposals of this nature, even if they represent radical departures from the status quo, seem to be surprisingly uncontroversial—provided that discussion focuses on the abstract desirability and effectiveness of solutions within a longer-term perspective (OECD 1997).

The difficulties of agreement would, of course, be immensely greater when it came to the second step of designing ways for getting from here to there—from the divergent status quo conditions and political constraints of individual countries to a functionally superior and more convergent model of the future European welfare state (Esping-Andersen 1996). But here, the Community might take advantage of the fact that structural and institutional heterogeneity, while extremely great across all member states, is not universal. As Harold Wilensky, Peter Flora, Gøsta Esping-Andersen, and others have shown, European welfare states can be grouped into institutional "families" that share specific historical roots, basic value orientations, solution concepts, administrative practices, and whose path-dependent evolution has required them to cope with similar difficulties in comparable ways.[14] Without going into any more detail here, within the present European Union it is possible to identify at least four such "families."

14. See, for example, Wilensky (1975); Alber (1982); Flora (1986); Esping-Andersen (1990); Alber and Bernardi-Schenkluhn (1991); Castles and Mitchel (1993); J. Schmid (1996).

1. Scandinavian welfare states, which are mainly financed from general tax revenue and which emphasize generous income replacement together with universally available and high quality public services, including public health care
2. Continental systems with relatively generous, income-maintaining social transfers and health care financed primarily from employment-based social insurance contributions, and with a relatively low commitment to social services
3. Southern systems, which represent less comprehensive and less generous versions of the Continental model
4. The British-Irish system, which emphasizes egalitarian and tax-financed basic pensions, unemployment benefits, and health services, while leaving other forms of income replacement and services to private initiative and the family

These groupings are certainly not clearly separated from each other. The Netherlands, for instance, combines elements of the Continental and the Scandinavian models. While Italy corresponds most to the Continental model, its health-care system was reformed along British lines in the 1970s, and it also shares some of the characteristics of the Southern model (Alber and Schenkluhn-Bernardi 1991). Nevertheless, there is reason to think that among the present members of the Union, there are relatively distinct groups of countries that share important aspects of their welfare state structures and institutions, that are likely to face similar problems, and that will therefore benefit not only from examining each others' experiences, but also from coordinating their reform strategies. If these discussions are managed and monitored by the Commission, it should at least be possible to initiate moves toward greater institutional convergence over the longer term.

Industrial Relations

Coordinated approaches would be equally valuable for the reform of industrial relations systems, where institutional differences seem to be even more important than in public or state-sponsored social policy areas (Crouch 1993). At present, pressures for reform are felt most acutely in Scandinavian and Continental systems characterized by corporatist arrangements at the sectional and national level and codetermination at the level of the firm. Since they are most highly institutionalized, they are seen to suffer from severe competitive disadvantages in comparison to the flexibility of purely market-driven Anglo-American systems. Nevertheless, corporatism and cooperative industrial relations have in the past benefited considerably from their capacity to control wage inflation and to raise industrial productivity (Scharpf 1991; Streeck 1992). These advantages are likely to be undermined as each country responds individually to present pressures for labor-market flexibility and unfettered managerial prerogatives(Streeck 1995; 1997a).

Given the institutional heterogeneity of national systems, there is certainly no chance for creating a universal European industrial relations regime that would institutionalize sectional corporatism in all member states or codetermination in the corporate structures of the *Societas Europea* (Streeck 1997). Yet it seems obvious that if reforms could be coordinated among the group of corporatist countries,[15] there would be a much better chance of defining and adopting path-dependent institutional changes that would increase flexibility while still preserving the advantages cooperative corporatism has enjoyed in the past.

There is reason to think, however, that a still heavier burden of adjustment must be faced by European industrial relations systems that are neither corporatist nor purely market driven. They seem to be at a competitive disadvantage compared to both countries with more flexible labor markets and those with more disciplined and cooperative unions, and will probably need to move one way or another —toward the Austrian or the British model—in order to increase their competitiveness and their attractiveness to internationally mobile capital investments. Again, it seems likely that the need for adjustment and the options available could be clarified, and the adoption of reforms facilitated, by coordinated approaches among countries that find themselves confronted with similar problems.

Needed: Opportunities for Sub-European Coordination

If the Amsterdam decisions on '"closer cooperation and flexibility" had allowed for the formation of groupings that comprise less than half of all member states, it might have been most promising to use the institutional infrastructure of the Community, and especially

---

15. One characteristic disadvantage of corporatist systems is their seeming complexity and lack of transparency for foreign investors, which is greatly increased by the variety of idiosyncratic national corporatisms. At a time when the importance of foreign direct investment is increasing, therefore, coordination could by itself increase the attractiveness of all corporatist systems.

the analytical and coordinate services of the Commission, to assist the development of social-policy and industrial-relations reforms which are suited to the specific conditions of groups of countries. At the same time, these reforms would represent convergent moves toward the common longer-term perspective of European welfare states. That would have been a most effective arrangement for counteracting any tendencies toward "competitive welfare dismantling." Moreover, and even more important, in the domestic politics of each of the participating countries, the reform of existing welfare systems could have benefited, in the face of ubiquitous opposition, from the legitimacy bonus of internationally coordinated solutions, and perhaps even from the legal force of EC directives.

At present, however, the institutional infrastructure that would most facilitate coordination is not in place. The heterogeneity of existing national structures and institutions, and of the specific problems they must face, is far too great to allow the development of *uniform* reform strategies. At the same time, purely *national* reform efforts are operating under constraints of international regulatory competition that are likely to allow only suboptimal solutions to be adopted by unilateral reform. Under these conditions, it is nevertheless important to point out that coordinated reform strategies among countries that share critical institutional preconditions are more promising, in principle, than unilateral coping strategies at the national level.

There is a need, therefore, for institutional arrangements that allow countries sharing similar problems to coordinate their reform strategies. Conceivably, some of these benefits could be achieved through Schengen-type arrangements outside of the institutional framework of the Community—but that would not only lose the organizational support of the Commission, it would also presuppose a greater degree of prior consensus among the participating governments than could be expected before the beginning of the analytical and conceptual work that must be done to identify common solutions. But perhaps, as was true of Schengen as well, if "closer cooperation" is initiated by some countries outside of the Community framework, then perhaps the next Intergovernmental Conference will again find a way of incorporating such arrangements in the constitution of the European Union.

References

Alber, Jens. 1982. *Vom Armenhaus zum Wohlfahrtsstaat. Analysen zur Entwicklung der Sozialversicherung in Westeuropa.* Frankfurt/M.: Campus.

Alber, Jens, and Brigitte Bernardi-Schenkluhn. 1991. *Westeuropäische Gesundheitssysteme im Vergleich.* Frankfurt/M.: Campus.

Bovenberg, A.L., and A.S.M. van der Linden. 1997. Can We Afford to Grow Old? Paper presented at the OECD High Level Conference *Beyond 2000: The New Social Policy Agenda.* Paris, 12–13 November 1997.

Castles, Francis G., and Deborah Mitchel. 1993. Worlds of Welfare and Families of Nations. In *Families of Nations. Patterns of Public Policy in Western Democracies,* ed. Francis G. Castles. Aldershot: Elgar, 93–128.

Crouch, Colin. 1993. *Industrial Relations and European State Traditions.* Oxford: Clarendon.

Ehlermann, Claus-Dieter. 1984. How Flexible Is Community Law? An Unusual Approach to the Concept of Two Speeds. In *Michigan Law Review* 82, 1274–1293.

Esping-Andersen, Gøsta. 1990. *The Three Worlds of Welfare Capitalism.* Cambridge: Polity Press.

Esping-Andersen, Gøsta, ed. 1996. *Welfare States in Transition.* London: Sage.

Esping-Andersen, Gøsta. 1997. Welfare States at the End of the Century: The Impact of Labour Market, Family, and Demographic Change. Paper presented at the OECD High Level Conference *Beyond 2000: The New Policy Agenda.* Paris, 12–13 November 1997.

Flora, Peter, ed. 1986. *Growth to Limits. The Western European Welfare States since World War II.* Berlin De Gruyter.

Garrett, Geoffrey. 1995. The Politics of Legal Integration in the European Union. In *International Organization* 49, 171–181.

Gerber, David J. 1994. The Transformation of European Community Competition Law? In *Harvard International Law Journal* 35, 97–147.

Giering, Claus. 1997. Flexibilisierungskonzepte für Europa. Arbeitspapier der Forschungsgruppe Europa. Centrum für angewandte Politikforschung. Universität München.

Golub, Jonathan. 1996a. Sovereignty and Subsidiarity in EU Environmental Policy. In *Political Studies* 44, 686–703.

———. 1996b. State Power and Institutional Influence in European Integration: Lessons from the Packaging Waste Directive. In *Journal of Common Market Studies* 34, 313–339.

Golub, Jonathan, ed. 1997. *Global Competition and EU Environmental Policy.* London: Routledge.

Grabitz, Eberhard, ed. 1984. *Abgestufte Integration. Eine Alternative zum herkömmlichen Integrationskonzept.* Kehl: Engel.

Haas, Ernst B. 1980. Why Collaborate? Issue Linkage and International Regimes. In *World Politics* 32, 357–405.

Hancher, Leigh. 1995. Case C-393/92, Gemeente Almelo and Others v. Energiebedijf Ijsselmij NV. In *Common Market Law Review* 32, 305–325.

Haveman, Robert. 1996. Employment and Social Protection: Are they Compatible? Paper presented at the OECD High-Level Conference *'Beyond 2000: The New Social Policy Agenda'.* Paris, 12–13 November 1996.

Héritier, Adrienne. 1997. Market-Making Policy in Europe. Its Impact on Member-State Policies. The Case of Road Haulage in Britain, the Netherlands, Germany and Italy. In *Journal of European Public Policy.* Special Issue, No. 4, 1997.

Héritier, Adrienne, Christoph Knill, and Susanne Mingers. 1996. *Ringing the Changes in Europe. Regulatory Competition and Redefinition of the State. Britain, France, Germany.* BerlIn: De Gruyter.

Holmes, Oliver Wendell, Jr. 1881. *The Common Law.* Boston: Little Brown.

Kapteyn, Paul. 1991. '"Civilization under Negotiation." National Civilizations and European Integration: The Treaty of Schengen. In *Archives Européennes de Sociologie* 32, 363–380.

Ireland, Patrick R. 1995. Migration, Free Movement, and Immigrant Immigration in the EU: A Bifurcated Policy Response. In *European Social Policy. Between Fragmentation and Integration,* ed. Stephan Leibfried and Paul Pierson. Washington: Brookings, 231–266.

Joerges, Christian. 1996. Das Recht im Prozeß der europäischen Integration. In *Europäische Integration,* ed. Markus Jachtenfuchs and Beate Kohler-Koch. Opladen: Leske + Budrich, 73–108.

Joerges, Christian, and Jürgen Neyer. 1997. Transforming Strategic Interaction into Deliberative Problem-Solving: European Comitology in the Foodstuffs Sector. In *Journal of European Public Policy.* Special Issue.

Langeheine, Bernd, and Ulrich Weinstock. 1984. Abgestufte Integration: Weder Königsweg noch Irrweg. Zur Auseinandersetzung über die Weiterentwicklung der Europäischen Gemeinschaft. In *Europa-Archiv* 39, 261–270.

Maduro, Miguel Poiares. 1997. Reforming the Market or the State? Article 30 and the European Constitution: Economic Freedom and Political Rights. In *European Law Journal* 3, 55–82.

Mattli, Walter, and Anne-Marie Slaughter. 1995. Law and Politics in the European Union. A Reply to Garrett. In *International Organization* 49, 183–190.

Mestmäcker, Ernst-Joachim. 1987. Auf dem Wege zu einer Ordnungspolitik für Europa. In *Eine Ordnungspolitik für Europa. Festschrift für*

Hans von der Groeben zu seinem 80. Geburtstag, ed. Ernst-Joachim Mestmäcker et al. Baden-Baden: Nomos, 9–49.

————. 1994. Zur Wirtschaftsverfassung in der Europäischen Union. *In Ordnung in Freiheit. Festgabe für Hans Willgerodt zum 70. Geburtstag*, ed. Rolf H. Hasse, Josef Molsberger, and Christian Watrin. Stuttgart: Gustav Fischer, 263–292.

Nicoll, William. 1984. Paths to European Unity. In *Journal of Common Market Studies* 23, 199–206.

OECD. 1994. The OECD Jobs Study. Facts, Analysis, Strategies. Paris: OECD.

OECD. 1996. Social Expenditure Statistics of OECD Member Countries. Provisional Version. Labour Market and Social Policy Occasional Papers No. 17. Paris: OECD.

OECD. 1997. Family, Market and Community. Equity and Efficiency in Social Policy. Social Policy Studies 21, Paris: OECD.

Rasch, Steffen. 1996. Perspektiven für eine einheitliche Zinsbesteuerung in der EU. In *Das europäische Mehrebenensystem. Mannheimer Jahrbuch für europäische Sozialforschung, Band 1*, ed. Thomas König, Elmar Rieger, and Hermann Schmitt. Frankfurt/M.: Campus, 315–331.

Reich, Norbert. 1994. The "November Revolution" of the European Court of Justice. Keck, Meng and Audi Revistited. In *Common Market Law Review* 31, 459–492.

Ross, George. 1995. *Jacques Delors and European Integration*. Cambridge: Polity Press.

Scharpf, Fritz W. 1991. *Crisis and Choice in European Social Democracy*. Ithaca: Cornell University Press.

————. 1994. Community and Autonomy. Multi-Level Policy Making in the European Union. In *Journal of European Public Policy* 1, 219–242.

————. 1996. Negative and Positive Integration in the Political Economy of European Welfare States. In *Governance in the European Union*, ed. Gary Marks et al. London: Sage, 15–39.

————. 1997. Employment and the Welfare State. A Continental Dilemma. MPIfG Working Paper 97/7. Cologne: Max Planck Institute for the Study of Societies. Available online: http://www.mpi-fg-koeln.mpg.de.

Schmid, Josef. 1996. *Wohlfahrtsstaaten im Vergleich. Soziale Sicherungssysteme in Europa. Organisation, Finanzierung, Leistungen und Probleme*. Opladen: Leske + Budrich.

Schmidt, Susanne K. 1997. Behind the Council Agenda. The Supranational Shaping of Decisions. MPIfG Discussion Paper. Cologne: Max Planck Institute for the Study of Societies.

Streeck, Wolfgang. 1992. *Social Institutions and Economic Performance. Studies of Industrial Relations in Advanced Capitalist Economies*. London: Sage.

————. 1997. Industrial Citizenship under Regime Competition. The Case of European Works Councils. In *Journal of European Public Policy*, Special Issue.

————. 1997a. German Capitalism. Does It Exist? Can It Survive? In *New Political Economy* 2, 237–256.

Sinn, Hans-Werner. 1996. The Subsidiarity Principle and Market Failure in Systems Competition. CES Working Paper No. 103. Munich: Center for Economic Studies.

Sinn, Stefan. 1993. The Taming of Leviathan. Competition Among Governments. In *Constitutional Political Economy* 3, 177–221.

Tindemans, Leo. 1975. Report on the European Union. Bulletin of the EC. Supplement 1/76.

Tsebelis, George. 1995. Decision Making in Political Systems. Comparison of Presidentialism, Parliamentarism, Multicameralism, and Multipartism. In *British Journal of Political Science* 25, 289–325.

Tsoukalis, Loukas. 1997. *The New European Economy Revisited.* Oxford: Oxford University Press.

Villeneuve, Robert. 1997. The Role of Public Services in Building European Citizenship. In *Transfer* 1/97, 98–118.

Wilensky, Harold L. 1975. *The Welfare State and Equality. Structural and Ideological Roots of Public Expenditures.* Berkeley: University of California Press.

Weizsäcker, Ernst-Ulrich von. 1989. Internationale Harmonisierung im Umweltschutz durch ökonomische Instrumente—Gründe für eine europäische Umweltsteuer. In *Jahrbuch zur Staats- und Verwaltungswissenschaft* 3, 203–216.

Wolter, Achim, and Rolf H. Hasse. 1997. Gemeinsame Beschäftigungspolitik. Überfällig oder überflüssig? In *Wirtschaftsdienst* 77, 386–389.

Part II

SOCIAL POLICY UNDER GLOBAL ECONOMIC CONDITIONS

4. Globalization and Social Policy in the Nation-State

Rudolf Dreßler and Heiner Flassbeck

The issues of "international competitiveness" and "investment location" are the stuff of economic policy debate—abroad as well as at home. American labor unions complain about the loss of 400,000 jobs because of NAFTA and about stagnating incomes among industrial workers because of import competition from developing countries. In France, the Netherlands, and Sweden, one can observe a loss of jobs attributable to foreign direct investment. There is anxiety about the hollowing out of Japan's industrial base due to the relocation of production to the newly industrializing countries of Southeast Asia. Even Korea and Taiwan face increased competitive pressure from the aspiring developing countries of the region. Yet, many developing countries in Africa and Latin America see themselves as victims of marginalization because their economies barely register in the burgeoning trade and capital flows. It is not only in the industrial countries—in the North—that growing trade and capital flows with the developing countries and the transitional economies are viewed with great concern. All sides fear that increased international competition between countries with starkly different wage and social systems will lead to growing pressure for adjustment.

A New Era of Globalization?

Globalization usually indicates growing economic interdependence among nation-states through trade in goods and services and the mobility of capital, technology, and labor. Since the late 1940s, international trade has been the driving force behind increasing international interdependence among the world's countries. This has been accompanied by a steadily increasing degree of openness among most national economies. Above all, Western European countries and the United States have globalized their trade in industrial goods. For a long time, the weight of market-integrated sectors increased in all the industrialized countries, and we can expect this trend to continue. National markets once essentially closed are opening and becoming exposed to international competition. Right now, state-protected monopolies in telecommunications, transportation, and energy are the sectors most affected. Banking, insurance, and other private services will also have to face stronger international competition in the future.

Two developments in recent years have strengthened the economic and political significance of globalization: the collapse of the communist system of power and the increasing reorientation of developing countries in the Asian-Pacific region and Latin America toward the Western model of economies and democracy. This has not, to be sure, led to a general acceleration of trade. In Germany one may even observe a temporary deglobalization of trade interdependence. Since the mid-1980s, the trend toward openness in the German economy has weakened; in the wake of unification, Germany's degree of openness even dropped temporarily (see Figure 4.1).

Figure 4.1 Degree of Openness in the German Economy, 1950–1994 (Export share of commodity production and import content of domestic commodity supply; in %)

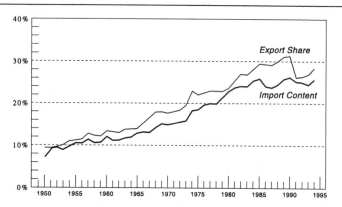

West Germany prior to 1991; all of Germany after 1991. Sources: Statistisches Bundesamt (Federal Statistical Office) and Estiates of DIW (German Institute for Economic Research, Berlin).

Liberalization of international capital markets, rapid progress in telecommunications, the introduction of new financial instruments, and the growing financial requirements of the threshold and developing countries have led to an extraordinarily rapid growth in worldwide capital transactions. Stock market quotations and long-term interest rates are determined more and more by international capital movements, harboring a speculative factor that should not be underestimated. This lowers the effectiveness of national monetary and fiscal policies in guiding macroeconomic processes.

Since the 1960s foreign direct investment has taken on greater importance for economic interdependence among industrial countries. In the 1980s it grew significantly faster than world trade and domestic investment. But with a share of barely more than 3 percent of domestic fixed capital accumulation among the OECD countries, foreign direct investment remains less important than international trade.

There is no global market. The labor markets of most nation-states are regulated by restrictive immigration policies. Today the share of residents born abroad is more than 10 percent of the total population in only three of the leading OECD countries. However, over the last several decades this share increased in most countries. It is an open question whether and how far international immigration movements contribute to a more rapid equalization of worldwide wage levels for simple jobs as compared to pure commodity exchange. In any event, there is little incentive for developing countries to open their labor markets, even if it is getting more and more difficult for them to control immigration movements.

Globalization As Political Choice

Globalization is not merely the result of technical progress and international competition but is also a political choice: the economic and political opening of an increasing number of countries—whether accomplished multilaterally in the framework of GATT and WTO, for example, regionally within the European Union, or unilaterally in Eastern Europe, China, Southeast Asia, and Latin America—has strongly facilitated cross-border flows of goods, services, capital, and technology. The increasing openness of national economies through the reduction of government-established barriers to trade and capital transactions was supported by the conviction that an open economy increases prosperity among all participating countries. Additionally, disappointment prevailed as a result of the expectations raised by the development model, which tried to ease the transition of less developed countries toward self-sufficiency by means of direct Western aid. Apart from that, the industrial countries did not even get close to reaching their self-proclaimed development goals (0.7 percent of GDP).

The Consequences of Globalization for the North

According to all available scholarly studies, it would be an inaccurate generalization to support the notion that competitive pressure from less developed countries in the South has forced the greater developed countries in the North to increase their productivity and simultaneously lower their costs. Just as unsustainable is the notion that unemployment in the North has hardened because of increasing competitive pressure. To be sure, labor-intensive sectors became subject to competitive pressure in the course of global structural change. Yet new sales opportunities have arisen in those sectors intensive in human capital and technology. For example, Germany was able to increase powerfully its exports to Southeast Asia, especially in machine tools, surface transport vehicles, and electrical and telecommunications technology. Particularly in the area of high value-added industrial goods, the industrial countries as a whole register high—and, in the end, even growing—export surpluses against the developing countries. If anything, this testifies more to an export of unemployment than of jobs.

In the wake of growing worldwide division of labor, however, the demand for less qualified industrial labor sinks in the North, while it increases in the South. The greater the weight of the developing and threshold countries in global trade, the stronger the tendency for industrial jobs that call for greater qualifications. The industrial countries must meet the challenge of this structural change if they want to enjoy the advantages of trade. But this is not a major cause of increasing unemployment in Western Europe and increasing income inequality in North America.

In the course of structural change, jobs in specific regions and sectors naturally disappear, while new ones arise in others. As a result, unemployment increases in specific labor-market segments, while it declines in others. This is how it has always been. In times of slow growth and high unemployment, however, the costs of structural change weigh more heavily than in times of major economic dynamism. As a result, there is greater pressure on economic policy to maintain jobs in specific regions and branches. Politicians comply with these pressures because they involve their political constituencies, but in the long run, this behavior will not accomplish much. The only result is that more and more tax money gets tied to subsidies.

What is decisive, in the final analysis, is how successful economic policy is at combating unemployment at home. Especially for Europe as a whole—with its small share of foreign trade—the main task cannot be improving external competitiveness. Above and beyond this goal, what is required is timely assessment of the consequences of structural change, identifying problem sectors and regions, and promoting sites for new sectors, especially services. In addition, incentives need to be given for greater intersectional and interregional mobility among employees. What is required is a positive adjustment policy that promotes and socially cushions structural change instead of impeding it.

The Consequences of Globalization in the South

The economic power of the South is significantly lower than that of the North. Economic exchange between North and South therefore has significantly greater meaning for the South, where 11 percent of the entire gainfully occupied population is employed in the export industry; and 10 percent of the entire capital stock of the South is financed by funds from the North, which corresponds to a mere 2 percent of the North's assets. Thus, the North carries a special responsibility for the economic development of the South: by means of open markets and unrestricted capital movement, the North eases the export-dependent industrialization of the aspiring threshold and developing countries and enables the creation of new jobs and growing incomes there. For the South, unrestricted access to the markets of the North is far more significant than development assistance ("trade, not aid").

The promotion of economic growth in the South is necessary not only for reasons of development policy but also of stabilization policy. The political influence of the highly populated developing countries is going to increase significantly in the coming decades. According to Western estimates, already by the year 2000 three dozen developing nations will come to possess weapons of mass destruction. The overwhelming majority of these countries will have disposition over a very young population, a result of rapid population growth. If the effort to create preconditions for the appropriate employment and growing income of these people does not succeed, the problem of large worldwide income differences can turn into a social and political explosive that should not be underestimated.

Social Dumping by the South?

The low level of wages and social services in the South is the precondition for its international competitiveness in labor-intensive sectors. It is the immediate reflex of a substantially lower level of development, and therefore of productivity, compared to the North. But the low level of wages and social services is often explained by other factors, such as the ban on trade union activity and work organization, along with nonfulfillment of minimal demands for the protection of health and human dignity. This affects child labor in particular. As a consequence, industrial countries frequently demand that developing countries observe certain social standards and pressure them to implement them through trade sanctions.

The ban on child labor and the freedom of association and collective bargaining are basic human rights codified in the Charter of the United Nations and the International Labor Organization (ILO). The North should therefore take a principled stand on the recognition of these human rights in all developing countries: by depriving military dictatorships of political support, by linking the granting of development assistance to social standards, and by insisting that aid be directed toward combating poverty. Trade sanctions are the wrong solution because they are in danger of being abused as a Trojan horse for protectionism in the North. It is no coincidence that the demand for trade sanctions increases when the South, in the course of industrialization, begins to export more labor-intensive industrial goods to the North. When the South's exports consisted chiefly of raw materials and agricultural products, working conditions in the mines and plantations of the South —always worse than in the export industries of the aspiring threshold countries—hardly commanded attention in the North.

As the South catches up economically with the North, not only will wages rise in the South but also social standards. Industrialization and the urbanization that accompanies it create new forms of economic and social insecurity that contribute to dissolving traditional family structures. The result is the emergence in the South—as already exists in the North—of a comprehensive system of social security (unemployment, old age, health, and accident insurance). This may already have occurred in many threshold countries. Meanwhile, those countries hesitant to improve the living standards of the broader population by restrictive employment and social policies are only able to achieve temporary competitive advantages. In the course of democratization, strong real-wage increases become inevitable, as was the case with South Korea toward the end of the 1980s. Such real-wage increases subject the economy to major competitive pressures that might have been eased only by earlier wage increases.

Social Dumping by the North?

Social dumping by the North to fortify its own competitiveness is not only unnecessary but also counterproductive. The North faces no competitive problem. Moreover, the international monetary system would not permit the North to further improve its competitiveness against the South by lowering wage and social costs, for this would lead to an even lower inflation rate, which would bring in its wake an upward revaluation of currencies that would quickly nullify the competitive advantage all over again. The experience of highly stability-conscious countries (for example, Germany and Japan) shows that they actually suffer from this kind of "overshooting revaluation," with significant adjustment costs for the domestic export industry. In addition, social dumping by the North endangers its social stability. In the long run, no open foreign-trade order can be maintained in the absence of social stability. And social dumping by the North creates the danger of undermining the preconditions for the international division of labor. This would be the worst of all the available options.

Job Export through Capital Export?

In their trade with the developing countries, the industrial countries are net exporters: they sell more to than they obtain from the South. This export surplus signifies the North's economic strength; its mirror image is a corresponding net capital export that allows the developing countries to finance their import surplus against the North. It goes without saying that, next to public development assistance and private credit, direct investment is also a component of capital export. With the liberalization of international capital markets and the opening up of many countries in the South, private capital transfer to finance the "import hunger" of these aspiring nations will assume greater importance. In addition to helping secure markets and raw material deposits, direct investment by the North in the South naturally also serves to transfer labor-intensive production methods. This is just another variation on the general theme of structural change. Whereas earlier entire sectors fell victim to foreign competitive pressure, today it is often just individual manufacturing sites. Managerial jobs, by contrast, remain in the North.

Taxing International Currency Trade?

The suggestion has often been made to put a minuscule turnover tax on international currency transactions. It is expected that such a "Tobin tax" would dampen speculatively determined exchange-rate fluctuations because the tax would be cumulative after frequent currency transactions. In addition, international organizations could expect to mobilize several hundred billion dollars to finance development assistance. The idea of limiting exchange-rate fluctuations is correct, but a turnover tax on international currency transactions is the wrong method. It presupposes a worldwide agreement that would be resisted by all the leading financial centers. In addition, a tax like this would merely increase the threshold for smaller speculative transactions; it would be ineffective in countering massive speculation against currencies like the British pound or the Mexican peso. Of central importance for an easing of currency fluctuations is stronger international coordination by the industrial countries in the areas of monetary and fiscal policy, which will make it difficult for international investors to reap rewards from inconsistencies in national economic policies.

The Causes of Unemployment in Europe

Labor-market developments on both sides of the Atlantic are unsatisfactory: whereas too few new jobs are being created in Western Europe, in North America there are too few well-paying jobs. Whereas long-term unemployment is overproportionate in Western Europe, in North America many job seekers are forced to accept part-time work.

High unemployment in Germany does not signify weakness in investment location but weakness in growth. If high unemployment meant weakness in investment location, the proponents of the "investment location debate" (*Standortdebatte*) could not explain why international comparisons show that the Western part of Germany had a significantly below-average unemployment rate—comparable to that of the United States—until the start of the 1990s. This perspective also cannot explain why Germany as a whole, in spite of the increased unemployment rate caused by unification, still fares better than France, Great Britain, Italy, Spain, and many small Western European countries.

The causes of high unemployment are neither rising globalization nor increasing "rigidity" in Western European economies. Globalization increased steadily in recent decades; in this respect, the opening of Eastern Europe has changed nothing. As a consequence, it cannot explain the jump in Western European unemployment resulting from the two oil shocks and the last recession. "Rigidity" in all of the Western European countries has reduced since the beginning of the 1980s, most recently as a consequence of introducing the single market in 1993, presumably the largest program of deregulation in recent decades. To be sure, the state continues to play a greater role in Western Europe than in the United States. Be that as it may, decreasing "rigidity" does not go along with an increasing level of unemployment.

The causes of unemployment in Europe lie elsewhere. During the 1980s all Western European countries—to varying degrees—pursued a policy of tight money; budgetary consolidation; tax relief for profits; and deregulation of commodity, capital, and labor markets. Under the pressure of high unemployment, the trade unions moderated their wage demands, especially in Germany. As a consequence of these developments, to be sure, returns on investment capital throughout Europe have strongly improved. However, labor-market developments disappointed expectations.

The recession at the beginning of the 1990s nullified all the supply-side efforts toward lower unemployment. Now the developments of the 1980s threaten to repeat themselves: high real interest rates put a brake on investment and increase debt service for public budgets. Growing mass unemployment, because of more social expenditures and fewer revenues, leads to further growth in public debt. Efforts undertaken toward budgetary consolidation become fortified on a Europe-wide level and nip every recovery in the bud. Wage moderation by trade unions dampens price increases but makes no effective contribution toward reducing unemployment when monetary and fiscal policies are restrictive.

European unemployment cannot be reduced if economic policy takes place only on the supply side and monetary policy is directed exclusively—and often without coordination with the rest of economic policy—toward the maintenance of price stability. To illustrate this point, year by year, high domestic savings are built up, but nobody is prepared to take on debt. Private households are unwilling because debt has no favorable result on incomes; businesses are not prepared to assume debt because demand expectations are bad and real interest rates are still too high; and finally, the state is not ready because of a European-wide effort to drastically reduce current deficits in order to fulfill the Maastricht criteria. Foreign countries are all that remain! All European countries are keen on getting foreigners to take on debt, and so they attempt to create the preconditions for this by lowering costs and reducing social expenditures. This cannot bode well. Europe as a whole cannot solve its problems in this fashion because foreign trade's share of domestic product is smaller than 10 percent, and other countries are not prepared to accept this. An upward revaluation of European currencies or a collapse of the world trade order through competitive devaluation would be the consequence.

The short- and medium-range solution lies in Europe itself and is quite simple: either we succeed in getting businesses to invest by forcing down interest rates, or government will have to give up the attempt to reduce its debt out of concern for destabilizing the demand side even further.

Consequences of Unemployment

High unemployment not only threatens the continuation of the European integration process, but also gives impetus to new miracle cures. The teaching of protectionism à la Buchanan, Le Pen, and Haider promises to increase national prosperity by partially closing off one's own country. Historical experience actually teaches us that this can only lead to a reduction in both domestic and foreign incomes. The view that one could improve international competitiveness and preserve one's own living and social standards by making deep cuts in the social safety net is just as bleak. This can actually put social stability in danger without allowing "competitiveness" to increase. Both teachings lack an economic foundation. Nevertheless, it appears as though high unemployment and weak growth provide these demagogues with a political and social foundation.

Our appraisal of the current situation finds it should be reversed: it is not a reduction of integration into world markets that reduces unemployment. Rather, easing unemployment with appropriate growth policies is the precondition for preserving and continuing the level of integration already achieved. If this becomes endangered, it is not only the prosperity of the North that will suffer, but also that of the South—with unpredictable political consequences.

5. Consequences of Globalization for Women

Ulla Schmidt

Economic and social systems at both the national and international levels are currently caught up in a rapid and critical process of change. This does not mean, however, that in the age of globalization national economic policies are powerless and that there is no latitude left for policy action. On the contrary, national economic policy has the task of paving the way into the twenty-first century in such a manner that women and men can contribute on an equal footing with their creativity, their talents, and their qualifications.

The center-right government in Germany has reduced the concept of globalization to a debate of wage costs and is using it as a strategic instrument for dismantling the welfare state. This domestically motivated instrumentalization is leading to economic instability, mass unemployment, and growing inequalities in living standards and opportunities in life. Downward adjustment is producing a highly divided society, in which democracy, justice, and equality are under threat. With increasing frequency the welfare state mandate contained in our constitution is being called into question on the basis of "world market constraints."

The welfare state, as defined in Germany's Basic Law, pertains to structural and institutionalized solidarity, a necessary response to the inequality that is inevitably created repeatedly in a free market environment. For this reason social justice is needed constantly; in other words, we need government intervention to create equality of opportunity and a just distribution of wealth. A society that reduces its citizens to purely economic factors will not succeed. We need decent housing, decent working conditions, equal access to education, training, information, as well as culture; and women should have equal participation in all of these decision-making processes.

Not all of today's predictions about the future society, when the digital revolution has been completed and we have a developed state of globalization, will come true. But the trend toward requiring only 20 percent of today's labor to produce the same amount of goods and services describes the threat posed to social solidarity and the need for a policy to achieve a larger measure of social justice.

Germany cannot avoid taking part in the epoch-making process of economic globalization. And the fact of the matter is that the country derives major advantages from it, given that this process promotes economic and cultural exchange between nations. Cultural and traditional habits are modified by the influences of economic and social factors. Economic and cultural exchange that is supplemented by politically forward-looking regulatory instruments is particularly advantageous for women. Globalization is creating a need for global regulatory policies. This includes regulations for trade, the financial markets, and environmental protection, as well as for the equality of women and men.

Something new can develop if democracy and progress are viewed as a global challenge in conjunction with the equality of women. This does not contradict the social changes being brought about by globalization. Instead, it would seem absolutely necessary that reliable political and economic structures be developed on the basis of global framework conditions for women and men. Global trade is ill-fated if left to develop of its own accord, something that is being allowed by an increasing number of governments, including the Kohl government.

Globalization calls for political intervention to make the associated risks controllable. The market is an indispensable organizational principle for economic activity but cannot be for society. No company can be successful without a functional, buoyant social environment with values, morals, humanism, compassion, and equality of the sexes. Only then will globalization constitute an opportunity for women and not a risk.

Globalization is not a gender-neutral phenomenon; it has different effects on men and women. Thus it can be used to promote gender-specific divisions or to overcome them. In the 1970s and 1980s there was a considerable decline in the number of jobs typically held by women. A large-scale, globalized movement began in the garment industry in which labor-intensive mass goods were and continue to be manufactured in low-wage countries. Since then the Thai economy has shown impressive growth rates of 7 to 8 percent annually. It is primarily women who work in those production sectors (textiles, leather goods, and jewelry) that have now been moved abroad. Southern Europe, North Africa, the Far East, and Latin America have moved into the global marketplace on the basis of low wages paid to women and the low level of social welfare costs involved.

If considered an opportunity, globalization must also be seen as an opportunity for the Newly Industrialized Countries (NICs) and Third World countries. If we don't succeed in creating the right conditions for adequate employment and rising incomes for women and men equally, then we could have a socially and politically explosive situation on our hands. In this context, the debate on international social clauses is of particular importance and played a key role at the last World Trade Conference in Singapore.

Opinions vary on what form social clauses or social standards might take. Some call for bans on child labor and forced labor, or the lifting of bans on trade union activities. Others cite minimum standards for job security, health care, and old-age pensions. Women's organizations, in particular, advocate minimum social standards because women's jobs expose them to considerable health-related and environmental risks. Other vital issues include maternity leave guarantees, sexual harassment protection, and employment security. We already know today that globalization produces winners and losers—winners because more women are working in the export industry and in the services sector, losers because of increasing job market deregulation and the growing numbers of women living in poverty. The percentage of unemployed women in the OECD countries is nearly twice as high as for men.

Even though Germany currently has the best-qualified generation of women in its history, women are being crowded out of the job market; more women are unemployed than men. For years, the labor market has been divided into groups of insiders and outsiders, and women are generally outsiders. This is evidenced by the sharp rise in the number of part-time jobs that pay 610 Deutsche marks a month (with no social security) and in the amount of undeclared employment, both of which are for the most part traditionally women's domain. Millions of women are thus unable to make enough to live on, and many will become welfare recipients when they are out of work or beyond working age.

For years women have seen their jobs erode and a decline in government social welfare benefits, alongside a trend toward providing "more jobs for the boys." The laws protecting employees against dismissal have been suspended for small companies, which primarily employ women. Three social criteria in connection with dismissals were introduced for larger companies: the employee's length of service, the employee's age, and the employee's family obligations. Because men are still considered the primary breadwinners for families for 75 percent of German families (one reason for this being that women are paid, on average, 25 percent less) and men generally have an uninterrupted job history, they have a distinct advantage. Women are faced not only with the stereotype of traditional roles but also with wage discrimination, which has a double effect. And as if that weren't enough, maternity leave is now being met with a 20 percent reduction in wages. This means that women in low-income jobs who have problematic pregnancies may not earn enough to survive. Thus the process of marginalization and withdrawal of public support that began with social welfare recipients, the jobless, the disabled, and young people in search of job training opportunities affects women also.

Such a policy is potentially explosive. Without a fair distribution of employment and equal opportunity in education and culture, without eliminating gender discrimination and improving the financial status of families, our democracy would be threatened because there would be no social justice. New thinking and policy changes must amount to more than various degrees of deregulation. We need a renewal of social infrastructures, not their destruction. We need to strengthen our social safety net instead of boring holes into it. We need to expand our investment in education and research instead of reducing it. Globalization implies a reasonable international division of labor, flexible responses to changing conditions of the world market, but more than anything else, it implies the reliable funding of research and the quick turnaround of ideas into new and marketable products. There are dormant resources in the areas of innovation and qualification that need to be used. Qualification requirements, such as the ability to engage in team efforts, the ability to analyze problems, and the ability to make decisions regarding the implementation of technological developments —fit a profile attributable to women in particular. One thing is certain. Without continuous training of the workforce and an employment-focused labor policy, it will be impossible to cope with the challenges globalization poses.

Social Democrats want competition and international economic exchange. But we want it to benefit all women and men and not just a few groups. Gender equality is just as much a part of modern society as is social security for all citizens. This does not contradict economic globalization; on the contrary, it safeguards a productive and stable society. Such an objective calls for equal participation of women and a fair distribution of employment, which means reducing the work hours on existing jobs and redistributing the work more equitably. This would also change the conditions for policies relating to women. We face new challenges with regard to the political, economic, and social participation of women on the basis of gender equality.

Like all other industrial societies, Germany is becoming a service-oriented society. The decline in the number of industrial-sector employees and the rise in the number of service-sector employees are characteristic of this change. These are prime examples of globalization, fueled by the use of information technology systems and the provision of information-related services. In these times hopes turn to new businesses. Each successful business startup creates an average of four new jobs. Given this equation, we would need 500,000 new businesses in Germany just to cut the current unemployment figure in half.

Another quality of globalization can and must be that of sustainable development. It is obvious that environmental pollution does not stop at national borders. Environmentally compatible growth constitutes both an opportunity as well as a challenge to create its framework conditions. We need jobs with a future, jobs that will combine economic success with social and ecological objectives. These objectives address the needs of today's generation and will not pose a threat to future generations. In terms of emerging economic and technological changes, this means that the prospects for the future lie in the high-tech sector. New products and production processes are being developed and highly skilled jobs are being created. Jobs in other sectors will be lost, in particular, production jobs that place low demands on the employee's qualification level. These employees will have to be retrained in order to qualify for other jobs. Lifelong learning is going to become an additional challenge for labor and education. Thus, we will need to make use of existing reservoirs of expertise, qualifications, and creative potential among women. Globalization creates a need to shape labor, economic, and social policies with women in mind. The following measures would enhance the possibility.

Equal Opportunity through Mainstreaming

For years the European Community has fought discrimination against women in the labor market. It has promoted the integration of women into the job market with specific affirmative action programs, which finance campaigns and projects that fight female unemployment, encourage women in management positions, and promote the compatibility of family and career. The current Fourth Program of Action (1996–2000) is aimed at achieving equal opportunity through "mainstreaming."

This approach requires gender-specific perspectives and analysis in all policy areas, programs, and campaigns. It is necessary to consider the differing conditions, situations, and needs of women and men in all policy areas. This applies to planning, implementation, and evaluation activities as well as to the programs' applicability to Europe, to the other industrial nations, and to the developing countries. A gender perspective formulated in this way realizes equal opportunity cannot be achieved by a separate policy for women. "Mainstreaming" leads to gender equality only if all policy measures and concepts have positive effects for women.

A supplement to affirmative action measures, mainstreaming is one of the principles applied by the European Structural Fund, the EU's largest source of funding. Innovative projects are financed with government resources such as taxes. A key objective is to create jobs by women for women. An outstanding example of such a project, which depended entirely on government funding, is a business center in Berlin called *WeiberWirtschaft*. With a total floor space of 5,500 square meters, it is the largest cooperative in Europe for women-owned businesses. The cooperative now has roughly one thousand members who have purchased shares ranging in value from 200 to 50,000 Deutsche marks. The membership also includes women from India, Spain, the United States, and other countries. The entrepreneurial presence of some fifty female business owners forms a core of economic potential that has created some two hundred jobs for women in the areas of general services, manual trades, manufacturing, culture, supplementary training, social services, and rent-subsidized housing. The business center sets an ecological example by integrating areas for work, commerce, and recreation under one roof. The building offers women stable rent levels, joint use of office equipment, joint advertising, and space for conferences, seminars, and exhibitions.

My next example shows that while men are still looking for a way out of a problem, women have often already found a solution. It regards the German textile industry, which is in a crisis because more and more manufacturers are moving their production sites to developing countries or to Eastern Europe to take advantage of lower wage costs. In Eastern Germany there has been a considerable loss of jobs in the industry. Of a previous 300,000 jobs (70 percent of them held by women), there are only 49,000 left.

A group of these unemployed female textile workers studied scientific reports and found that some 30 percent of young people under the age of eighteen suffer from allergies to certain types of textiles. The only remedy to this is ecological products, such as untreated natural fibers. These women decided to develop a new niche market and started producing natural-fiber clothing for children. Their company, YoYo-Kid, now sells its children's clothing on the European market. The startup was possible only with assistance from the European Structural Fund. There is no lack of women with courage and ideas, but there is a lack of money for getting started (and there are no private donors or sponsors for ideas in Germany).

Equality in the Job Market

In Germany, affirmative action is a voluntary choice for private-sector companies. We Social Democrats have long called for our government to introduce mandatory affirmative action laws in the private sector. The current government continues to reject regulatory interventions and to promote free enterprise. This makes it difficult for women to participate in the workforce on an equal footing. We need to pass laws ensuring that women with the same qualifications are given preference in hiring wherever they are underrepresented. In addition, all business promotion and structural policy measures should be linked with affirmative action policies targeting women, creating skill-enhancing training opportunities and skill-requiring job opportunities.

Equal Opportunity in Vocational Training

Like young men, young women want good career training and a profession that matches their interests and abilities and gives them financial independence. There are more than 380 recognized professions, but half of our young women train in only seven of them. The most common choices are sales clerk, office clerk, hairdresser, and dental assistant. These professions all have something in common: low pay during training. After training is completed, there is little or no chance to advance, and the pay remains low. Professions with more potential, such as those in the field of information and communication, in tourism, in the metalworking industry, or in the electrical industry, are open to young women in name only.

The Need for Women in Science and Academia

Even after a careful search we find very few women in Germany who are in a position to exert prime influence on policies concerning science and academia. During the past twenty-five years, the percentage of women who qualify for professorial positions has risen from 5.2 percent to 13.8 percent. Yet this is not reflected in the actual hiring of women as professors. Despite affirmative action laws, men hold 94.8 percent of the full professorships at German universities. In fact, the percentage of female professors continues to decline.

This fact is even more serious when we consider that the equality of women in science and scholarship will be one of the prerequisites for breaking down obsolete structures and ways of thinking. The qualifications and creative potentials women can contribute will be indispensable in achieving a climate of innovation.

To enable women equal participation in research and development projects aimed at bringing about resource-friendly products and their production, universities must be granted latitude to develop affirmative action policies, which will succeed only if supported by the proper legal framework. The qualification and personnel systems at universities must be restructured so that more women are hired. This can be done best if universities use affirmative action guidelines in all evaluation procedures. This also applies to subject-specific and interdisciplinary research on women and gender relations. Additionally, we need a system of incentives and sanctions to implement affirmative action measures for women that can be used to influence university-wide and department-specific funding.

Business Startups by Women

In Germany currently 880,000 women own businesses. A woman heads one out of every four companies, and one out of three was founded by a woman. Self-employment is an opportunity that women have long seized. By the year 2010 the number of self-employed persons is expected to double. It is all the more important that women participate in this wave of business startups on an equal footing. Whether in Germany, elsewhere in Europe, or in North America, women tend to undergo the same experience. Banks do not take them seriously, and they have trouble raising the necessary startup capital. Although Germany has numerous state government programs offering loans under favorable conditions, a business startup campaign for women is nonetheless needed to balance out the disadvantages that exist with regard to startup capital, equity capital, and venture capital.

Fair Distribution of Paid and Unpaid Work

The redistribution of gainful employment is an important aspect of family friendliness. In Germany we have widely varying worktime structures—some people work very long hours and others very short hours. Equal distribution of worktime between genders is difficult to achieve. Men do not have time to do housework and take care of children, whereas women tend to operate on the fringes of the job market. For this reason we support flexible worktime options on the basis of weekly, monthly, annual, and working lifetime accounts. This addresses individual needs and makes it easier to coordinate family and work. At the same time, this proposal permits redistribution of employment between insiders and outsiders.

For example, BMW (one of Germany's major automobile manufacturers) saved jobs and created some 7,000 new jobs by introducing a four-day workweek. Although flexible hours reduce individual workers' incomes, our objective is to create jobs that provide social security for as many people as possible. In turn, this will increase the overall income and prosperity of our families.

Many major companies have developed new worktime systems to help employees balance job and family demands. Hertie, a large German department store chain sponsors management training courses and information campaigns promoting "active fatherhood." A number of companies favor making "family friendliness" an assessment criterion for management personnel. This is not only to support women and families; smart managers know that anyone who does not take his or her family's needs seriously can not be trusted with leading company employees.

We hope employers everywhere will soon be looking for managers who are professionals both at work and at home. The family-friendly index developed in the United States is an excellent example for Germany to follow. It should not be implemented in isolated instances intended only to promote corporate image, but rather out of conviction and on a regular basis. It would be prudent to establish a thirty-hour workweek for women and men. Although many people would have a considerably shortened workweek, many unemployed people would find new employment opportunities, and many women would enjoy equal employment opportunities. German employers resist the idea of reducing the workweek to thirty hours, but a standstill on labor policy will not get us anywhere in the long run.

Professionalization of Household Services

Germany has debated for years about how to structure programs that are friendly to women and families. These programs primarily involve childcare and household-related services that help relieve the heavy burden women bear when they choose to work and have a family at the same time. But there are also elderly people who need help in their everyday lives—with their shopping, when going to see the doctor, or in cleaning their homes.

Some three million women who work in private households for low wages (less than 610 marks a month) provide relief. Newspapers run ads for household assistants reading "Wanted, a jewel for our household." However, when it comes to unemployment, sickness, and old age, these "jewels" usually come up empty handed. For this reason we Social Democrats want these household assistants to be employed by service agencies who give them social security coverage as well as sufficient pay, and we want private households to buy the services they need from the agencies.

Government subsidies are needed so that the households in question will be able to afford assistants. Service agencies would have to charge 25 marks an hour to be able to provide social security for their employees. This is too expensive for the average household, so we propose a subsidy of 10 marks for each hour worked. This amount would be offset by hiring unemployed people with few skills to work in the service agencies, where they could acquire more skills. This program makes sense because support for the unemployed would cost the government even more money.

Prospects

The social consequence of these measures will be the equal distribution of employment, pay, education, time, and power between women and men. With these democratic reforms, women can gain from the advantages of globalization. The trend toward a service-based society (trade, transport, communications, banking, insurance, personal services), the trend toward an information and knowledge-based society, and the trend toward a highly skilled society (organization, management research, development, training and consultancy) can be used to address affirmative action issues for women and equal opportunity issues for women and men. If and when women with high-level skills enter the "mainstream" of economic and social life, then the chances are good that there will not be a backlash against the opportunities globalization offers.

"Gender democracy" is a challenge and a change of perspective that is long overdue as we enter the twenty-first century. Men and women will require a new sense of solidarity because they will have to pursue gender democracy jointly. The earlier and more methodically this strategy is pursued, the sooner women will be protected from the globalization trap.

Thinking globally and acting locally will demand a certain amount of reorientation, not only for our society, but for all societies. We need a perspective on progress that will bring us together. In the future it will be important for women and men to insist on or to defend their fundamental democratic rights in the context of the global developmental process. All nongovernmental organizations must promote this process, so that stereotypical, traditional thinking will not be reinforced but rather broken down. It is time to terminate an unwritten social contract that lists the social inequality of women and men as a basic element. We need a social contract that will strengthen solidarity between women and men. In working life, in social relations, in social affairs, and in government, both women and men's experiences must be included in all decision-making processes equally. Only when we have both social equality and gender equality can every woman and every man share in shaping the future.

Part III

LABOR-MARKET POLICIES AND GLOBALIZATION

6. Industrial Relations in an International Economy

Wolfgang Streeck

The question of economic internationalization's impact on relations between employees and employers not only touches on a barely manageable assortment of individual issues, it is also an eminently political question. It concerns the future no less than the present, and practical possibilities as much as observed facts—the interpretation of which all too easily reflects wishful thinking. Real opportunities to legitimize fundamental interests and fulfill distributive demands depend on how the question is answered. The question affects more than the role of trade unions. It touches equally (and simultaneously) on the future of twentieth-century politics' most decisive organizational form, the nation-state—in which all existing systems of industrial relations are firmly embedded.

The Social Democratic trade union, "leftist" (in the broadest possible sense) discussion about the consequences of internationalization is taking place in the face of a radical challenge from a newly emboldened camp of market-economy advocates in scholarship, economics, and politics. This camp portrays globalization of the economy as a dramatic watershed and demands an equally dramatic liberation of the market from political and institutional regulation. Now, liberal demands for reinstating the market are anything but new; to many this raises the suspicion that economic internationalization is only being put forward as a new justification for the

Reprinted with the permission of the author from "Globalisierung der Wirtschaft, Standortwettbewerb und Mitbestimmung," a publication by the Friedrich-Ebert-Stiftung, Bonn.

pursuit of old interests or that internationalization itself is either exaggerated or a complete invention.

Equally far from novel is the assertion that free markets are not only the most efficient means of allocation, but also (*eo ipso*) the most socially fair such mechanisms, which is why deregulation would prove useful to everyone, including those who are supposedly protected under regulation. What is new, however, is how the liberal camp today regards what it has always seen as the inefficiency of regulatory interventions in the market as of a national character. Supposedly, political intervention in the marketplace leads to substandard factor allocations (growth losses and a decline in the international competitiveness of firms producing nationally), as well as to social injustice (high permanent unemployment figures and growing inequality between the employed and unemployed). Political intervention encounters national limits, whereas economic forces act increasingly internationally and can thus, in a sense, disappear from the national economy (at times, to its detriment).

As far as I can see, the neoliberal view about the consequences of economic internationalization has elicited two basic Social Democratic trade union responses, one pessimistic and one optimistic, each provable in its own right.[1] The pessimistic response, which is strategically barren, resembles neoliberalism in the way it diagnoses a growing disjuncture between the tendency of markets to expand globally and the national nature of political institutions. Neoliberalism, in response, maintains that the capitalist economy should withdraw—irreversibly—from the social and political controls it withstood for the decades following World War II. However, the pessimistic argument holds that this has already happened.

Accordingly, there has been increasing commercialization, commodification, and economization of spheres of life previously spared market influence. This leads to pressure on those social welfare standards ("social welfare civil rights") that previously secured living conditions higher than what would have been allotted to the broad masses by the market. These standards would have to collapse under

1. A third reaction, especially widespread in some traditional circles of the former "left wing," consists of declaring the new relations to be the demagogic-ideological mystification of "the Henkels and Lambsdorffs," thereby denying them their reality. This misinterpretation is promoted by the manner in which the aforementioned present "globalization" as a kind of dictatorial superperson concerned with pushing through little projects like cutting sickness pay down to 80 percent. Of course, this can merely explain—though by no means excuse—leftist tendencies to deny reality, which incidentally display some interesting points in common with the Social Democratic "Keep it up!" attitude toward modernization.

the strain of increased competition, as would the institutions and organizations—especially wage bargaining and trade unions—that previously pushed such standards through in opposition to the market. The ultimate consequence of the internationalized economy's reinstallation of what Karl Polanyi called the "market's Satanic mills" is what has been designated by the catchword "social dumping": the competitive deregulation of national political-economic regimes resulting in a general loss of social security, a sinking living standard for a growing number of people, a decline in social cohesion, increasing inequality, and the like.

By contrast, the optimistic Social Democratic response to the challenge of internationalization—which, so far as I can see, is becoming increasingly the majority position—looks for company in what is sometimes termed the "liberal" or "OECD consensus." This is the broadly shared conviction that the internationalization of product and factor markets is not only unstoppable but should also be actively promoted for the benefit of all. Protectionism is rejected as simultaneously stupid and unethical (it's not possible; and even if it were possible, it would do more harm than good—and even if it did some good, it would harm the weaker among us).[2] Doubts about the compatibility of trade and social welfare are countered by reference to the interwar period, in which economic nationalism is said to have led to the world economic crisis and ultimately to World War II; or by reference to the fact that these doubts are shared by populist-nationalist movements like LePen's or Buchanan's. This way, the democratic-internationalist tradition of social democracy helps ensure that it can latch on to economic liberalism.[3]

Where the social-liberal position differs from the neoliberal one—and what constitutes its special character—is its completely different estimation of national policy's role. At the center of Social Democratic globalization optimism lies the suspicion that national

2. Even those who are expecting "social dumping" as a consequence of internationalization do not, as a rule, have a protectionist alternative to free trade. That something can lack an alternative and yet possibly prove fateful is admittedly a premise with hardly any programmatic political prospects even if it is true. The art of programmatic politics consists not least of all in being able to persuade others that what cannot be changed is also desirable.

3. The interwar period and fascism also play an important role in the world image of the pessimists. For them, the fragility of liberal democracy and international stability in the 1930s is largely explained by the way that nationalists at the time, in an already largely internationalized economy, could not satisfy their citizens' demands for securing minimal social welfare standards and so fell into the hands of radical, demagogic movements offering nationalistic, internationally aggressive pseudo-solutions.

economic policy intervention in an internationalized economy can heighten the competitiveness of the home economy, both by means of an industrial policy that creates infrastructure as well as through a social policy aimed at securing social balance ("social peace as a factor of production"). Competitive deregulation becomes improbable in light of economic superiority postulated for national systems that can provide companies producing on their territory with an efficient infrastructure and a satisfied and therefore cooperative workforce. Both require political intervention—ranging from policies on research and technology, through labor-market and social-security policies, all the way to guaranteeing effective opportunities for participation at the workplace. Instead of compelling social dumping and a Thatcherite disengagement of politics from economics, the new competitive conditions put a premium on a modernizing economic and social policy as it might best be pursued by—needless to say, undogmatic—social democrats. By the same token, the new competitive conditions require systems of industrial relations in which strong trade unions and works councils provide for an effective balance of interests (a balance also accepted as fair by employees).

Nonetheless, the expectation does not always hold that international competition will strengthen, rather than impair, the role of national policy, including national social welfare policy. On the one hand, Social Democratic optimism about modernization proceeds from this assumption: it is healthy to fashion working and living conditions in a socially responsible way, and a relevant policy of economic competitiveness for the nation-state is therefore not only politically possible, but also economically necessary. On the other hand, one simultaneously insists that in an internationalized economy it is not nation-states but businesses alone that compete with each other. What characteristically remains open is the question of whether this is intended as an empirical description or a normative goal. This open question is therefore anything but meaningless because both neoliberals and social dumping pessimists imply that separating economic and system competition has become impossible given increased international mobility among factors of production. (Although the former see the impossibility of separating the two kinds of competition as the most important vehicle for the deregulation they desire, while to the latter the same assertion represents an unavoidable consequence of how social-welfare institutions are lagging behind market expansion, a lag ultimately attributable to the general decline in social-welfare standards they fear.)

In the worldview of the Social Democratic modernizers, the mechanism that prevents (or is meant to prevent) intrastate system competition—and to prevent the undermining of national policy capacities—is international cooperation. Here, too, there are conspicuous differences with the two other positions. Those expecting a dismantling of the welfare state as a consequence of economic internationalization do not believe that cooperation between persistently sovereign individual states is capable of excluding institutional system competition and a race to the bottom. In their analysis of international politics, therefore, they emphasize the lack of supranational integration and an associated permanent fragmentation of political sovereignty vis-à-vis an increasingly integrated economy.

The neoliberals share this assessment in principle, but they welcome its implied connection because for them supranational integration amounts to a restoration of a governmental regulatory monopoly leading inevitably (and anew) to market distortions. Supranational state formation is therefore rejected by them in the name of the healthy competition of national institutions and policies in the international marketplace, and (whenever this helps their case) in the name of defending cultural diversity, national traditions, and political democracy, as well as on behalf of such values as decentralization, subsidiarity, and debureaucratization. Cooperation and coordination between independent nation-states is envisioned as a superior alternative, especially when the possible results of such cooperation can be pinned down institutionally to an additional, mutually operated opening of international markets.

The Social Democratic modernizer's position more or less explicitly recognizes the impossibility of supranational state formation (not least of all owing to liberal-conservative resistance) and, as a result, cautiously appropriates the liberal values of national diversity and political decentralization (as of free trade). At the same time, however—in case (for some reason, and in spite of its fundamental economic functionality) the internationalist welfare state should still come under international deregulatory pressure—the Social Democratic modernization strategy promises itself and others that it will defend the interventionist welfare state at the national level. That defense is to be undertaken with the assistance of the very cooperation between sovereign nation-states that the social dumping pessimists regard as an inappropriate technique for preventing system competition (and which the neoliberals have even selected as the vehicle for market expansion and deregulation). To say it squarely, what is supposed to happen in the neo-social-democratic world view of international cooperation, as an alternative to simultaneous protectionism, supranational integration, and deregulation, is that the national interventionist state would be secured. This would be accomplished by having the participating states renounce system competition and put themselves in a position where their respective home economies could use national social-welfare and industrial policies to create international competitive advantages at a high level of social welfare.

In the following, I will associate myself with neither the social dumping thesis nor with Social Democratic modernization optimism (the latter not at all). Many of the familiar notions of the leftist internationalization pessimists underestimate the inertia of political institutions and therefore the length and complexity of the corrosive process we should expect. They especially disregard the important fact that this process, owing to different institutional conditions, runs differently from case to case, so that it does not necessarily lead to international convergence. The optimistic Social Democratic position, by contrast, suffers (1) from playing down the political range of those changes that have already happened in the world economic environment surrounding national policy (partly for the sake of its ability to link up with the liberal consensus and partly so as not to exclude itself from the only kind of action that seems possible); (2) from overestimating the indispensability of an intact social infrastructure for the profitability of "shareholder value" capitalism; (3) from vastly overestimating the possibilities of international cooperation to prevent political and social system competition, especially given how the Social Democratic optimists places their own hopes in a politics of enhancing national competitiveness; and (4) from generally and fundamentally underestimating the revolutionary effects of system competition, already well underway, on the relationship between the economy and politics established in the postwar period.

Economic Internationalization and National Politics

I shall begin with a few short theses laying out the relationship between economic internationalization and national political institutions. Then I shall move on to the effect of internationalization on industrial relations, first at the national and finally at the supranational level.

The neoliberals who are pushing for deregulation, just like those on the left who fear for the future of regulated capitalism, have occasionally let themselves be persuaded to describe the internationalization of the economy as a recently occurring and radical epochal rupture. Among various voices of reason, but also among those who insist that absolutely nothing has really changed, this has opened up a discursive niche for objections against the so-called globalization thesis, which they quite properly deem a catastrophe theory.

1. Thus, there can indeed be no doubt that trade and finance were already highly internationalized in the nineteenth century and in some phases during the interwar period, and that corresponding quantitative indicators from today (at least, at first glance) do not appear dramatically higher than they were back then.

2. Unquestionably, it is just as true that the internationalization of the economy does not start primarily developing as globalization, but rather as regionalization within the three world regions of America, Asia, and Western Europe. This can be picked up from the data showing that trade and foreign investment still, for the most part, take place between developed countries or within their three regional blocs. For Germany this means (among other things) that cheap wage competition from the former Eastern Bloc or East Asian countries (so far) plays a negligible quantitative role.

3. Furthermore, the internationalization of the economy (however this is understood) has, at least so far, not led to an international balance among levels of social-welfare expenditure or among the social-security and industrial-relations system structures. There are also almost no indications that this will be the case anytime soon.

4. It is equally incontestable that success in world trade did not necessarily depend (at least in the past) on a low level of social security. On the contrary, for a long time the most successful countries on the world market (apart from Japan) guaranteed very high social welfare services (Germany, Sweden), while notorious permanent losers in international competition, like Great Britain and especially the United States, had only medium-level or even very low-level social-welfare burdens to carry.

5. It is equally empirically demonstrable that labor costs are not the only decisive factor when multinational enterprises select a

business location. The local infrastructure and the kinds of productivity gains it facilitates seem to be just as important, as is the need to use production close to the final point of sale as a way of reacting to customers' changing requirements or of avoiding trade barriers.

6. Finally, it can be convincingly demonstrated that even the most deregulated markets require rules in order to function. This means that the liberation of markets from previously restrictive rules is typically accompanied by a renewed regulated production, so that liberalization of the world economy, in a certain sense, actually coincides with growth in regulatory activity—witness the World Trade Organization or the European Union.

To conclude from all this that everything has basically remained the same, however, would be a mistake. The economic and social capacity of national politics to act depends on power relations between social groups as well as on the extent to which these groups count on governmental services (whether social welfare, technological, or some other kind) to pursue their interests. Both these things have to change before the mobility of productive factors across borders can increase asymmetrically. To the extent that there are growing opportunities for capital to exit from national contexts it finds unfavorable, there are declining opportunities for (much less mobile) labor to force conditions on capital for the sake of its profits and society's cooperation. (As with labor, so are there diminishing opportunities for corporatist and governmental institutions constituted on a national basis.) This changes the political terms of trade within each one of the participating national systems, even when the final result is not a migration of capital abroad. The latter would be the result of employee organizations and governments realistically recognizing the altered power relations (numerically expressed in the secular rise of returns to capital and the lag in real wages) and then reacting to these with preemptive concessions.

There are structural as well as institutional reasons for the fact that the potential international mobility of capital has risen considerably over the last two decades. These include an acceleration and accumulation of gradual developments that have slowly been taking effect for some time, as well as political events or technological breakthroughs that ratified and accelerated the gradual change preceding them. Something appearing to be even more important than the (growing) competition on increasingly internationalized commodity markets is the internationalization of the capital market, of production systems based on a division of labor, and of the companies that have been allowed and forced into being by (among other things) the digitalization of production and information systems. Here, especially progress in logistics and communications technology has made possible an (until recently unimaginable) international expansion and coordination of investments, production sites, and contracts, whose obvious economic advantages have forced nation-states to open their borders more than ever before to flows of capital, contracts, and trade.

One may doubt whether these nation-states had any choice in the matter, if only because the dissolution of Bretton Woods was the last point at which the postwar possibility disappeared for pursuing economic policy in an internationalized economy as a matter of national policy. At the heart of the order conceived at Bretton Woods stood an organization for the international monetary and fiscal system that had given participating nation-states, under the hegemonic leadership of the United States, a high degree of mutually reinforcing capacity for action to guide their economies. The nation-states were assigned the task of securing the conditions for maintaining (within their respective countries) what was later designated the postwar compromise between capital and labor. The major objective of this social contract was a political full-employment guarantee. The policy machinery available to nation-states for keeping this promise consisted above all in an anticyclical Keynesian economic policy at home and was embedded abroad in a cooperative free trade and currency regime guaranteed by the United States, as the strongest political and economic power (a system aptly characterized by John Ruggie as "embedded liberalism").

The postwar system of internationally coordinated national full-employment policies was aimed at enabling nation-states (for the sake of their own domestic social cohesion and political stability) to exempt a minimum level of social equality and material provision—in other words, of social welfare rights—from national and international economic competition. This way the market economy, free trade, democracy, and the welfare state were made compatible for the first time, and (social-) democratic politics was in a position where it could protect voters from the vicissitudes of the world market. This was something that the interwar period's extremists had demagogically promised, and which liberals today once more declare to be either unnecessary or too costly.

With the disintegration of the Bretton Woods institutions, however, the benevolent international environment that national Keynesianism needed to render more good than harm also declined. Today, much of what happens within the borders of a single country depends directly on events taking place outside the country and is not guided by domestic policy measures. In place of internationally flanking for a national full-employment and social-welfare policy, we find a previously unattained degree of international interdependence. This subjects national institutions and policies to international competition in a manner unimaginable just a few years back.

It is no longer possible to undo the obsolescence of those national borders restored from time to time in the course of the postwar nation-state's home and foreign-policy domestication, or to undo the heightened mobility (economic, technological, and institutional) of capital. Relations that until recently could be treated more or less as static have become dynamic and contingent. Today, not only demand but also supply can migrate from one national context to another. The nation-state and the employees it represents electorally can count upon "their" capital—on their investments, places of manufacture, and factory orders—less so than ever. Instead, they must actively solicit these. Some of the consequences for national politics are already noticeable to a great extent; they amount to a development that can be summarized in slogan-like fashion as the transformation of the postwar welfare state into a competition state.

(1) Along with the growing mobility of capital, there has been a loss in the capacity of national policy to impose social obligations on companies and investors if these have not already been undertaken. What replaces obligations are incentives, such as for the continued use of production centers suitable for motivating cooperative behavior out of self-interest. This shifts the emphasis of state policy away from the exercise of sovereign power in the name of a democratic popular will and toward the service-like creation of favorable conditions for entrepreneurial conduct, conditions that have to be more attractive than what other states are offering.

(2) As a result of intrastate competition for the favor of internationally mobile investors, the taxability of capital is declining. The visible expression of this trend may be observed in all countries' efforts to lift financial burdens from companies and employers by reforming taxes and social-welfare contributions. The result is that public expenditures for infrastructure and social-security increasingly have to be financed solely by consumers and employees, while

capital, which is consistently improving its vagabond life, is increasingly released from its duties to social solidarity.

(3) Social-welfare policy increasingly has to justify itself by the contribution it makes to national competitiveness. Insofar as one of its goals consists of reducing the difference between winners and losers in the market, social policy has to demonstrate that this heightens (or at least does not inhibit) productivity. Beyond that, it is not possible to defend continuing the welfare state (or cutting it back only gradually) by reference to social conflicts one might otherwise expect, conflicts that would be equally damaging to national competitiveness. When there is conflict, the anticipated losses in productivity and production would have to be greater than the cost relief coming from cutbacks. In addition, when conflict does get more intense, it is becoming increasingly acceptable to shift the cost for business to a different national context.

(4) The state itself—its efficiency and effectiveness—is also becoming a competitive factor. States that are embedded in an international market economy are under pressure to become lean—so that, among other reasons, they can rescind taxation of capital on their territory. An important consequence is that the state apparatus becomes less and less disposed to be a site for employment that is socially regulated, sealed off from the market, and therefore secure. This is especially true for those who are going to be dismissed into the private sector as a result of competition and forced rationalization; afterwards, they are no longer at the disposal of the state as instruments of a hidden social-welfare policy. This means growing burdens that actual social-welfare policy must shoulder, just when the resources that could be mobilized for this purpose are declining.

(5) The same effect emerges from the way international competitive pressure on government policy compels nation-states to reduce budgetary deficits, draw down debt, and make fighting inflation a higher priority than reducing unemployment. The criteria laid down in the Maastricht Treaty for participating in the European Currency Union ratify this development; it is therefore no accident that the Treaty does not forbid states to try reaching austerity goals at the cost of the employment level. Governments of nation-states whose economies are integrated into an international economy have essentially two constituencies, their electorate and the markets. The latter vote daily and in a publicly effective way about whether the economic and fiscal policy of a country deserves confidence. This question is always answered in the negative when

even the mere suspicion arises that a government might tolerate an expansion of the public budget or inflation on behalf of goals like full employment and social justice. Insofar as the policy of sound money dictated by international capital markets costs employment, the burdens shouldered by national social-security systems increase just at the time (and for the same reasons) that the means at the disposal of these systems are diminishing.

(6) The most important means states have when they compete for capital is the buildup of an infrastructure that enhances productivity. This applies especially to countries whose governments strive for a high and balanced level of wages and incomes and who do not want to give up on regulating economic activity on their territory in a socially and economically acceptable way. To the extent that these kinds of political goals scare off investors, they need to be balanced by a national infrastructure that can attract investments by lowering unit costs. In developing such an infrastructure, nation-states have considerable political leeway, something that can be quite properly invoked as an argument against those who assert that economic internationalization spells the end of national politics.

At the very least, however, one needs to take into account how internationally mobile investors can play one country off against another, thereby lowering their contributions to building and maintaining any single country's infrastructure. As a result, not only the costs of social security, but also those of national infrastructure policy must increasingly be carried by employees, who are less mobile and have a stronger interest than investors in seeing investments happen in their country rather another one. In light of the general pressure on public finances, this leads to increasing competition for the same resources between productivity measures and social security, further narrowing the leeway governments have for social policy.

(7) International cooperation between competition states primarily serves the simultaneous and mutual dismantling of national market borders that could prevent integrating a country into new market connections and production systems allowing for prosperity. Cooperation going beyond "negative integration" is, however, improbable. There is a special limit to the kind of "positive integration" that would neutralize the potential competitive advantages of certain countries and thereby turn potential competitive advantages into real ones. This kind of integration is bound to remain limited in scope so long as nation-states prevent their own incorporation into a supranational state. This ties national policy to a new type of multilevel policy in which the supranational level

essentially sets up markets that nation-state-level policy must then accommodate competitively.

(8) From the perspective of the nation-states tied to an international system of market-opening multilevel policy, liberalization of their national economies is the logical answer to economic internationalization. Politically, liberalization relieves the nation-state of burdensome assignments—especially the political guarantee of full employment—which, following the decline of the international postwar order underpinning it, the nation-state has proven unable to safeguard. To the extent that internationally concerted liberalization may be portrayed as a strategy to secure or restore national competitiveness, it can even help renew the legitimacy of the nation-state that has been damaged by economic internationalization. In the meantime, governments in all the Western democracies have learned to portray their own tendency to abdicate in favor of the market as the only promising economic policy that remains in the national interest—witness the impending common abdication of monetary policy to a European Central Bank committed only to monetary stability and international financial markets. The more that the state's capabilities for action to accompany privatization and the opening of markets exist only on paper, and the less that defending this capacity seems to remain a precondition for social stability, the easier it is to get over the loss of these capabilities. Overall (under conditions of market-opening multilevel policy) the highest priority of economic and social-welfare policy for national competition states must be making sure that each national economy is made fit to compete internationally for markets, commissions, investments, and the general confidence of market forces. Fundamentally, all policies and institutional structures have to meet the test of whether or not they contribute to this goal.

The tendency to transform the welfare state into a competition state is no less real just because it is being achieved step by step. And nothing is changed by arguments like the one that the employment level in most developed countries would tend to be even lower without internationalization, that foreign direct investments frequently serve to capture markets rather than to cut costs, or that different societies (such as Great Britain and Sweden) can and did select different paths of transformation. Arguments like these do not alter how the internationalization of advanced capitalism's onetime national economies has so fundamentally transformed the capacities of nation-states to act that one may speak of a gestalt switch in national politics. Ultimately, its origin lies in a transformed micropolitics of national institutions in international markets, shaped by asymmetrically distributed exit opportunities for the major factors of production. These increasingly determine which adjustments have to be performed by national and which by international politics, as well as which goals can or cannot be pursued within the framework of the possible.

Social dumping is an unfortunate concept because it aims above all at short-term changes in the investment behavior of businesses. Much more important for the future of the welfare state, however, are the long-term changes in politics that have been accepted in order to avoid such changes in investment behavior. The permanent pressure exerted by growing capital mobility and high unemployment produce lasting changes in the quality of political compromises and decisions because of the way that pressure works step by step over the long run. To change or reconstitute the postwar welfare state into a competition state, it is completely unnecessary for 80 percent of German investment to leave for Portugal or the Czech Republic tomorrow; it suffices for current policy to be confronted with how investments abroad are growing faster than domestic ones, while foreign investments at home either stagnate or recede. Social systems change from the margins.

Social democratic hopes—to control international capitalism at the end of the twentieth-century cooperation, which had socially been done successfully for certain aspects of and at certain times in postwar national capitalism's history—are aspirations worthy of every honor. But the difficulties are widely underestimated—perhaps because neither the national basis for social solidarity nor its necessary embeddedness in an international hegemonic regime was particularly conscious of, or sympathetic to, the Social Democrats. Today especially, "actually existing" international cooperation amounts to a set of alliances for liberalization of the type represented by projects of the European internal market and currency union. And the market value of the kind of social peace created by Social Democrats has taken a sharp dive. That does not mean that companies would not always prefer, in principle, to have the concessions they have been urging be irrevocably preserved as a product of voluntary insight, surrendered without a fight. But the tax on capital yields still considered acceptable for the sake of financing a social balance has become noticeably smaller. As Olaf Henkel (head of Germany's major industrial association) has never tired of emphasizing, no one today is striking in England or America, countries where there is no codetermination and (almost) no welfare state. Businesses, too, are slowly getting accustomed to the new circumstances, especially since the remnants of the old system (whose costs have already been as good as written off) still yield some profit. A renewal of this system, however, would have to go against the trend, and the means whereby this could happen are not yet recognizable.

From my perspective, I would like to outline the most important developmental tendencies to which the national systems of industrial relations are subject, both inside the national competition states now forming and in their new international context. I am assuming that these new political and economic conditions, which have taken effect everywhere to the same extent, nonetheless touch upon nationally embedded collective labor relations in ways that vary from country to country. For obvious reasons, my remarks will refer especially to rich countries like Germany, where the issue is defending (under changed conditions) high social-welfare standards, a relatively balanced wage and income level, an extended welfare state, strong trade unions, and a tradition of state guarantees for corporatist self-regulation.

Industrial Relations in the National Competition State

Intensified competition in almost all markets and capital's increasing opportunities to extricate itself from overly demanding national systems of regulation are the most important factors determining industrial relations at the national level today. The result is not necessarily de-unionization and individualization, the goal Margaret Thatcher envisioned in Great Britain; even there, things have not quite reached this point (yet). A variety of developments and reactions are imaginable, but they are all dictated by growing competition among nationally constituted societies for investment capital and jobs.

(1) Basically, companies' increased ability to extricate themselves from any national regulatory framework curtails the latter's ability to make commitments. To the extent that companies can migrate away from regimes that threaten to burden them with unacceptable commitments—whereby out-migration in the broadest sense also includes short-term shifts in the site of production—states and trade unions tend to be satisfied with voluntary agreements as a substitute for the imposition and implementation of binding rules. These might also consist of getting already existing obligatory rules to be modified informally, or of no longer insisting on enforcing them.

As a consequence, originally obligatory systems of rules transform themselves into voluntaristic ones, in part underhandedly. Because voluntaristic systems of industrial relations cannot extend the internal rules they developed equally to all companies participating in the market—which would result in removing these rules from competition altogether—it is in the nature of voluntaristic systems to show more regard for the competitive interests and needs of individual companies. This can be portrayed as progress in the direction of greater flexibility and competitiveness, or it can be depicted as a contribution to denationalization and debureaucratization. What causes this, however, is the way companies that have become more mobile can increasingly withdraw from being subject to rules that do not suit them.

(2) Voluntaristic systems of industrial relations lead to less uniform results than obligatory ones because they leave more room for the free decisions of the participants and permit stronger agreement on regulations for special conditions in individual cases. In these systems, as a result, the relative situation of the participants is determined less by institutions and more by the market. To the extent that industrial systems of rules lose the capacity to create obligations and to standardize, their capacity for redistribution is also diminished. This necessarily leads to a heightened polarization of working conditions across sectors, companies, and labor and product markets, and therefore to heightened inequality among employees. The best examples are Great Britain after the abolition of the industry-wide wage and the United States after the end of pattern bargaining.

Germany's obligatory system of codetermination has at least attempted to guarantee codetermination as an equal right of industrial citizenship for all employees. By contrast, concepts of participation that are voluntary and peculiar to each business (as is the dominant pattern in the Anglo-Saxon countries and is becoming more popular in Germany) proceed from the assumption that the forms and opportunities for participation available to employees vary widely according to job. The assumption is also that these participatory forms and opportunities are fashioned procompetitively, i.e., that they can and must be justified by a positive contribution to the company's competitiveness.

(3) Competitive pressure on product markets increasingly leads companies to reject systems of rules deemed particularly unacceptable when they prevent turning the employment relationship into an object of business strategy. More than ever before in the history

of postwar capitalism, the market—which internationalization has extended far beyond the jurisdiction of national regulatory systems—lets the way human labor is used become (again) a source of competitive advantage and disadvantage. In all developed industrial societies during the last decade, therefore, companies have been making an effort to regain control over personnel policy in the broadest sense (including personnel costs) as parameters of strategic company policy. Especially as a result of the "Japan shock," what matters most is finding ways to make the deployment of personnel lean, i.e., more intensive and economical. This typically happens inside companies when decisions on the deployment of labor are delegated as much as possible to decentralized levels responsible for outcomes on their own authority. For these decentralized units, consequently, an incentive emerges to develop situational specific decisions about personnel policy, sharply tailored to the units' special requirements.

Obligatory systems of social regulation that take no account of special conditions in the individual profit centers of flexibly reorganized businesses and business groups pose obstacles, and so provide an opening to the demand for flexibility. Faced with growing opportunities for capital migration, states and trade unions turning a deaf ear to these demands do so at their peril.

(4) A variegated picture also results from comparing different national paths of development. The spectrum of reactions to the new economizing and individualizing pressures ranges from Thatcherite attempts to smash the unions with the aim of restoring managerial rights to the formation of national and firm-level coalitions for competition and modernization encompassing trade unions. Sometimes both approaches are pursued alongside each other within the same society, perhaps in different branches or companies.

And even where change does take place with union participation, it always amounts to decentralization of industrial relations and to their liberalization, in the sense of greater emphasis on voluntary (in place of obligatory) solutions, as well as of greater leeway for the individual enterprise. These make industrial relations more destandardized and, compared to the past, more strongly shaped by situationally specific competitive pressures. Society-wide social contracts are increasingly dissolved in favor of firm-level agreements, and the public or quasi-public regulation of employment relations tends to be replaced by a private one. The principle underlying institution building in industrial relations thereby becomes less and less one of implementing industrial citizenship rights throughout society, and more and more a principle of minimizing transaction costs.

(5) In any event, industrial relations in the competition state fall under the shadow of high unemployment. The nation-state robbed of its Keynesian leverage is no longer in a position to support trade union interest representation through full employment by the state. High permanent unemployment together with simultaneous flexibilization and decentralization of industrial relations can lead to trade unions becoming representatives solely of those who are employed. Their interests in employment security are not always easily reconciled with the interests of the unemployed, who want to gain access to employment. At the same time, firm-level union organizations run the danger of becoming socially acceptable comanagers of downsizing. Attempts to escape these problems through a policy of labor redistribution are limited by cost barriers, both among companies and social insurance carriers. In addition, they run into difficulty to the extent that companies that have become more mobile find it easier than ever before to leave regimes that commit them to shoulder burdens of solidarity and that, for example, seek to force them to cope with the difficulties of organizing an uninterrupted flow of production when per capita labor time is going down.

(6) Some of the new business strategies are human capital-oriented, in the sense that their pursuit requires a high level of skill, motivation, and integration for the labor force. For traditionally cooperative trade unions like the German ones—but increasingly, too, among traditionally conflictual unions like both the Italian and Anglo-American kinds—this has awakened hopes for a successful defense (or even first-time implementation) of a social-welfare model combining high wages, relatively little social inequality, and social security for all with effective collective opportunities for participation. Resemblance with the hopes of Social Democratic modernization optimists are not accidental. It is assumed

  a. that market strategies for labor and products requiring an expensive cultivation of human capital from companies are, under today's technological and economic conditions, more profitable in the long run than strategies tied to lowering of social-welfare standards, and not just because of transition costs made higher by conflict;

  b. that a human capital-oriented way of doing business requires a measure of consensus and inner involvement on the side of labor power that cannot be had without union representation and institutionalized social security—and, moreover, that this way of doing business relies on a public social-welfare infrastructure that no single company can set up on its own;

c. that companies wanting to make the most for themselves out of the new economic conditions must have a long-term interest in a stable social order in which independent trade unions are accorded an indispensable modernizing role; and

d. that the fulfillment of such a role will allow the trade unions to achieve general social welfare interests, especially the interest in social balance, going beyond what the market would require or affect on its own.

Whether such hopes will be fulfilled only the future can show. The fact remains that there are hardly any well-formulated alternatives to the different varieties of human capital-oriented trade union productivism currently in circulation. Nonetheless, it is possible to register some doubts, based on experience, about whether we might not be expecting too much here. In what follows, I want to depict these doubts.

(7) Even where trade unions participate in firm-level and society-wide coalitions for competition and modernization, they lack extensive opportunities to make the human capital-oriented variants of adjustment to the world market obligatory for the entire society, and therefore lack the ability to generalize the human capital model beyond individual firms or branches. Like the nation-states themselves, nationally active trade unions increasingly need to count on incentives to pursue their goals in an internationalized economy. Less and less can they fall back on social obligations. Especially if they are going to push companies toward pursuing adjustment strategies that are socially acceptable and (where possible) depend on union cooperation, trade unions have to make concessions in advance. (These concessions would have to be in the area of institutional and personnel infrastructure, and with the purpose of making the social balance that unions seek acceptable.) This is what lies behind the protestations (which have lately become stereotypical in all Western countries) that every native workforce makes about how unusually well trained, flexible, and ready to cooperate it is.

A social-welfare infrastructure policy like this has to be distinguished from a social-welfare cohesion policy of the kind pursued by the German and Swedish trade unions in the past, where the aim was to provide everybody in society with skilled work, closing the gap between the market's winners and losers using political means.

This policy also availed itself of the opportunity to exclude low-wage employment (or employment under poor working conditions) in which any collective right to a voice (as guaranteed by generally binding and demanding regulations on the terms of employment) might be lacking. At the same time, companies ready to do business in a manner consistent with a socially regulated capitalism were guaranteed lasting support from trade unions and work councils, including a safeguard for social peace on site.

Today, in light of high permanent unemployment and companies that have become more mobile, regulatory intervention at the national level that once excluded socially unacceptable company strategies—such as maintaining profitability by downsizing or by spreading wage categories widely across skill groups—is becoming harder to achieve. In place of the cooperative disciplining of capital that is characteristic of welfare capitalism in the postwar years, we increasingly find a policy of economic incentives, of which it can only be hoped that they are used as desired.

(8) Human capital-oriented production methods not imposed on companies through obligatory rules or left open to business as its sole option only come about when voluntarily chosen by company management as the most profitable alternative. The result of (what is to this extent) their voluntaristic character is that they show up simultaneously with and alongside alternative entrepreneurial concepts in which human capital plays a smaller role. Where institutional possibilities for generalizing socially desirable production concepts are absent, the danger arises that these will remain isolated (restricted to "islands of excellence"); in this way, they contribute as much to social polarization as to social integration.

In addition, continued use of a human capital-oriented production method lacking institutional support always depends on continuing to appear more competitive and profitable to the employer than the alternative methods. This threatens to make the social situation of the employees and the role of the trade unions depend on each company management's good will or superior insight into its long-term interests (or those of the company)—or even dependent on having the long-term interests of the company or its management take priority over any short-term interests (whether management's or labor's). Moreover, it does not contribute toward more bargaining power for trade unions and works councils, if a cooperative company strategy set on a voluntary footing can be revised at any moment.

(9) In addition, it is by no means certain that human capital-oriented company strategies are possible only with the participation

and support of unions dependent on the company. In all developed capitalist societies today, we find the phenomenon of the highly competitive and socially highly integrated company (typically in new branches like microelectronics) that offers its labor force first-class working conditions (including opportunities for workplace participation) while at the same time strictly avoiding subjecting itself to wage agreements, for the sake of its flexibility. At least some companies of this kind seem to have succeeded at using advanced methods of human resource management to integrate their core employees into a cooperative entrepreneurial culture. This gets the employees to reject union mediation and renders the company broadly immune to union organizing attempts.

Even in countries like Germany, companies today need not necessarily fear being unable to cope with industrial conflict because there is no union, or worry about losing their employees' trust for lack of autonomous union representation. Today, it often seems as if the competitive pressure of world markets and the ever tangible dependence of each workforce on the company's success affect how the employees' consensus and their readiness to perform work—not just mechanically, but with personal involvement—can be manufactured by many companies in-house (so to speak), or even made into a condition of employment; often, it seems as if union mediation is no longer required. To this extent, it must seem dubious to entertain the notion that the heightened consensual requirements of modern production methods offer trade unions an opportunity to exchange their contribution to the company consensus against the power to shape and regulate business and society.

(10) Only on certain conditions is it also possible to rely on companies' interest in profit for human capital-oriented social partnership. Based on the last few decades' experience, there can be no doubt that even the most demanding and socially acceptable production methods can be profitable, and that companies accepting union regulation and social security as part of their way of doing business can be successful. However, as the impressive recoveries experienced by numerous American and British companies in the last few years have shown, this hardly means that company strategies involving less social partnership need be inferior. The capital yields reached by the leading Anglo-American companies are, in any event, not lower than German and Swedish profits; on average they are even higher.

Another consideration speaking in favor of the Anglo-American solution to the profit problem is the way they are less strenuous.

Thus, a company with a personnel policy that dispenses with the distinction between core and marginal staff and that offers comparable conditions to all employees can also probably earn well, even today. But there is also a lot of evidence indicating that the company could do the same with a dualistic personnel policy that would be less expensive technically and less costly economically. Since companies' increased mobility favors their moving production from demanding to less demanding regimes—either by shifting production to another country or by renegotiating flexibilization at the previous production site—in the future one can expect that more and more companies will find life somewhat easier for themselves in countries with demanding regimes.

Although it may be true, it does not help knowing that a cooperative business strategy might tend to secure the long-term interests of a company better than less demanding concepts of production aimed solely at short-term interests. The willingness of a company to renounce short-term in favor of long-term advantage has to do, not least of all, with its rootedness in native ground. Long-term profitable adjustment to local regulatory systems that make it difficult to reap short-term, opportunistic profits is adjustment that only becomes rational when there is no opportunity for exit, or when the transaction costs of repeated entry and exit are too high. In any event, it matters fundamentally more to investors (shareholders) that they get very high returns from numerous successive short-term investments than high returns from a single long-term investment.

There is a great deal of evidence testifying to how the ongoing development of capital markets and the further decline in transaction costs will lead to a global hunt for high short-term profits by investment capital (or, indeed, by investment capital just made newly available). As a consequence, turnover among companies and jobs would increase and, most likely, social stability would decline. The latter, however, would only happen locally, so that investors operating on a global scale could evade the costs by shifting to different locations. It is entirely appropriate to entertain doubts about the macroeconomic rationality of this kind of "hit-and-run" capitalism. However, such doubts cannot prevent the individual investor from maximizing his returns by rapid shifts in his portfolio "for as long as supplies are still available." Moreover, because political and public power is fragmented nationally, the opportunity to draw practical consequences from these kinds of doubts is practically nil.

(11) On the whole, the internationalization of markets makes it impossible for societal actors at the national level to demand that companies make a contribution to society's integration a condition for their own domestic social integration. In this way, the integration of firms and of society as a whole increasingly diverge. Companies can hope to win the consensus and cooperation of their staffs without being called upon to match this by achieving a good society (that is, a society satisfying the claims of the majority for justice and equal liberty). As the examples of the United States and Great Britain demonstrate, even companies with such demanding methods of production can be profitable when the surrounding society is divided, the social-security systems are drying out, and the public infrastructure is crumbling. Private wealth does not require social balance, nor is the latter a necessary consequence of the former; if this were so, the United States would be the most developed welfare state in the world.

The South Side of Chicago has never prevented anyone from investing his or her money in the United States and making a good living there. Even when the American trade unions were quashed, it by no means deterred foreign investors, including those accustomed to German-style social partnership; if anything, this attracted them. Today big international companies command enough resources to establish the internal conditions necessary for the application of progressive production methods on their own; they are less reliant on assistance from politics or the trade unions. American companies, too, can build up a workforce with a high skill level. Admittedly, they do this only when they can be sure the skills they are providing are only useful in-house, and so they do nothing to improve opportunities for employees on the external job market.

By way of summary, it can be said that intensified competition on all world markets has impaired the capability of all nationally delimited systems of industrial relations to standardize job regulation in different branches and firms with an eye toward achieving social equality and solidarity. Above and beyond that, the new migratory options of financial and industrial capital cause incremental change in power relations on the labor market, which is expressed in distributive relations revised to favor capital as well as in diminishing chances for putting general and formal rules into effect. The result is an increasing voluntarism and growing diversity to industrial relations, increasingly negotiated by its immediate participants in accordance with each and every company strategy in the shadow of the market.

This means that industrial relations in developed capitalist societies are becoming not so much deregulated as flexibly re-regulated, with company-specific requirements for higher competitiveness advancing to become the highest (and frequently the only) criterion for making rules. In contrast to this, traditional viewpoints about the defense of rights, the democratization of work, and the prevention of societal divisions move into the background. Taking these into consideration as part of business strategy has less of a chance to become a condition for trade union and societal cooperation with the interests of investors, who may increasingly choose between different national societies and who are no longer dependent on a particular society. This is also fundamentally true for highly developed and highly regulated systems of industrial relations such as Germany's, in which a long tradition of successful social partnership sees to it that change will take place slowly, from the margins inward. Nobody can exclude the possibility that systems like these, especially the German one, can find ways of asserting themselves even under these novel conditions. Yet, it is not clear just now exactly how this could happen.

Supranational Industrial Relations

The prospects are slim for using compensatory institution building at a supranational level to restore the commitment making and redistributive capabilities of national systems subjected to the pressure of extended markets. They are just as slim as the prospects for an incorporation of national systems into a unified, harmonizing supranational system. Insofar as supranational industrial relations are in the process of formation, they reflect the new conditions transforming national systems much more strongly than the traditional structures of national systems.

Just like supranational institutions in the intrastate field, institutions in the realm of labor relations are also overwhelmingly voluntary in nature. Their inability to bind authoritatively makes it largely impossible for them to prevent participating nation-states from entering into regime competition with each other; to this extent, they obey the same logic of multilateral liberalization that broadly determines international politics among states. Corresponding to this, what has been taking shape in supranational labor relations over the last several years has been, in the first instance, organized along company lines and justified above all by its contribution to the competitiveness of the company in question (or, in any event, not justified by how it regulates competition).

(1) On the supranational level, there is simply no state that could make negotiations between the parties to collective bargaining generally binding beyond company limits. Not least of all for this reason, there are virtually no negotiations of this kind. The European Union's weak "nonstate" is especially poorly placed to further the ability of the collective bargaining parties to act and organize on a supranational level in a manner even approaching what (for example) the German legislature can do with its laws on wage bargaining and codetermination. The content and history of, say, the EU directives on European Works Councils demonstrate that the European Union is almost totally incapable of issuing rules for industrial relations that would add anything substantial to what multinational companies are ready to negotiate voluntarily.

The absence of a supranational state with the ability to shape policy means that the organizational assistance trade unions desperately need at the supranational level will fail to materialize. Likewise, effective public pressure on employers to make them capable of reaching collective decisions and to agree to negotiations at a higher level than the individual company will fail. This cannot be attributed to lack of good will on the part of the European Commission, and probably nothing else might have been possible given the national cleavages within European business society, which does nothing to alter the fact that supranational industrial relations in Europe are largely state-free—meaning, above all, decentrally organized and market driven. Even the rudiments of a corporatist regime type available after twenty years of trying are practically meaningless compared to what is available in national welfare states. And previous developments do not give any cause to expect that this might change in the foreseeable future.

(2) This is especially true given how the national systems incapable of protecting the supranational system from mutual competition are subject to steady corrosive pressure forcing them to restructure themselves in ways conforming to market competition. This process—and not the construction of a European corporatism (possibly incorporating national systems, or at least protecting them against each other) that has hardly progressed beyond a rudimentary level over the last two decades—is the determining factor in Europe today. There is much evidence testifying to how this process will move forward quickly enough to make supranational protection of national systems unnecessary, for lack of a critical

mass, and well before this would be even remotely possible politically and institutionally. To this extent, the same dynamic of liberalization is at work in European industrial relations that are shaping multilevel policy between states.

How poorly the emerging European system of industrial relations is positioned to restrain competition between national systems is demonstrated by the example of the European works councils. These are nothing more than an international annex to their respective national systems of interest representation on the job; the latter remain formally untouched by the EU guideline. In substance, this means that national regimes with high and obligatory standards of worker participation remain under pressure emanating from the possibility that production will be moved to a neighboring country where the codetermination rights of the workforce are less well developed. The consequence is that works councils and trade unions in strong regimes increasingly have to avoid taking full advantage of their rights, lest they run the danger of drawing short in the competition for jobs.

In the German case, there is the additional factor that the largely voluntary European works councils are merely anchored in labor law and not in company law. This means that German codetermination on the company level remains permanently deprived of the protections against competition it might offer if extended to Europe generally. Indeed, the promulgation of the guideline on European works councils stimulated thoughts of reviving the European Union's old projects for a European business law. Previously, these had always failed because the kind of worker participation at the company level that Germany pushed for proved unacceptable to employers and most European governments. The new recommendations now point toward staying satisfied with a future European corporation law that makes reference to the European Works Council. In the medium term, this could make the survival of German company-level codetermination depend on its competitiveness in the eyes of the investor, for whom any possible long-term stabilizing effects of company-level codetermination might lose value. As a result, the gradual movement of companies toward a European corporate structure, with or without flexible codetermination, could turn company-level codetermination of German provenance into a remnant system, similar to what became of codetermination for coal, iron, and steel in Germany.

(3) The kind of industrial relations now emerging at the European level is company-based, not branch-based; to this extent, the

European works councils also fit the trend. Within big multinational corporations, too, there will not be any integrated wage negotiations in the near future. But it is imaginable that companies will use the European works councils and their international personnel divisions when informal and voluntary consultations going beyond the minimum required by the EU directive start to replace binding negotiations. In the medium term, this may give rise to framework agreements that would make a particular company's international human capital strategy more legitimate and internally binding.

The unavoidable consequence of this would be a further weakening of the old national industrial relations systems' ability to integrate companies operating on their territory into a regulatory pattern equally binding for all. This would have to make the Europeanization of industrial relations a factor that would further weaken the regulatory and generalizing capabilities of national systems by offering big, trendsetting companies the opportunity to use the Europeanization of their human capital policy as a means to withdraw gradually from national systems. As a result, collective labor relations in Europe on the whole would become more voluntary in that the gradual withdrawal of leading companies from national systems would be a kind of transition of several regimes relatively capable of enforcing norms and obligations to a single regime granting companies broader leeway under the shadow of competition. It therefore seems realistic to assume that the regulatory patterns established in this fashion at the supranational level might break through to a national level still subject to competitive pressure, and the current trend to liberalize industrial relations will be strengthened.

In light of the weaknesses characteristic of international institutions in industrial relations, caution should be exercised against raising hopes for effective international cooperation among unions to restrain system competition. The much more likely alternative to a de-unionization of European national economies (which seems initially less probable on the Continent) is the incorporation of trade unions into national modernizing coalitions with the objective of making production conditions at home more attractive for domestic and foreign investors. International cooperation would then primarily serve to facilitate an external defense for playing off national advantages in infrastructure; by its very nature, this cannot go far.

Correspondingly lax, and also nationally centered, are those international networks that almost all national trade unions use in their attempts to extend their organizational reach beyond their respective countries' borders. In this case, European peak associations and supranational institutions serve above all as infrastructures in which the foremost observation posts for all the different national labor organizations mesh together. European integration is not (at least not now) capable of suspending competition among the national systems; instead of putting the brakes on the procompetitive restructuring of national systems, it tends overall to accelerate this apparent trend. Nationally organized trade unions can, and increasingly do, attempt to offer their services as comanagers for this purpose; how and under what preconditions they can become more than a fifth wheel on the wagon of competitive restructuring remains an open question.

However, even if unions are indispensable (and not just for a transitional phase), the danger always remains that the contribution that union interest representation could make to the realization of social goals (like the prevention of excessive inequality) might decline because national trade union policy in international markets becomes too caught up in the competition imperative. Conceivably, the practical and strategic problems indicated here are not unsolvable, but initially they have to be recognized and described as ruthlessly as possible. Hopes placed in a socially benevolent automatic dynamism for the profit motive—in companies that understand their interests correctly, bank on long-term profits, and thus welcome union influence and social security—are probably misplaced. Equally misplaced is the expectation that the erosion of commitment-making capabilities by national regimes will be balanced, so to speak, by the creation of a decentralized and debureaucratized "citizens society" with a socially responsible entrepreneurial culture to match. Markets surely do not work this way.

7. Globalization—Risks and Opportunities for European Labor Policy

Jürgen Hoffmann and Reiner Hoffmann

Starting Points of Policy

"Re-embedding" As Political Objective

Trade unions are challenged in national labor markets by "disembedding" and globalization; through the increased flexibility of large firms on international labor markets and the high flexibility of capital, companies are taking increasing advantage of exit options relative to national investments and thus are able to evade national regulatory systems and trade union demands. Therefore, the balance built into the continental European political and economic systems between wage labor and capital, and in particular the characteristic "Rhenish capitalism" tied to the welfare state, is coming under massive pressure. Capital's cooperative disciplining is disappearing. Even the threat of relocation can destandardize industrial relations and differentiate them according to the degree of relocation options. Moreover, a wage policy based on solidarity, a regional wage agreement, and a social cohesion policy can be evaded.

First, political starting points must be developed (not just by and for trade unions) that hamper utilization of the exit option or lead

Reprinted with the permission of the authors from the series "Discussion- and Working paper," Nr. 97.04.01 (Brussels, April 1997), a publication of the European Trade Union Institute in Brussels. References for this chapter are on page 135.

the tendency in socially acceptable directions by means of resistance ("voice" option) and demands placed on regulatory systems at the national and European level. Second, such a policy must intervene in the economic and social restructuring process to keep open future activity regarding social infrastructure. Third, a policy of social cohesion must be connected with national and international redistribution, if the result is to be more than internal social division and differentiation and a new form of external social closure at the supranational level.

Europe As Production Site

There is no such thing as a uniform economic area called the European Union, even if the single market long ago became reality or is about to become one. We can distinguish four areas of economic regulation (hereafter referred to as regions), which can be further differentiated in terms of the various national economic structures and regulatory systems:

1. The Northern European region (Finland, Sweden, Denmark), characterized by high labor productivity in industry and successful niche production on the world market. This region is characterized politically by a social democratic welfare state model and is thus distinguished by a high welfare state sector, whose industrial relations (to varying degrees) are part of this statistic regulatory model.

2. The region of "Rhenish capitalism" (Western Germany, the Benelux countries, parts of France, and northern Italy). This region is identifiable by a highly productive, export-oriented, and (previously) successful Fordist production model (high-quality, high-skill, high-wage production), whose regulatory system, especially in Germany, is characterized by corporatist structures, a functional connection of industrial and bank capital, high labor standards, and a high share in the welfare state's social product and social security.

3. The region of the EC's "southern enlargement" (Portugal, Spain, Greece, and, in economic terms, southern Italy), with economies that are still strongly agrarian and have regionally dominant traditional social structures. This region is also characterized by high-productivity islands (individual companies or entire districts centered around large urban centers such as

Barcelona), which function more as subcontractors to the productivist core of Europe.

4. Great Britain and Ireland, where Great Britain in particular is characterized by the separation of industrial and financial capital and the brutal conquest of a mature economy by Thatcherist radical market policies. These policies resulted in a drop in the standard of labor, forced the unions and collective bargaining systems into a corner, and reduced and partially privatized the social-security system and state infrastructure policy (education, science, public health).

Yet the difficulty in treating the Europe of the EU as a single whole stems not only from these differences regarding economic preconditions and forms of regulation at the level of the European regions; it also lies in the fact that the differences within the various national systems themselves, not least of all due to the actors' reactions to globalization processes, are large and becoming larger. A growing eclecticism at the management level is now becoming possible because the systems of industrial regulations are becoming harder to enforce and less capable of harmonization. At the same time, there is a widening gulf between large capital flows, which are geared toward the international market, and small and medium enterprises, which are geared toward the domestic market. To find starting points for policy in this increasingly complex spectrum—without claiming to deal with every aspect—we will outline various aspects of the relationships between globalization processes and European economies, concluding our presentation at the international level of regulation.

The Countries of "Rhenish Capitalism" and Social Democratic Statism under the Pressure of Globalization

On the basis of the above, it is the first and second types of region in the EU that will be bound to endure particular problems with the globalization processes already described—characterized by high labor standards, corporatist associations, and associations of states and cooperative business cultures. In this regard, it is sensible to analyze in greater detail especially those regions characterized by the "threefold formula" of high-quality, high-skill, and high-wage production. Particularly at the political level of the EU and OECD finance ministers, precisely these forms of regulation are held responsible for "Eurosclerosis" and are meant to be changed through deregulation and liberalization. This will happen if it is determined that wage negotiation systems need to be decentralized and made more flexible; minimum wages lowered and deregulated; and the state sector trimmed down, made more flexible, or privatized.

As a result of phenomena associated with economic crises, this political assessment is being given added force in the classical Western and Northern European high-productivity regions and sectors mentioned above. In these regions high-quality production based on the high productivity of a skilled workforce and high wages is coming more clearly under pressure worldwide from competitively priced products. This development is also associated with the trend toward internationally standardized preconditions for production as a result of the impact of modern communications and information technologies. In major sectors like the automotive industry, the focus is no longer on high-quality competition based on ("immobile") system-related knowledge, but on price (and hence cost-related) competition. At the same time, as a result of globalization, the functional and productive relationship that exists between sectors as well as between large, high-productivity, and world market-oriented companies and small and medium-sized enterprises producing for the domestic market—and in some cases as subcontractors for these large companies—is becoming looser and even threatened. This is because companies geared toward the world market can now, based on comparative cost-related advantages, internationally procure inputs and company-specific services based on outsourcing and global sourcing, and thus escape redistribution mechanisms on the domestic market (via wages and prices).

This is why the various bodies of national legislation (especially in Germany) are now coming under pressure. These companies and sectors, which had previously enjoyed an (indirect) share in the large firms' success on world markets, often have very labor-intensive and wage-intensive production and thus bear the largest burden of non-wage costs (which go toward financing social-security systems). At the same time, in the German system it is these very firms that are most involved in the training of skilled workers. And this split between large and small or medium-sized enterprises is promoted by an economic policy that does not support the productive, often regionally fixed ties, but is based on the productivity-related success of the large firms.

In this connection, an innovative regional and structural policy would be a sensible starting point for a policy that does not maintain old structures, but promotes new, post-Taylorist economic structures and immobile factors of production, a policy that raises the regions' capabilities for interlinking and thus makes them economically more attractive, and that also combines this new attractiveness with new social and ecological regulations ("regulation of flexibility"). It is precisely the promotion of post-Taylorist enterprises and regions that could be a starting point, as well as a political objective (a proposition addressed in greater detail below). An urgent accompanying task—and one which would have to integrate economic, social, and ecological responsibilities—would entail the political reform and promotion of basic research, of scientific and educational knowledge, as well as relevant knowledge transfer.

In addition, the systems for levying social-security contributions, in the countries where these are financed through insurance systems focused on earnings-related income, primarily constitute a burden on the cost factor of labor, which results in the costs of this factor increasing with the need to finance growing social problems. At the same time, it is this very factor that declines proportionately as production becomes more capital intensive. For economic reasons—i.e., not only for the social policy reason of preventing discrimination against those who lack, or have not had the opportunity to obtain, gainful employment—there already seems to be an urgent need for a reform of the bases for tax assessment and the medium-term transition to a tax-financed social-security system.

The Regional and Enterprise Strategies of Globalization

The prevailing policy of most national governments in the EU is one of locational competition, which sees the lowering of wage and nonwage costs, profit taxes, and the deregulation of industrial relations as suitable means to achieve more growth, higher employment, and balanced state finances. But such a policy, which leads to an international race to lower costs, not only endangers the future of one's own productive base through cutbacks in spending for material infrastructure and education/ training and a reduction in individuals' security of expectations; it also jeopardizes social cohesion. Yet, paradoxically, this policy makes itself increasingly open to extortion through the politically implemented expansion of companies' exit options. Obviously, such a policy starts from the premise that the capital being courted—and it must be courted—is fully liquid and transitory.

In contrast, we believe that the possibilities for capital to evade national and social constraints through financial investments are not so unlimited as assumed. First of all, the financial sector's returns are naturally linked to real production, thus to the expenditure of labor in the capitalist production process. However, this connection only imposes itself on the participants, including workers, through monetary crises, stock market crashes, and other breakdowns (and thus threatens those who obtain a surplus in production through careful management equally as much as financial jugglers and global players). In addition, productive capital cannot be simply transformed into financial investments; it is fixed to the location. Some German employers, for example, who presently fear for the social consensus in view of strikes and their high costs, obviously value highly the German location (and Europe) with its high productivity; and they might demand cost-reducing reforms and restructuring programs (in social security as well) whose political advisability would be questionable. However, they will not risk any destruction of this highly productive and profitable situation by provoking large-scale social conflict.

At least for the foreseeable future, the high productivity of regional centers in the countries implementing Rhenish capitalism prevents any type of global sourcing from becoming a mass phenomenon and thus leading to waves of dismissals. In developed capitalist economies, a productive type of production today involves more than the wage-cost factor of a skill area; rather it involves the regional networks of small, medium-sized, and large firms; university science centers; the high production knowledge produced in the educational system; a developed infrastructure; a high standard of regulation of labor and of social security; and above all, high social and political stability. These regional locational factors, on which the high productivity in continental Western European countries is still based, can certainly be extended through global sourcing, but they cannot be replaced.

The productive "embedding" of companies in such economic and social networks of the region also prevents us from assuming that capital has unlimited mobility. In fact, conversely, it could be concluded from the market turbulence and currency instabilities accompanying globalization and the "disembedding" process, and from the trend toward more complex products and shorter innovation cycles, that being embedded in a regional network promising continuity is an important precondition for innovation by companies. Such an embedding promises productive potential and realized expectations on the sole basis of which it becomes possible to play in a globalized competition: the return to regional potentials here becomes a precondition for coping with global challenges.

Moreover, the currently predominant policy of a race to lower costs fails to recognize central problems of restructuring regional policy or it misses their solution. Large parts of the previously successful Fordist-Taylorist production model in Western Europe—if they do not want to remain trapped in Taylorist forms of production—face new and highly competitive buyers' markets and must simultaneously develop new productivity resources. This is a problem not solved through a policy of naive cost reduction; in fact, its solution is hampered. The restructuring of companies and regions toward flexible and interlinked production, more flexible mass production, and flexible specialization, requires an active structural and skills policy that is highly region-oriented, one which raises the interlinkage capability of regional structures and their skills potential. After all, these "high skill-high trust" organizations compete in a different and clearly more benign world than their Taylorist rivals. The policy implications of this are that governments can move their economies onto higher growth paths by encouraging technological diffusion, innovation, "good practice" management techniques, and the development of appropriate infrastructures for the information society.

Learning societies and knowledge-based firms are the key to success. It is not deregulation that is needed here, but re-regulation in the sense of new, intelligent regulations that link companies' interest in flexibility with the individual's flexibility needs. These regulations also link the opportunity for more participation and a more ecological production with protection from the risks of greater flexibility and higher skills at the same time that they prevent sociopolitical marginalization. Social, economic, and ecological sustainability will thus raise companies' confidence and survivability and, in the long term, ensure them more chances in the face of the globalization process:

> In this scenario labor-market deregulation is not a central issue. International functional flexibility of workers in line with changing work organization is much more important to firms. Flexibility to "hire and fire" looks at best irrelevant and at worst could encourage the low

wage/low skill route to competitiveness. The challenge for OECD countries is how to move the whole of their societies and not just an elite on a "high route to competitiveness." (Evans 1997, p. 11)

The fact that for individual firms this path toward a low wage-low skills production is an attractive alternative in the process of restructuring is evident by a German example: in the opinion of various industrial sociologists and politicians—besides the already mentioned tendency to adopt a "shareholder-value" business culture—at least some firms, under the pressure of intensified international competition, are inclined to halt their successful restructuring process. This is done with the help of skilled labor (the "production intelligentsia") and aimed at flexible production open to participation. It favors a "neo-Taylorism" in which unskilled and semiskilled activity, corresponding to a policy focused on short-term wage-cost reduction as the answer to international competitive pressure, forces back the position of modern production labor ("production intelligence"). But the result of such a policy would mean that the long-term situational advantage of high-paid skilled labor, which also provides high-skill quality production and is cooperatively bound into industrial relations, is wasted. In addition, the possibility of sustainable productivity development is sacrificed on the altar of short-term efficiency considerations. A policy supported by trade unions and works councils to prevent this business strategy would yield social modernization effects.

The Europe of the European Union As an Opportunity in the Globalization Process

The development of trade flows and of direct foreign investment shows that globalization occurs not in a single gigantic leap, but as a process and in individual waves. In the globalization process, the EU can be fully viewed as a possible reference model because, despite all sociopolitical shortcomings, it is not a neoliberal free trade area. It should not be forgotten that since its beginnings European integration has been essentially directed by economic interests and has been primarily an economic and market alliance. At the same time, however, political motives have always been present, as evident in the founding of the European Coal and Steel Community. However, the single market was first of all intended to improve the competitiveness of European companies under the pressure of world market competition. It was a program to encourage competition, to break out of the encrusted economic, technical-industrial, and social structures of the so-called Eurosclerosis. The supply shock caused by liberalization was intended to promote the return of European companies to technological world leadership.

The economic and social effects of the single market have often been exaggerated, although it can be assumed that they accounted for a substantial share of the nine million jobs created in the EU from 1986 to 1990, a substantial proportion of which were, however, destroyed in the recession of 1992–93. Similarly, this temporary success cannot obscure existing structural deficits. European industry on the whole has indeed been able to improve its position in slower growth markets, but it has a clear deficit in the sectors and fast-growing markets belonging to high-tech production. With the presentation of its White Paper (European Commission 1993), the European Commission has provided a substantial, albeit contradictory, contribution to the debate. It comes to the following conclusion: "The Community's industry has improved its position on slow growth markets ..., whereas its results have deteriorated on markets with a high added value, such as office automation, computers, electronics, optical instruments, and medical and surgical equipment. Structurally, it therefore does not meet the requirements of the markets of the future."

A conclusion drawn from this maintains that to raise the interlinkage capability of modern production associations and contribute toward improving systemic competitiveness, trans-European networks should be built and developed in the fields of telecommunications, transport, and energy infrastructure. The Community-wide creation of information superhighways should bring spatially separated businesses together into strategic alliances and promote the interlinkage capability of modern production associations, thus systematically promoting immobile production factors. Trans-European transport networks and energy systems should modernize the EU's infrastructure and simultaneously build bridges to Eastern Europe and North Africa. The challenging, but ecologically entirely feasible project can also make a concrete contribution to solving the European employment crisis. However, under the pressure of the Maastricht convergence criteria, the financing of individual projects (investment volume of 524 billion ECU) is a wholly unresolved problem.

Contrary to the neoliberal view that Europe's economic system is not competitive because of its high wages and social-welfare benefits, in its White Paper the Commission arrives at a more mixed assessment: in contrast with a low-wage strategy within the EU, and thus counter to the path taken by the United States, labor costs are not at all the sole factor determining international competitiveness. Sharp fluctuations in labor costs are the consequence of massive exchange-rate fluctuations in the bilateral exchange rates of the ECU, dollar, and yen. In addition, it is argued that wage differentials relative to the new industrial countries are so huge that they can hardly be overcome through wage reductions or a low-wage strategy for the purpose of achieving any sort of competitive advantage.

A second path is thus proposed, one corresponding to the spirit of the European social model. According to this, the growth in real wages should be one percentage point below the growth in labor productivity. In connection with the Maastricht convergence criteria, especially with the reduction of public budget deficits, private investment activity should be clearly stimulated—a course ultimately at odds with the neoliberal illusion that more employment automatically results from greater private profits. This course also overlooks the fact that the profitability of investment Europe-wide since 1982 has steadily grown and that not only are real wages a percentage point behind productivity growth, but that (employed) workers have already had to accept real wage cuts in stages. This gives too little thought to the fact that productivity growth is not only part of the problem's solution but part of the problem itself; it furthers division in society (the dissolution of social cohesion) and the accompanying growth of unresolved environmental problems.

The Commission's recommendation to lessen the labor-cost factor through a clear reduction in nonwage costs in the form of wage taxes and social contributions seems more effective in this case. A clear reduction could break the above-noted vicious cycle in which the costs of this factor rise with the financing of growing large-scale unemployment, while at the same time it is precisely this factor that declines due to a growing capital intensity of production. This is even linked to environmental measures.

> The CO_2 energy tax proposed by the Commission should—independent of its other justifications—be one of the most suitable possibilities for compensation in order to reduce labor costs. The uniform taxation of capital revenues at source, as the Commission proposed back in 1989, would also be a possibility for compensation. (Commission 1993, p. 20)

The future skills supply of labor should be of major importance for Europe as a production site, with respect to both international competitiveness and the modernization of labor markets and individuals' opportunities for self-realization. The EU White Paper notes among other things that the employment system no longer meets the requirements, which have clearly changed under conditions of globalization. Recovering and preserving the competitive position and lowering unemployment require a skills profile of workers that is adapted to innovations of work-organization technology, one that ensures high productivity and correspondingly high incomes and can contribute to company-internal and company-external flexibility required as part of new production concepts.

> The introduction of more flexible and open training systems and the development of individuals' adaptability are becoming increasingly necessary; for companies as well, to enable them to better utilize the technological innovations they have developed or purchased. (Commission 1993, p. 132)

The European Commission's employment report for 1995 estimated the dynamic of structural changes of labor markets to be 10 percent. This means that each year 10 percent of all jobs are replaced by new ones requiring a higher, or at least changed, skills profile. The breakneck introduction of new technologies makes previous skills increasingly obsolete. Allan Larsson (of the European Commission's DGV) believes that about 80 percent of the technologies currently in use will be outmoded in ten years. At the same time, however, 80 percent of European workers for the year 2007 are already in the labor markets. It is thus only proper to call for a broad advanced training offensive to which trade union qualification demands would be directly connected. According to the European Commission's assessment, the universities—among others—must play an increasing role in developing new opportunities for further education, for which they must receive the corresponding resources. However, a further contradiction occurs here resulting from the restrictions of the Maastricht convergence criteria: instead of promoting the necessary development of education systems, national culture, and science ministries are subjected to the cost-cutting dictate of their finance ministers.

The Commission's recommendations for an innovative labor policy are also contradictory. The reduction of the workweek is described as a "wrong path," in particular because it hampers internal flexibility and thus the promotion of productivity. In general, however, it is not denied that work time reductions in recent years have made a clear contribution to employment security and job creation. In the Netherlands, for example, half of the 30 percent rise in employment can be attributed to the reduction in average work time. Against this background, new forms of work time policy are recommended, which consist of various elements, such as flexible retirement rules, modulated working times during the year, and expanded part-time models. In contrast to the neoliberal mainstream, it is fully recognized that innovative work time concepts could increase companies' innovation capability and, in combination with new forms of work organization, contribute to enhanced productivity. However, thus far this has not led to the Commission proposing corresponding directives for an innovative work time policy.

Special attention should be paid to suggestions related to an interconnection of skills-enhancement and working time:

> In view of constantly growing productivity, and to achieve a better distribution of employment, there should be a further reduction in working time and a balance between working time and training time, although it is still not known how quickly and under what conditions this will occur. New paths are opening up to couple working time organization with the development of training. (Commission 1993, p. 133)

This provides fully concrete connections for a trade union work time policy. The fact that work time must today be adopted as a theme in the context of one's total working lifetime is nothing new to trade unions either. Refinement of a working-lifetime concept, in which various elements such as training and continuing-education time, part-time work, and part-time retirement, sabbaticals, and parental leave are systematically interconnected, could be a promising starting pointt for the redistribution of paid work. At the same time, a substantial contribution would be made to the compatibility of family and career.

The fact that an effective employment policy exclusively at the national level can no longer be successfully managed under the conditions of globalization and European integration was finally—and belatedly—recognized at the 1994 EU summit in Essen (Germany). Better coordination of labor market policies and agreement on employment policy priorities (promotion of investment, raising the employment intensity of growth, lowering nonwage costs, active labor-market policies, and improvement in measures on behalf of problem groups of the labor market) are all aimed at making a concrete contribution to modernizing labor markets. The first successes have indeed been realized; yet many EU member states, citing the EU's employment policy priorities, lean toward a further deregulation of labor markets and a dismantling of social-security systems. Despite all the positive beginnings in the direction of a European social union, it must not be overlooked that to date this essentially involves a market integration in which economic interests clearly predominate. Through persistent large-scale unemployment and the further dismantling—in place of a necessary innovative reform—of social-security systems, a deep crisis of legitimization threatens the EU, which can jeopardize the political and social integration process over the long term.

If the EU really wants to establish itself in global competition as a role model, then the opportunities must be utilized that arise in the Intergovernmental Conference aims at reviewing the Treaty on European Union. Among other things, this includes further democratizing the EU institutions and strengthening the European Parliament, adopting fundamental social rights in a future European constitution, and anchoring an active European employment policy in the treaty. A deepening of the integration process with the revision of the treaty will finally equip the EU for the historically and politically necessary enlargement to include the new democracies in Central and Eastern Europe. Above all, however, such a revision of the treaty could give the EU an image as a unified actor in the globalization process, one that can intervene on behalf of an international regulation of unleashed global and money markets according to principles of democracy and solidarity.

Regulation Opportunities at the International Level

Even if trade unions, in contrast to national governments and the European Union, have hardly any chance of exerting influence at the global level because of their limited sanctions potential, which is tied to labor markets, they can nonetheless bring their weight to bear in the form of support for internationally operating organizations and in international negotiation systems. Ultimately, for the regulation of global financial markets and trade flows, this is the final level at which concrete possibilities already occur. Thus, already today, beyond regional arrangements (such as the EU), we can recognize the beginnings of international regulation that approaches the above-cited goal of a political, social, and ecological re-embedding of global economies, and that can thus be taken up by a policy for representing trade union interests as well. Consequently, there are international regulations governing world trade and capital flows in the form of (currently very inadequate) international agreements (Rio, Montreal); in the World Trade Organization (WTO), OECD, and ILO; and at the financial policy level of the International Monetary Fund and the World Bank, although until recently these last two have themselves substantially promoted unleashing.

But at the same time, these organizations contain institutional preconditions for such regulation. Especially at the level of international conferences on trade agreements, basic rights in labor relations (freedom of association, wage rights, prohibition of forced labor and child labor, nondiscrimination) and human rights are becoming increasingly accepted as absolutely essential in negotiations—with consequences:

> The fact that in January 1997 the OECD has been ready to censure the Republic of Korea—a new member—for not living up to commitments on freedom of association and collective bargaining given when joining the organization, is highly significant. It did not happen in the case of Mexico's membership in the OECD and would have been unthinkable even five years ago. (Evans 1997, p. 19)

Behind this are not only national governments, but also—especially evident in the disputes over the NAFTA treaty—the beginnings of international players in the form of nongovernmental organizations (NGOs), which initiated processes of re-embedding through internationally coordinated protest actions (public information campaigns, consumer boycott actions, occupations, and the like). However illusory and dangerous it may be to expect quick results, it would also be highly problematic to represent these beginnings as condemned to failure per se.

International forms of regulation are also being discussed for "casino" capitalism and have a chance to be realized. At least within the framework of the European Union, an effective barrier has been established against EU-internal speculation with a common currency—notwithstanding the undeniable problems associated with the manner of introducing the euro without accompanying social policy. In addition, the potential for extortion by individual multinational companies can be blocked through harmonization of tax systems that should be internationally demanded (ecological tax reform) and regulatory policy. Moreover, regulating short-term financial transactions (which, as noted above, account for up to 80 percent of total transactions) and raising their cost (such as through the project for a "Tobin tax") could reduce the risks of the international liberation of financial capital.

Besides the Tobin tax there are several proposals to throw sand in the wheels of international finance. However, these proposals—ranging from minimum reserve requirements for "hot money" in national banking centers, to international agreements on capital taxes, to international regulation of banking and financial center activities—all face the problem of "free-loader" behavior by individual nations. Ultimately, the question here will be settled by whether it is possible to obtain a majority of states—still to be developed—to prevent such free-loader options or to achieve international cooperation and/or sanctions. Or, the question arises as to the extent to which social movements and organizations in those countries exploiting the free-loader option can generate social pressure internationally. In this regard, this is also a question of the achievement of civil and social liberties, and thus a genuinely trade union-oriented question.

Globalization of the Economy, the European Union, and Trade Union Policy in Europe

The recent strikes in Germany, France, and Denmark have shown that the trade union and company players are regionally not so helplessly subject to globalization pressures as the horror scenarios on globalization suggest. For example, it appears that the resistance to reductions in the continuance of pay in the case of illness has currently forced capital owners and managers to an understanding of the necessity that the model of Rhenish capitalism cannot be simply written off without serious financial losses in the short term. This could be one basis for a new social contract, which would not only have to be defined economically but also socially and ecologically and would support the resistance of social movements to the destructive consequences of globalization. In defensive actions to protect social rights, trade unions would then also have the function of using pressure to point out to companies what is necessary in the long term.

However, such a policy of the offensive defense of Rhenish capitalism and the defense of high labor and social-policy standards in Europe in connection with work time reduction policies would mean that the reasonableness of these rules systems themselves would have to be reviewed in light of economic and social changes. This also means giving support to innovation in companies and regions in terms of the above-cited restructuring and in terms of a social and ecological organizational policy, without losing sight of what is economically necessary. Such a (supply-oriented) organizational policy can then be a sensible way out of the globalization trap at the regional level, if innovations are socially and ecologically regulated in the European connection as much as possible. This, not least of all, would require from individual trade unions substantial concessions on ecological demands as well as cross-sector and international social solidarity. Over the long term, however, this policy could preserve the European production sites and labor markets in the ecological necessities (sustainable development) and social transformations they face and—however paradoxical it may sound —thus even act in an economically sustainable manner. But with growing integration in the European single market, such a policy of linking resistance and organization presupposes international coordination of national trade union policies.

The fact that trade union internationalism of the late 1960s and the 1970s was often little more than a theoretical exercise and did not go beyond familiar trade union rhetoric was due not only to the familiar labor market and organizational limits to international solidarity, but also to a situation in which nation-states, under the Bretton Woods currency regime and the conditions of Keynesian class compromises, could ensure the unions relative political influence and social policy achievements. The pressure of globalization and the threat of an erosion of national industrial-relations systems create not only the familiar risks (developed above), but also entirely new opportunities for trade unions to bring their organizational structures and areas of operation out of their national limits. This is surely a high-risk venture, but probably one without alternatives if they want to go beyond previous declarations and their inherited songsheet and impose limits on capital in internationalized markets and political arenas.

The still-pronounced regional disparities in the European single market often hamper a strategically agreed behavior of trade unions. For example, differences in levels of labor productivity between Germany and the Benelux countries on the one hand and the agrarian economies of southern Europe on the other represent obvious barriers to a unified strategy of trade union interest representation. Added to this are considerable differences in organizational structures, the degree of organization, political-ideological orientation, and the political cultures of the national trade unions in the EU; the latter is also true of differences between national firms, associations of firms, and labor-policy relations.

In addition, the role and function of the government are of decisive importance with respect to labor relations in general and agreement on income policy in the framework of macroeconomic regulation of the economy in particular (to the extent that this is determined by policy at all). For example, for agreement on income policy, for which the government establishes the legal framework (procedural and substantive regulations), three variants exist, practiced in Europe in differing manners: first, an interventionist income policy with restrictions on wage freedom (for example, in Belgium); second, a limitation on the possibilities for influencing collective wage agreements through neoliberal strategies (for example, in Great Britain); and third, the orientation toward neocorporatist management; or the coordination of economic and social policy with collective wage agreements (found in the Netherlands and the Scandinavian countries, and partly in Italy).

In almost all Western European countries, government influence over labor relations is, to differing degrees, characterized by the pressure of employers for further decentralization of wage negotiations, a direct reaction to the possibilities offered to businesses by the globalization process. However, differences here should be noted:

> A decentralization of collective agreement negotiations can take place in an uncontrolled (unorganized) or controlled (organized) manner: the former means that decentralization occurs as the consequence of the collapse of the regulatory power of the level above. Controlled decentralization occurs when the wage associations of the levels above delegate certain regulation powers to levels below, yet maintain a certain control over this level. (Mesch 1995, p. 25)

With respect to the changes in the designated negotiation levels in Western Europe, classification into five groups is possible: (1) countries in which the status quo could essentially be preserved (the Netherlands, Finland, and Spain); (2) countries in which uncontrolled decentralization and the dismantling of regional collective wage agreements could be achieved; (3) countries in which controlled decentralization and indirect coordination of sectoral negotiations have developed (Germany, Austria, Denmark, and Sweden in part); (4) countries featuring recentralization (Norway); and (5) countries in which simultaneous centralization and decentralization can be observed (such ambivalent developments are particularly notable in Italy, France, and Belgium). This list alone shows that we cannot speak at all of a linear trend toward uncontrolled decentralization, but rather that while globalization has indeed put pressure on trade union wage negotiations in regions and sectors, very different and flexible answers have been found or are being sought that respond not only to the economic decentralization trend in the globalization process but also to the complex needs of trade-union members and enterprises as a result of social modernization processes in the EU member states.

The challenges facing both national wage systems and the general framework conditions of trade-union interest representation against the background of socioeconomic structural changes (modernization of society, pluralization, and individualization) in Western Europe largely coincide. Despite similar problems, only the beginning of a convergence, in other words, a unification of national labor relations, can be observed. Respective national labor relations differ strongly from each other, and identical or similar problems are dealt with very differently. This divergence in labor relations has considerable consequences for a future-oriented Europeanization of industrial relations. In particular, under the conditions of a currency union, trade-union wage policy runs the risk of coming under additional pressure.

This is true not only for the public sector, which is already facing the pressure of restrictive budget policies today. Against the backdrop of different production levels, the achievement of economic and monetary union (EMU) will subject national labor markets in almost all sectors to substantial competitive pressure through the elimination of exchange-rate adjustments: "If exchange rates no longer equalize the economic levels of different countries like a system of canal locks, then wage and other labor costs take on this lock function, and the trade unions will take over the role of the lock-keeper" (Altvater and Mahnkopf 1993, p. 246). Claus Noé argues similarly, noting that without an institutionally safeguarded wage and incomes policy there will arise a "common Europe of money and capital," but not one of labor and employment. The hopes connected with EMU by parts of the employer camp and in conservative circles have been very clearly expressed by a member of the German central bank committee: "The power of national wage cartels will be further eroded" (Noé 1996, p. 44).

European trade unions are not far from a convergent and coordinated wage strategy and a coordination of national negotiations, which would be a necessary and appropriate answer to the processes of Europeanization and globalization. Although the European Trade Union Confederation (ETUC) was already advocating closer cooperation in this field a number of years ago in a discussion paper on the prospects for European wage negotiations (ETUC 1993), national trade unions are only now beginning to understand that there is no alternative to Europeanization. The urgency of the problem of a stronger coordination of wage policy at the European level is clear from the interventionist wage policy of the Belgian government. Following the failure of a national employment pact, it dictated by regulation that the development of wages and salaries had to be based on average wage increases of the neighboring countries of Germany, the Netherlands, France, and Luxembourg. This was nothing more than a government-ordered coordination and Europeanization of wage policy.

The need to act is obviously enormous already before the entry into force of the third stage of EMU. In particular, the sectoral level must be given decisive importance; despite all differences, it represents the central negotiation level in the EU member states. European trade-union associations have indeed intensified their exchange of experience on trends in wage policies through conferences and wage policy committees, but the outlines of a coordinated wage policy are not yet evident. For example, neither mutual participation in national wage commissions nor mandatory coordination of collective wage agreement demands is yet established practice of European trade unions.

The recent discussions in the European Metalworkers' Federation in particular offer prospects in this connection. Future coordination of wage policy in the metalworking industry is to be organized on a mandatory basis in a three-stage procedure. This includes: (1) the participation of member associations of other EU member states in the sessions of wage commissions; (2) joint discussion and preparation of minimum standards of wage policy; and (3) an "accountability obligation" when jointly agreed wage rules are not implemented. For example, joint wage-policy goals could be agreed on in the areas of ensuring real incomes and work time policy. Such a strategy does not amount to the centralization of wage policy at the European level, to which there is no correspondence in most European countries. In addition, no legally regulated European wage autonomy is required for such an approach, even if it is justifiably demanded by trade unions.

The essential aim here is to link productively the variety of regional and international economic and social structures and traditions in terms of framework wage regulation, rather than unify them according to the old pattern of making demands. The goal that European wage policy should aspire to is not unification (in the sense of a "hierarchy option"), but coordination and regulation of diversity. At the European level, such an approach would first of all be capable of providing wage-policy regulation of the dirigiste system(s) of industrial relations created by globalization, on which a mandatory rules system could then be progressively built. However, such a system requires not only action- and conflict-capable trade unions, but also wage-capable employers' associations. Thus, success for the trade unions at the European level is essentially dependent on whether the trade unions again succeed, as at the start of industrialization at the local and national level, in operating as midwives of European employers' associations (especially at the sectoral level).

In the future, European works councils might play a pioneering role in the Europeanization of industrial relations. After a corresponding proposal for a directive was blocked for over twenty years in the Council of Ministers, the adoption of the directive on the establishment of European works councils can certainly be considered a success for European trade unions. Before the adoption of the directive in September 1994, there were only forty European works councils (EWCs) based on voluntary agreements. The need for a legal framework can be seen clearly in the substantial dynamic movement unleashed by the directive. The directive was used as the basis for over four hundred agreements concluded from September 1994 to September 1996. In all, some 1,300 European concerns fall under their scope. The EU directive can be considered an indication that the European Union is fully capable of adopting mandatory rules on the creation of a European industrial relations area.

The processes of Europeanization (at the political level and in the European single market), internationalization of production, and the globalization of financial markets for the first time are directly confronting all EU trade unions with the need to develop international organizational structures and international solidarity as well as with the demand for policies governing international regulation (for example, the money markets). So, in one way or another, internationalism is becoming a very concrete issue, going beyond mere Labor Day speeches. Or put in sociological terms:

> In the debate on globalization the world's understanding of itself is becoming realistic. It conveys the view that there is no genuine externalization of the consequences of actions, and that after the conquest of the global space significant progress is only possible through intensification of qualitative innovation and equal opportunity. (Wiesenthal 1996, p. 52)

In view of the juncture of social modernization and economic globalization processes, this involves developing new forms of intracompany, intercompany, sociopolitical, and international regulation to defend against socially and ecologically disastrous externalization processes and to protect and develop a socially rational skills and production structure in Europe.

Such a policy necessarily stands in opposition to the short-term efficiency imperatives of parts of capital and the business culture predominating there. And trade unions must become aware that they themselves can be participants in such externalization processes, in labor markets, and in environmental issues. A reflexive innovation in this sense could then be very capable of helping to lead trade unions out of the globalization trap. The question is not how to strengthen the European situation at the expense of international social justice and the ecology, but how innovation is to be socially and ecologically regulated so as to nationally and internationally achieve social justice and environmental sustainability over the long term.

For trade unions at the sectoral, regional, and international levels this must more than ever involve binding together, by means of compromise, the contradictory interests that will inevitably emerge in the process and that are bound to be exacerbated by the various positive and negative effects of globalization (unity lies at the end of this difficult process but is certainly no self-evident precondition based on a fundamental contradiction). Coordinating networks will therefore have to be organized not only from above, at the ETUC level; they will also have to be developed regionally and internationally as networks from below. The trade-union policy task would then be the organizational safeguarding of these networks and the provision of financial and communications assistance. This option would not entail a strengthening of individual unions through mergers, nor the transfer of hierarchical trade-union organization models to the EU level; rather, the simultaneous presence of modernization, Europeanization, and increasing ecological concern calls for a strengthening of the powers of the trade-union movement, beyond the sectoral context, at company, regional, and international levels; though the sectoral context—together with the corresponding subsectors of the labor market and their sanction potential represented by the possibility of strike action—must remain the unions' firm foothold.

In the EU, beyond the limits of national and European labor markets, trade-union policy must increasingly take on the task of halting the social collapse of this society, the threat of the loss of social cohesion through globalization, regional competition policy, and the computerization of work. Trade unions must also re-anchor in society a concept of solidarity—which is based on individualism and which moves beyond a quasi-forced collectivism—as a self-selected goal and a general standard. For the future of trade-union success stands or falls on the continuance of standards of solidarity in European society. Yet for a new trade-union policy, seizing the opportunities of social processes of change would also mean that they not only avert risks and speak to people in their misery, but that they also notice and support their members in their strengths, that they develop and promote their individual and collective opportunities for social emancipation. To only support the resistance to government and business policies currently erupting in the EU's core countries would mean that they themselves would fall for the policy of the short term to which businesses are now so devoted throughout Europe. For however necessary these battles may be in order to defend the living standard of individuals and to realize well-understood long-term interests in a productive and innovative European production site, it is also true that the Europe of the EU will maintain itself through change alone (which must include social and ecological change).

In addition, in the long term a solidarity-based policy orientation of trade unions going beyond partial labor markets can only be achieved by linking the interests of the economically weaker and economically stronger countries, the interests of the winners and losers in globalization, and by linking wage interests with the defense of life outside the company and the economy; in other words, with environmental interests. And this effort toward social solidarity and ecological reconstruction will only be possible—however paradoxical this may sound in view of ecological development—if Europe as a production site remains economically productive at its core.

But as Ulrich Beck has rightly noted, such a policy aimed at averting the risks posed by globalization includes also—and above all—the right of freedom of defense, enshrined both nationally and internationally, against the pressure exerted in Europe by the process of globalization and by bureaucratic-technocratic complexes. Such a right is a prerequisite for the development of democratic public opinions and the power of trade unions to resist the apparent and actual material constraints of the global and money markets.

References

Altvater, E., and B. Mahnkopf. 1993. *Gewerkschaften vor der europäischen Herausforderung.* Westfälisches Dampfboot, Münster.

Commission of the European Communities. 1933. Growth, Competitiveness, Employment. White Paper, Bulletin of the European Communities, 6/93, Luxembourg.

European Trade Union Confederation. 1993. European Collective Bargaining—ETUC Strategy. Guidelines for Collective Bargaining and Prospects for the Development of the Social Dialogue. Document adopted by the Executive Committee. Brussels, 4 March 1993.

Evans, J. 1997. Welfare, Security and Economic Performance—Public Policy Overview. Paper prepared for the International Progressive Policy Conference in Brussels, 2–5 March 1997.

Mesch, M. 1995. Sozialpartnerschaft und Arbeitsbeziehungen in Europa. Manz, Wien.

Noé, C. 1996. The Maastricht Process Is Marginalising the Unions and Employers, in ETUI (1996). *Collective Bargaining in Western Europe 1994–1995.* Brussels.

Wiesenthal, H. 1996. Globalisierung – Soziologische und politikwissenschaftliche Koordinaten eines unbekannten Terrains. Berliner Debatte INITIAL No. 5/96.

Part IV

FOREIGN POLICY CONSEQUENCES OF GLOBALIZATION

8. German Foreign Policy in the Context of Globalization

Rudolf Scharping

Foreign policy in the traditional sense no longer exists. The once clear dividing line between foreign and domestic policy has become blurred. Crises in and around Europe and the resulting instabilities directly impact conditions at home. Although the consequence of foreign problems, such conflicts are often enough perceived as internal threats. Foreign policy today is synonymous with economic policy, social policy, environmental policy, monetary policy, financial policy, and domestic policy.

German foreign policy should be guided by four fundamental objectives. First, it should promote peace; second, it should advance democracy and respect for human rights; third, it should foster a sustainable concept of prosperity; and fourth, it should work toward comprehensive security. We should pursue these objectives by peaceful means, prioritizing prevention and an equitable balance of interests. It is in Germany's own enlightened self-interest to aim for a European Union capable of acting globally, for stable international relations, in particular between the EU and the United States, and for a strengthening of multilateral and international organizations.

During the period of East-West confrontation, the old Federal Republic of Germany was subjected to the strategies of the Western powers, who later became its partners. West Germany was kept under control but simultaneously protected from the communist threat. This circumscribed the scope of action and responsibility of German foreign policy. The integration of West Germany into both the West's collective security structures and its framework of foreign policy interests—a process initiated by the victorious Western powers but then actively supported by West Germany itself—enabled us to prosper economically and build a stable democracy under the protective shield of the Atlantic alliance. We had both limited responsibility and limited sovereignty.

Since German unification, we alone have been responsible for our policies. Germany's new status and enhanced power, the upheavals as Eastern Europe moves toward democracy and market economies, the dissolution of the Soviet Union and the challenges it poses both for NATO and for the EU—these are merely a few examples of the complex recent transformations. These changes are forcing Germany to reassess the underlying tenets and guiding principles of its foreign policy and redefine its interests. If a country is to assert its interests, then it must also shoulder responsibility. In view both of its historical legacy and its enhanced power since unification, Germany shoulders responsibility first as a country exerting major influence on international relations; and second, as the target of expectations from its European partners, NATO, its other European neighbors, the countries of the South, and international organizations.

In light of our country's recent and past historical experience, a number of basic tenets of German foreign policy can be identified, which, established in the old Federal Republic, have continued to prove their value today. Germany belongs irrevocably to the West. Germany's integration into the European Union and NATO—associated with Konrad Adenauer—not to mention its transatlantic ties, constitutes the unshakable pillar of our foreign policy.

The policy of détente—associated with Willy Brandt—laid the groundwork for an end to the Cold War. Based on dialogue, confidence building, renunciation of force, cooperation, and a fair balance of interests, détente helped create a set of policy instruments that even in the context of today's changed world orient our foreign policy when responding to the varied conflicts in and around Europe and promoting peace.

Against this background, and in view of increasing globalization, Germany should demonstrate both self-confidence and self-restraint in shaping its foreign policy. We should openly expound our interests and assume our international responsibility, which has increased proportionally to our enhanced international weight. But we should seek to balance our interests with those of other countries, in particular within our alliances and our membership in international and multilateral organizations.

A foreign policy of this kind corresponds to Germany's current situation. We face considerable international expectations and are expected to play a constructive role in international relations. At the same time, however, we are subject to the fear, especially among our European partners and neighbors, that Germany might again seek domination, even hegemony. Especially in the eyes of its allies and neighbors, Germany's history remains a critical variable. Were we to ignore this and think only nationally, we would lose all maneuverability in the foreign policy sphere.

Given our historical legacy and the challenges to come, four objectives must be at the forefront of German foreign policy.

1. We want to work toward a stable peace, and we consider international stability to be the most important precondition for achieving a secure future for our country and any other.
2. Human rights are a universal and inalienable element of human dignity. In our view, promoting respect for human rights and advancing democracy are the best ways to preserve peace.
3. We are committed to comprehensive security, that is, security based on political, economic, social, cultural, and environmental cooperation.
4. We are willing to share in the creation of sustainable prosperity, which stresses the interdependence of our own prosperity with that of others, and which ensures social solidarity, both in Germany and in our relations with other countries. A sustainable model of prosperity also calls for sustainable national and international policies.

Our efforts to achieve these four objectives must be guided by three fundamental principles. The first is integration and cooperation, the second conflict prevention, and the third, risk provision.

We are committed to integration and cooperation. European integration is the result of an unprecedented political learning process and is the twentieth century's most valuable legacy. It encompasses far more than common economic interests. The European Union is an expression of the specifically European concept of civilization, culture, and community. It is much more than a single market. In the long run people will not support the European Union if they fear that free-market forces threaten rather than protect their interests. Thus, deepening and widening the European Union and promoting cooperation with the new democracies in Central and Eastern Europe, including Russia and Ukraine, offer the best means of building stable and enduring peace in Europe. To continue the process we must foster and further develop the transatlantic partnership. In economic and technological terms, Europe and North America are partners but also competitors; yet strong transatlantic ties are cornerstones of the stability in Europe, and Europe must play a greater, equal, role in this relationship.

The second principle, conflict prevention, is the best way to avoid the use of force, given the increase in socioethnic, regional, and interstate conflicts. The third principle, provision for risk, remains necessary. Since the end of the East-West conflict, we have made great gains in terms of security; there has been substantial disarmament and cuts in defense spending. Yet, we must continue to prepare for future risks by ensuring our ability to defend ourselves, both at the national and alliance level. We will also have to assume new tasks in providing military support as part of international peacekeeping missions.

Since 1989/90, military security policy has lost its preeminent position in international relations. It has been superseded by economic policy, "geo-economics," and other global developments. Economic globalization and the emergence of a global market economy present enormous opportunities for Germany and for Europe. As one of the world's leading and most highly developed economic regions, the European Union can exploit the openness of markets and the increasing level of economic interdependence by expanding its ties to the dynamic economic regions of North America, Latin America, and Asia. This will lend substantial impetus to growth and technological development. And we should expect that relations between countries will become increasingly subject to international law—in the form of multilateral regimes and global regulatory instruments designed to safeguard free and fair competition, ensure a peaceful balance of diverging economic and social interests, preserve a healthy environment, and maintain our common welfare.

We should not overlook how increasing interdependence also exposes our continent to the problematic side of reciprocal relationships. Conflicts elsewhere in the world have a direct impact on Europe; jobs in Europe are threatened by dynamic growth in rival economic regions; environmental destruction and threats to the ecosystem impair our quality of life and that of others; we are exposed to international crime, terrorism, and drug trafficking; uncontrolled population growth and refugee flows from the poorer or less developed countries bring more and more people to Europe in search of protection and livelihood; the spread of weapons of mass destruction and the export of arms to antidemocratic or terrorist regimes pose a threat to European security.

Neither Germany nor any other European country will be able to take advantage of opportunities or cope with risks on its own. It is essential that Germany promotes the European integration process so that the EU can translate our common economic interests and joint economic strength into political action and thereby exert influence on global political developments. More than merely asserting our competitive position toward other major economic regions, this presupposes that Germany and the European Union are capable of modernizing their economic and social systems while at the same time supporting multilateral organizations to better regulate international relations.

The increasing importance of economics also affects the transatlantic relationship. The Washington Treaty remains a solid basis for Euro-American partnership and for American engagement in Europe. In the long run, however, given the reduced significance of traditional security policy, this treaty will not sufficiently ensure the vitality and strategic quality of transatlantic relations. These relations have long since acquired economic, political, ecological, technological, and cultural dimensions. The New Transatlantic Agenda adopted at the US-EU summit in Madrid in December 1995 outlined a number of initial steps in these areas. However, their implementation has until now proved difficult.

The Madrid Summit conclusion that preserving and promoting transatlantic prosperity is the key to shaping transatlantic relations in the post-Cold War era and into the twenty-first century requires more resolute support. An integrated transatlantic economic area is a worthwhile objective, even if it progresses only in small steps. If there is a European answer to globalization, it is integration, which includes economic and monetary union. The introduction of a single currency is imperative, as is compliance with the conditions set out in the Maastricht Treaty. Monetary union gives Europe a chance to hold its own in international capital and currency markets—this is particularly in Germany's interest. The Deutsche mark's role as a key international currency is overtaxing our economy. Germany is politically and economically too weak to bear the consequences. Recent years have shown that the permanent overvaluation of the Deutsche mark's external value reduces German industry's export opportunities, eliminates any gains in growth, and destroys jobs. A single market and a single currency will not suffice as the foundation of European integration; we also need harmonization of fiscal, financial, and economic policy, and a joint pact for employment and growth.

Control mechanisms should be introduced in international financial and currency markets and limits imposed on destabilizing currency speculation and financial transactions. We should not forget the havoc wreaked by international speculation in Europe in the early 1990s. Especially after the introduction of the euro, we need to foster cooperation among the dollar, yen, and euro zones; considering the regionalization trend within economic areas such as the EU, NAFTA, Mercosur, and the Asia Pacific Economic Cooperation (APEC), we must be able to exert a greater influence on global capital and foreign exchange markets.

Multilateral trade policy should focus on establishing a stable framework for the world economy. German foreign policy and the European Union should work to ensure that the World Trade Organization is able to enforce the agreed upon multilateral rules. Besides promoting further liberalization, the WTO should devote its efforts to establishing an internationally binding competition code encompassing sanctions for violations, minimum ecological and social standards, and codes of conduct regarding subsidies and the fight against corruption. To further underscore European Monetary Union, we must strive within the OECD as a whole to harmonize our tax systems by introducing minimum tax rates on companies and their investment income. This will eliminate harmful tax competition between countries and the risk of distorting trade and investments posed by such competition.

We cannot develop global regulatory mechanisms without strengthening the United Nations, the most important instrument for coping with global problems. The organization must be reformed and given broader power in development and social and environmental policy. The United Nations must improve its efficiency and obtain a degree of financial autonomy. Additionally, there remains an urgent need to reform the UN Security Council. A regional balance must be established in its permanent membership. Because a European seat is at present inconceivable, Germany should be given a permanent seat on the Council; this mandate is understood primarily as European.

The United Nations has done a great deal to combat poverty and hunger, confront development and population issues, and contain global environmental risks. These efforts absorb some 70 percent of the organization's resources. In Germany, however, the United

Nations has often been perceived primarily as responsible for peacemaking and peacekeeping operations. The sharp increase in the number of conflicts worldwide makes it clear that the United Nations can take the most effective action before an armed conflict erupts or once fighting has ceased. The UN's blue-helmet missions in particular have helped to stabilize peace. To make such missions even more effective, Germany should firmly support the establishment of so-called standby troops at the United Nations and ensure corresponding training and operational readiness within the German Armed Forces.

In recent years, experience with wars such as those in Somalia and the former Yugoslavia has shown that the United Nations is not capable of halting fighting on its own. Yet, it is the only authority with the right, on a case-by-case basis, to give an alliance or a regional organization such as the Organization for Security and Cooperation in Europe (OSCE) or the Organization of African Unity (OAU) a mandate to re-establish peace. Germany should also make a contribution—commensurate with its international weight and responsibility—to peacekeeping within the framework of the United Nations.

Now that the East-West conflict has ceased, our country is no longer exposed to a military threat; instead, we are surrounded by friends and partners. This is a particularly fortunate and historically unprecedented position for us to be in. But new instabilities and violent conflicts have arisen in Europe and on its periphery. The old fear of aggression from outside has been replaced by the fear of threats from within. Generally speaking, Europe is witnessing a conflict between two opposing forces: integration on the one hand and renationalization on the other.

Regarding this conflict, first there is the question of Russia's future role in Europe. Russia's present period of profound upheaval will continue for some time, and its direction remains completely uncertain. The West must seize every opportunity, however small, to influence developments in Russia to ensure that it establishes close ties with the West. The future of the Commonwealth of Independent States (CIS) largely depends on developments in Russia. It is unknown whether these countries will achieve internal consolidation and become stable independent states. It is in the European interest that Ukraine, in particular, remain independent and that the countries bordering the Caspian Sea also preserve their sovereignty—not just because of their energy resources. Especially because of the precarious situation in Bosnia-Herzegovina, the Balkan region from Croatia to Turkey is likely to remain an area of conflict for quite some time. Europe needs to bind these countries more effectively into Western structures. The same goes for the Mediterranean region.

These geographically definable conflicts and instabilities have a variety of causes—ethnic, cultural, religious—that must all be given careful consideration. We can no longer draw a clear dividing line between traditional domestic policy and traditional foreign policy: the many Muslims living in Europe today constitute a heterogeneous social grouping with multifaceted political and religious views and interests. They are thus both an enrichment and a challenge for the democratic and constitutional states of Europe and for the Western culture of the Enlightenment. I suggest that we promote a broadly based and clearly focused political and cultural dialogue designed not only to foster religious and ideological tolerance but also to actively defend human rights and ensure that Muslims living in Europe uphold our democratic order.

The notion of an unavoidable clash of civilizations points in the wrong direction. Common global action requires agreement across cultural divides. Fundamentalism can be found everywhere. None of the world's great religions constitutes an obstacle to people and nations living together in peace. An intercultural dialogue is an essential part of a foreign cultural policy aimed at fostering liberty and democracy and overcoming stereotypical images of the "enemy."

The Treaty of Amsterdam adopted by the European Council in June 1997 represents a step forward for the EU, but it is not enough to meet the challenges of the future. If Europeans agree that European integration is a civilization project extending far beyond the purely economic domain; if they agree that European integration is a historically unprecedented process bringing peace, democracy, freedom, prosperity, and social security; if, in other words, it is this European civilization that is at stake, then institutionalized routine and formalized Council meetings will not suffice to keep pace with the unfolding challenges. If we do not succeed in appealing to people's emotions and reinforcing their conviction that only in Europe and only together do they have a prospect of a peaceful future, the danger exists that enthusiasm for the European project could wane. And the decision-making machinery in Brussels, characterized as it is by red tape and a lack of transparency, would ultimately be unable to prevent Europe from drifting apart.

Europe's governments and policymakers must agree on a model to guide their endeavors: the vision of a European Federation as an effective global player. Already imperative in objective terms, if properly fleshed out, such a vision could also convince and inspire the people of Europe. This means addressing issues such as supranational democracy, a European charter of basic rights as the core of a common European constitution, and reform of the European Parliament, which would involve, for example, the creation of two chambers—one to represent the citizens of the European Union and one to represent the EU's member states.

The EU Commission's Agenda 2000 is a guideline for the eastward enlargement of the EU. By identifying the first group of Central and Eastern European applicant countries to enter accession negotiations, the Commission has helped to further strengthen and stabilize their transition to democracy and a market economy. Still, it would have been preferable to begin negotiations with all the applicant countries (the "regatta approach"). While continuing to differentiate among the applicant countries in terms of their internal reforms, such an approach would have avoided opening the wide dividing line between the first possible applicants and the remainder. It is in Europe's best interests that the countries that are not now part of the first group do not feel discriminated against or excluded. It is thus crucial that the European Union pursue an accompanying strategy designed to help these countries prepare for EU membership and to support their efforts to implement democratic reforms and achieve economic stability. Alongside NATO and EU enlargement it is advisable to establish other forms of regional cooperation to deal with specific questions of security and development in the region concerned—this is already happening in the Baltic Sea area. Such regional cooperation is crucial to creating stability and security throughout Europe.

A particularly urgent task facing the EU's Common Foreign and Security Policy is that of bringing stability to the Balkans by helping to resolve border and minority disputes peacefully while supporting reforms aimed at consolidating democracy, the rule of law, and market economics. The Peace Stabilization Forces (SFOR) will have to remain in place for several years. This means that for several years Germany will continue to contribute to the forces deployed under SFOR's mandate.

No consideration of German foreign policy and the evolution of a European foreign policy would be complete without a brief mention of Germany's relations with France. Franco-German relations have always played a prominent role in the development of Europe. And the Franco-German friendship has always been a driving force behind European integration. By acting jointly to defend their common interests, France and Germany have often ensured major progress on the road to European integration. But in recent years, their joint actions have become less effectual. There is now a strain in Franco-German relations, though it receives little public attention. Both countries are being forced to redefine their role in the post–Cold War era and to establish a new balance in their mutual relations; this is bound to produce friction. Yet, when this process is compounded by errors of political judgment, it becomes more difficult and fraught with risks. Differences of opinion emerge that can become a burden for both countries and for Europe as a whole. Both former Prime Minister Eduard Balladur and current Prime Minister Lionel Jospin have proposed that a new Elysée Treaty be negotiated. This is in my view a promising and important initiative, because for Europe a great deal depends on the development of relations between France and Germany and on the judicious involvement of other European countries in their friendship.

Since the end of the East-West confrontation and the collapse of the Soviet Union, the need for protection against a military threat has been replaced by the need for stability, both in political and in security terms. Under these new conditions, NATO has continued to play its role as the cornerstone of the transatlantic partnership, as an anchor of stability in Europe, and as a basis for America's indispensable engagement in Europe. NATO was quick to recognize changes in the political climate and initiated a comprehensive process of reform. It will remain a defense alliance, but one that will also have to contribute to its members' collective security. NATO operations not covered by Art. 5 of the North Atlantic Treaty require a mandate from the UN or the OSCE if they involve military enforcement from the UN Security Council.

The decision made by NATO at its 1994 summit to strengthen the European component within the Alliance—thereby increasing the European share of Alliance tasks and burdens with the aim of creating an equal and equitable Euro-Atlantic partnership—must produce practical results. France must be encouraged to rejoin NATO's military structure.

NATO's decision to admit the first group of Central and Eastern European countries, made at the Madrid Summit in 1997, will have a direct impact on the stability of democracy in the future new member states and will also help to create a more secure environment for foreign investors in these countries. Precisely because of these wider implications, NATO must remain open to those countries that share the political values enshrined in the transatlantic alliance and that fulfill the political and military requirements of membership.

With the signing of the NATO-Russia Founding Act and the NATO-Ukraine Charter, NATO has opened the way for further progress in building a cooperative security structure in Europe. Security for Ukraine and the inclusion of Russia are essential elements in the construction of a pan-European peace order. We can only achieve collective security together with Russia. Thus with confidence building and comprehensive cooperation in mind, the NATO-Russia Founding Act must be implemented with the utmost resolve. But it must not be allowed to diminish the importance of NATO or erode the cohesion of the Alliance.

The OSCE is the only body whose membership includes all European countries (as well as the United States and Canada) that share in the responsibility of ensuring Europe's security. By virtue of this unique quality, the OSCE will remain irreplaceable. German foreign policy must work resolutely to strengthen the OSCE and above all to enhance its effectiveness and its operational capacities. Further steps toward disarmament must be taken within the OSCE framework.

In the future, German foreign policy must concentrate on shaping and strengthening European foreign policy. We need a Europe capable of acting globally as an equal partner of the United States.

9. Germany's Role in International Affairs and Global Economic Interests

Christoph Zöpel

Globalization and Economic Development in Germany

Germany's media, scholars, politicians, and public are discussing the relationship between the country's economic development and global changes—as are their counterparts in many other countries. This discussion soon gives rise to the question as to what role one's nation is to play in the international sphere and how a nation-state, in this case Germany, can shape its economic policy in light of the effects of globalization.

The debate continues; three years have passed since the publication of the first books on the subject, some of which are well founded, others of which have merely received widespread media attention. For those interested in facts, some questions regarding economic globalization have been answered with relative certainty. Germany's economic problems can also be objectively analyzed within the context of the globalization debate. Yet basic differences in economic strategies remain. These differences boil down to whether one believes in the notion of "competition among countries to attract business investment" or "supranational policy."

Germany in International Comparison

Before looking at these differences in more depth, let us first examine Germany's economic problems:

- Since 1991 the number of employed has been falling, from 36.5 million to roughly 34 million in 1997. The unemployment rate has climbed from 7.3 percent to 11.5 percent, with an average of over 4 million employable people out of work in 1997.
- Public budgets are under strain. In the mid-1990s the overall tax ratio climbed to a record 42 percent. Of that, taxes accounted for 23.5 percent and social security contributions for 18.5 percent. At the same time, the budget deficit has reached a record level. Accordingly, the share of public spending, which pays interest on the debt, rose to 11 percent in 1996.
- Tax revenues also are shrinking, placing additional burdens on social security systems.

The most frequently discussed causes of this trend are the diminishing competitiveness of the German economy and insufficient economic growth. These causes are in turn traced back to the high tax burden and an environmental policy that is too stringent.

Let us now compare these data with the major economic indicators of other countries.

1. Average Growth Rates from 1980 to 1990

US	2.7 %
Japan	4.0 %
Germany	2.2 %
Great Britain	2.6 %
France	2.2 %
Sweden	2.0 %

2. 1996 Unemployment Rates

US	5.4 %
Japan	3.4 %
Germany	10.8 %
EU	10.9 %
within the EU	
Spain	22.2 % (highest figure)
Luxembourg	3.1 % (lowest figure)
Great Britain	8.2 %

3. 1995 Overall Tax Ratio According to the OECD Method of Measurement

US (1994)	27.6
Japan (1994)	27.8
Germany	39.1

3. 1995 Overall Tax Ratio *(continued)*

    within the EU

Denmark	51.7 (highest figure)
Sweden	50.2
Great Britain	35.2
Portugal	33.9 (lowest figure)

(Germany's figures for items 1–3 are significantly less favorable than those of the United States and Japan, but within the EU they are about average.)

4. It is difficult to find reliable indicators on environmental pollution and policy. Internationally, German environmental policy is considered successful. Pollutants in major emission categories have dropped considerably. However, CO_2 emissions, which present a problem for global climate policy, are still high. According to a theory advanced by Denis and Donella Meadows in their study for the Club of Rome, which was discussed worldwide in the early 1970s, environmental protection is one cause of limited economic growth.

To measure the effects of the four above indicators on economic competitiveness and export volume, let us consider (a) foreign investments, and (b) import/export ratios. In comparing import and export rates, it is useful to distinguish by country or country groups. We can thus garner information about competition among economies that are at different stages of development. For Germany, the countries of particular interest are the formerly communist countries of Central and Eastern Europe and the countries of Southeast Asia. Figures show that imports from these country groups to Germany are low; indeed, Germany continues to enjoy export surpluses with these countries.

A comparison between the United States and Germany reveals significant differences in the above categories. While Germany has a distinctly better position in terms of per capita exports, the United States is stronger in the foreign-investment category. It is, however, doubtful whether the differences can be traced back to the globalization of trade relations.

Global Trends and Economic Strategies

The globalization of trade relations is a long-term process that has been gaining momentum since the formerly communist states began integrating into the world economy in 1990. The increase in world trade from 12 percent to 16 percent has, however, had fewer effects on the macroeconomic situation in highly developed countries than has been discussed. From a structural point of view, this increase is due more to trade in raw materials and industrial commodities than to trade in services.

Yet, the importance of globalization extends well beyond international trade in a narrower sense. Globalization is the result of scientific discoveries, technological innovations, and entrepreneurial activities. It is, above all, the consequence of perpetually new information technologies and the accelerated movement of goods and people. Transistor radios can be used at any spot on earth; aircraft enable increasing numbers of people to travel to richer countries.

Globalization thus encompasses every sphere of human relations—labor and production, social circumstances, leisure time, and culture. This globalization of virtually all human social relations is irreversible and will continue to increase. A kind of "global society" has evolved from globalization. Highly developed democratic societies perceive this global civil society as desirable, yet it will always be a society with political institutions and players. Thus, globalization represents a challenge to politicians and to politics as a whole.

For centuries politics has been defined as the concerted effort of initially urban, then later territorial, societies to protect themselves against threats and to organize their economic and social coexistence. Now politics has become a global effort. But just as the politics of territory-states and, following the Peace of Westphalia, that of nation-states did not make political action at the city level obsolete, neither will global politics replace the politics of states and groups of states, such as the European Union. It is therefore worth asking (1) which problems are based on differences in each country's circumstances, thus requiring a tailored policy; (2) which problems demand a global policy; and finally (3) what are the different consequences of global policy in various countries?

The primary indicators revealing global differences are

- life expectancy and thus the age structure of the population;
- the levels of gross national product, employment, growth, and productivity;
- the structure of the economy by sector.

Life expectancy and age structure of the population Perhaps the most serious change in highly developed societies is that since the end of

World War II the life expectancy of the population has increased by roughly ten years, well beyond working age, to nearly eighty years on average. At the same time, birth rates have dropped; in some countries they are below the death rate. This demographic shift has caused social-security payments for retirement and health care to grow. It will place a heavier burden on the future working population, in other words, on today's youth.

Relief for the working population could come from immigration and high employment. The highly developed nations will have to rely on immigration in the longer term if they want to structure their populations in such a way that the active workforce can bear the burden of the elderly. The different age structures of Europe and the Middle East make this strategy easier; indeed, it is a means of social balance between these two regions. The situation is similar between North and Latin America.

Gross national product, employment, growth, productivity Rising employment is essential in the short term. To this end, many believe it is critical for Germany and Europe to eliminate weak growth. Specifically, a growth rate well above productivity would be necessary to spur employment. The question is whether such a rate is possible.

A comparison between Europe and the United States shows that average annual productivity gains between 1974 and 1995 were 2 percent in the EU and 6 percent in the US Conversely, average growth rates were

	1980–1990	1990–1994
in Germany	2.2 %	1.1 %
in the US	3.0 %	2.5 %
in Japan	4.1 %	1.2 %

Population trends are significant in this comparison. From 1980 to 1994, the population in the US rose from 228 million to 261 million, and in Germany from 78 million to 82 million. It is plausible to attribute the US average annual growth rate of 1 percent to the 1 percent average annual growth in population. Average annual growth in the US workforce was 1.3 percent from 1980 to 1990 and 1 percent from 1990 to 1994.

Structure of the economy by sector In this comparison between Germany/Europe and the United States, the sectoral composition of the economy becomes relevant. These countries are experiencing the transition from an industrial to a service-based society. Here the differences between the United States and Germany are particularly pronounced. The proportion of wage earners in the service sector is roughly 80 percent in the Unites States as opposed to roughly 60 percent in Germany.

Rising employment combined with lower productivity gains, a phenomenon occurring in much of the US service sector, is sometimes associated with lower wages, but above all with wage differentiation, which in turn leads to an unequal distribution of wealth and social tensions. The call for wage differentiation in Germany, however, is aimed not primarily at transforming the country into a service-based society but at maintaining a high industrial export content. Yet it remains doubtful whether in fact a high level of industrialization can be preserved in this manner. It is more probable that unemployment will rise as a result of high productivity gains in the secondary sector due to downsizing in the industrial sector itself and too little demand for labor in the service sector. Thus, the strategies for economic growth, which have not been quantified and are being promoted throughout Europe are up for discussion. Their effectiveness is doubtful. The limits to growth seen in the early 1970s, in fact, are not attributable to finite resources and environmental restrictions but to the impossibility of achieving exponential growth at the same consistently high rates. The slopes of the economic curves of more highly developed economies bear out this theory: rates are falling.

The real reasons for limited growth are (1) structural market saturation, particularly in the case of basic products, and (2) the limited capacity of densely populated areas to absorb accumulating material capital in the form of housing, machinery, infrastructure, and so on. In international comparison, countries must virtually start out at different economic levels and have disparate growth rates to be able to harmonize variances in their development.

Excessive, unrealistic growth expectations can lead to an economic policy that anticipates these rates and consists primarily of investment borrowing. When these expectations are not met, governments go into debt and private businesses and financial institutions collapse. As proof, the high public budget deficits and interest burdens in many EU countries are one consequence of this illusion about growth; the recent financial turbulence in Southeast Asia is another and primarily affects the private and banking sectors.

The current competition among countries to attract business investment creates a breeding ground for this type of illusory thinking about growth, even if it does manifest itself primarily as a race to lower public levies, wages, and environmental standards. Based on the logic of market economics, whereby prices for production factors and other things—labor and public infrastructure, social security, environmental protection—are harmonized, this competition will only lead to a race to the bottom. The growth effects most likely will not materialize due to the lack of demand from low wage earners and social-welfare recipients.

What will occur are social conflicts and ecological damage. In the analysis of American development, the connection between social inequality and crime becomes increasingly evident. According to labor-market researcher Gerhard Bosch's findings, crime has risen dramatically in the United States over the last fifteen years as lower incomes have fallen. It has become increasingly financially attractive for low wage earners to drop out of the labor market and earn money by dubious means. Bosch also investigated the fiscal repercussions of high crime rates using California as a case in point. In 1995 for the first time California spent more on prisons than on higher education. The proportion of public spending for higher education fell from 12.6 percent in 1980 to 9.5 percent in 1995. In the same time frame, spending for prisons rose from 2 percent to 9.6 percent.

With respect to ecological damage, the situation in Germany is favorable and reassuring when compared internationally. The major problem here is that highly developed nations as a whole serve as an economic role model, with global effects. One does not need to have a knowledge of science to rank the air pollution in cities like New Delhi or Cairo as barely tolerable. And it is no coincidence that financial and environmental crises have coincided in Southeast Asia. Permanently high exponential growth has environmental repercussions. An economic policy based on illusions about growth leads to a vicious circle of accumulating social and ecological problems and government inability to take fiscal action.

Global Policy

It is becoming clear to what extent economic, social, ecological, and cultural problems are global, or globally linked, and thus call for a global or international policy. At the same time, international policy is increasingly replacing foreign policy, which is inherently associated with the politics of sovereign nation-states. It is no longer a matter of asserting national interests over other nations but one of solving common problems and pursuing joint interests through a policy shared by many nation-states.

The Functions of Politics

This change has evolved from the historical nature of politics, which for centuries has had three inherent causes:

1. People could not defend themselves against violence alone and therefore came up with the notion of banding together. They have soldiers to fend off external enemies and police to combat internal ones.
2. People came to realize they could not lead economically, socially, and culturally prosperous lives without inventing certain common rules to manage their production.
3. People then recognized they needed rules for peacefully distributing among themselves what they jointly produced.

These three causes of politics have always existed and still do today: the need for security from enemies, rules for sufficiently managing joint production, and rules for distributing fairly what has been jointly produced.

For two hundred years there have been different answers on how to solve these three basic political problems. The ideas and forces that shape European politics can thus be divided into the categories "right wing" and "left wing." European and German Social Democrats belong to the great tradition of the European leftists. The four principles that differentiate left-wing from right-wing politics are:

1. Left means a fair distribution of wealth along with full employment and a social-welfare state; conversely, right stands for a market economy that needs a reserve army of workers and tolerates a situation where in the long run wealth is concentrated in ever fewer hands.
2. Left means continual democratization and emancipation; right means holding on to privileges, either of heritage, gender, or inherited property.
3. Left stands for internationalism; all people on earth are created equal. The right wants to reduce the world to the level of the nation-state and to the point of social exclusion.
4. The last quarter of the twentieth century saw the addition of the fourth principle: Left means actively supporting an intact environment; right accepts overexploitation at the expense of future generations.

The third principle is important in relation to the globalization debate: internationalism versus nationalism. The left wing, the workers movement, the unions, and the Social Democrats in Europe formulated this principle more than one hundred fifty years ago. At the same time, internationalism always has two important aspects, which could easily come into conflict. First, all people on earth are created equal. There are universal human rights, for which one must fight. Second, the first basic problem of politics, the need for security from external enemies, can best be solved if peace is maintained. Nothing is more secure than peace. This fact has prompted many leftists to become actively committed to pacifism.

Clearly these two aspects can be at conflict when it is necessary to fight for human rights. So, for example, leftists were drawn into the Spanish civil war in 1936 because the fascists wanted to squash human rights. But left-wingers could use pacifist reasoning to argue against deploying soldiers against Iraq or Bosnia.

These general aspects of diverging political goals lend insight into globalization and at the same time show why democratic left-wing parties in Europe have deduced from globalization the need for consistent international, or global, political action. Since the eighteenth century, globalization has been an intellectual and actual process. As a way of ensuring security and peace through internationalism, globalization is a political goal of the democratic left wing.

Stages of Globalization

With the discovery of Australia in 1605, the world became one. Intellectual and practical life across the world became increasingly interconnected in stages.

Stage 1

The postulate of universal human rights and the notion of lasting peace Immanuel Kant advanced these two axioms, which have lasting validity. The Enlightenment, Europe's greatest achievement, thus brought light into the world.

Stage 2

World War I and, after its end, the founding of the League of Nations The insight evolved that global institutions are necessary to ensure peace. The failures of the League of Nations contributed to the start of World War II and, thereafter, to the establishment of the United Nations, which has had increasing success since then.

Stage 3

Recognition of the universality of environmental and resource problems
The universality of environmental problems becomes most evident
in the danger posed to the climate by increasing CO_2 emissions.
The 1992 UN conference in Rio de Janeiro was an important
global-political consequence of this recognition.

Stage 4

*The global integration of financial transactions based on new information
technologies* It is this segment of commercial integration that is new
to economic relations, not the competition that threshold countries represent to the old industrial nations.

Now that the historically constant political goals of security and
economic welfare and the new goal of environmental protection
have become globalized, consistent political action is necessary
within the framework of a democratically oriented world order.
Watchwords of a democratic world order are

- reforming the composition of the UN Security Council
- expanding and integrating international economic organizations such as the IMF, the World Bank, and the WTO into
  global monetary and treaty-monitoring institutions
- forming UN environmental bodies capable of taking decisions

At the same time, global policy must necessarily be decentralized
and thus regionalized.

Effects of Global Policy on Germany

For Germany, this regionalization of global integration means

- consistent Europeanization, in other words, deepening and
  enlarging the European Union;
- European responsibility for internal security through conflict
  prevention or conflict resolution;
- coordinated European employment policy;
- harmonized European tax policy;
- European environmental standards;
- harmonization of the social-welfare state at the European level.

In the first step, the economic, ecological, and social deepening of
the European Union would create a uniform regional framework

for 57 percent of Germany's exports. In this area there would no longer be any serious distortions in competition due to differing taxes, social, and environmental standards.

In the second step, integrating those countries into the European Union could minimize income-related differences with Eastern Europe. As Eastern Europe vigorously promotes growth, economic levels will become harmonized, a factor important especially to Germany, which has long borders with Poland and the Czech Republic.

Eighty percent of German foreign trade is conducted with highly developed nations. Consequently, only 20 percent occurs with states where a type of competition that is perceived as dumping could develop in the environmental and social spheres. The competition coming primarily from threshold nations that many see as a particular threat affects only a small portion of German foreign trade, conventional industrial products in particular.

Global Policy and European Union

The euro and European employment policy are currently at the center of the European debate. The pros and cons of the euro are essentially concerned with economic stability. The central banks of highly developed countries have succeeded over the last ten years in following an effective policy of monetary stability. Europe must succeed in institutionally transferring that policy to a European central bank. Ruling out internal European exchange-rate fluctuations could make this monetary policy even more efficient than those pursued by the individual member states.

In retrospect, it is surprising that the German central bank has attained monetary stability despite the country's rising public budget deficits. Like other European states, until now Germany was unable to check this deficit-spending trend on its own. The stability criteria for the euro, especially the 3 percent limit on budget deficits, have brought about a change in European fiscal policy. Even countries such as Italy, which in the past have been politically assessed as unstable, have been able to meet the criteria. It is worth noting that the United States and Canada have been able to achieve this change in budget policy on their own.

Stable money and consolidated public budgets are key to a European employment policy. Such a policy must be pursued in tandem with the harmonization of tax and environmental policies. Then it will be possible to pursue wage and working-hour policies at the European level.

Prior to the EU jobs summit in Luxembourg at the end of 1997, conservative governments in particular, such as in Germany and Spain, defined employment policy as a national task. This would be understandable only if the competition among countries to attract business investment were deemed job creating, which it is not.

Together, Europe and the United States can shape global economic policy and global policy more effectively than they have done in the past. This will probably be easier in the economic than in the security sphere. Proposals for international policy, for global governance, exist.

Global Economic Policy

The past competitive situation between highly developed and developing countries—high wages and productivity here, low wages and productivity there—no longer applies to every sphere. Multinational companies can establish highly efficient facilities for industrial mass production anywhere in the world. Productivity gains thus level off. It is a task of international collective-bargaining policy to even out wage differences. Economic history since the beginning of industrialization shows that wage differentiation among economies always offers only temporary competitive advantages. The wealthier trading partners are, the greater trade among economies will be. So increasing prosperity in developing nations is also an advantage to industrial countries. For their own long-term benefit, therefore, highly developed countries must also promote importation from developing countries. Greater export possibilities for developing countries will encourage the import of capital and know-how to those regions.

Highly developed countries must increase their economic aid to developing countries. They should meet and renew their voluntary commitment to provide aid worth 0.7 percent of their GNP. This development aid must be used above all to improve the quality of immovable factors of production, such as worker training and infrastructure quality. At the same time, the competitive differences of the developing countries must be taken into account. The least developed nations lack the conditions that would simply enable them to export a sufficient amount of goods and services. That is why development aid is particularly needed for providing basic goods to the population, for training, and for infrastructure financing.

Development aid can be financed through cuts in other expenditures and the rechanneling of funds:

- The highly developed nations can do without many of the subsidies to globally active companies that are based on technology and industrial policies. Redirecting these funds would ease long-term world trade, from which highly developed and a few developed nations would benefit because of harmonized conditions for competition.
- Arms production and exports are largely dispensable. It is also necessary to shift these funds to economic aid for developing nations.

Globalization continues to instill fear in both highly developed and developing nations. The one group fears the costs of cheap labor; the other, the power of multinational companies with superior technology. The globalized economy therefore requires a global economic system. Standardizing global framework conditions and ensuring that countries strictly adhere to them are the crucial tasks of global economic policy. Framework conditions for the global monetary and capital markets constitute the most pressing need. Since the Southeast Asia crisis, there has been growing global agreement on this issue.

Regionalization of global policy is necessary not only with respect to the EU. Trade among developing nations is extremely low. Indicative are the trade relations in the Mediterranean region, between Europe and the Middle Eastern states. Arab states trade disproportionately more with individual European countries than they do among themselves. Therefore, particularly for the lesser developed countries, investment requires more closely integrated markets without barriers related to national frontiers.

Global Security Policy

Global security partnership can and must follow global economic policy. It will be easier if economic and social cooperation, as well as environmental cooperation, succeeds. A joint global system to achieve prosperity and common global rules for its fair distribution reduces violent conflicts. This was true during the formation of territorial- and nation-states. Why should it be any different for the formation of the "global state"? Military security then turns into internal security and law enforcement. It can begin at the regional level; continue in Europe and North America through security partnerships between regions such as Europe and the Middle East or North America and Central America; and end in a comprehensive global security partnership.

Luxembourg, Oman, Uruguay, and Germany, too, will have an easier time with this development than will the United States, China, India, or Russia. National sovereignty is dependent on the ability of a nation to defend itself against external threats. Yet it should evolve into prevention of violence and political protection against threats—benefiting small and large states whose borders are all the more open.

Part V

GLOBAL ENVIRONMENTAL POLICY

10. Global Environmental Management: On Measures of Climate Policy and How to Use Them

Udo Ernst Simonis

> *The neat resolution of a free market that so beautifully*
> *reconciles buyers and sellers does so far not reconcile*
> *growthists and earthists. Something new is needed.*
>
> —Nathan Keyfitz

The Political Context

In its 1995 report *Our Global Neighborhood,* the International Commission on Global Governance stated:

> There is no single model or form of global governance, nor is there a single structure or set of structures. It is, rather, a broad, dynamic, complex process of interactive decisionmaking that is constantly evolving and responding to changing circumstances.... Effective global decisionmaking thus needs to build upon and influence decisions taken locally, nationally and regionally....

This observation certainly holds as regards climate policy, so far the most elaborated field of global environmental management.

With respect to the formulation and implementation of such a policy, the Berlin Mandate, the most important concluding document of the First Conference of the Parties to the United Nations Framework Convention on Climate Change, adopted on 7 April 1995, postulates the following: "The Parties should protect the climate

---

References for this chapter begin on page 184.

system for the benefit of present and future generations of humankind, on the basis of equity and in accordance with their common but differentiated responsibilities and respective capabilities."
It continues: "The global nature of climate change calls for the
widest possible cooperation by all countries ...; developed countries [should] set quantified target limitation and reduction objectives within specified time frames, such as 2005, 2010 and 2020."
Finally, it states that "the process should begin without delay" (Berlin Mandate 1995).

As regards "joint implementation," an instrument which affects
both industrialized and developing countries, the Conference of
the Parties decided "to establish a *pilot phase* for activities implemented *jointly* among *Annex I Parties* and, on a voluntary basis, with
non-Annex I Parties that so request." During this pilot phase, a framework should be established "for *reporting* in a transparent, well-de-
fined and credible fashion on the possible global *benefits* and the
national economic, social and environmental *impacts* as well as any
practical *experience* or technical *difficulties* encountered" (Berlin
Mandate 1995).

The idea for the present article arose out of this complex context
of ethics and environment. The specific question to be answered is
the following one: what form should a future policy instrument for
the reduction of greenhouse gas emissions take if it is to enable
both *global environmental protection* and *global development*, while satisfying both the criteria of *economic efficiency* and *equity*? The answer,
which will be explained in the following, is: by creating a market
where, so far, no market exists, i.e., by introducing carefully designed internationally tradable emission certificates.

The Theoretical Context

Three main issues dominate the formulation of an international
greenhouse-gas regime, in the form of a "climate protocol" within
the Framework Convention on Climate Change that came into
force in 1994: *efficiency, equity*, and decision making under *uncertainty*. And three major policy instruments are discussed as regards
practical implementation of such a protocol: (1) introduction of an
international carbon tax and/or *carbon dioxide charge*, (2) *joint implementation*, and (3) *tradable emission certificates* (emissions trading[1]).

1. Incidentally, this is a concept for which twelve different names were found by
the author in the English literature.

The following discussion will cover all these instruments but will focus on the interactions between the equity issue and tradable emission certificates.

International Emission Charges

Pearce has summed up the arguments in favor of introducing a carbon dioxide charge or carbon tax as an instrument of a global climate policy (Pearce 1991).[2] As his central argument, he cites Baumol and Oates, who pointed out that a tax allows total emissions to be reduced at minimum cost (Baumol and Oates 1975). A given tax will induce emitters with low marginal avoidance costs to reduce emissions, while those with high marginal costs will find it more appropriate to pay the tax. In general terms, taxes use the market mechanism to adapt in an optimum way to the greenhouse problem, while direct government regulation can, in the individual case, be extremely expensive. In a comparative study on the US, Tietenberg established that the average ratio of "command and control costs" to "least-cost measures" was 4:1 (Tietenberg 1990).

Pearce adds four further advantages of a carbon tax. First, the revenue gained allows other taxes to be replaced (neutrality of effect). Second, the potential revenue opens up possibilities of substantial resource transfers from North to South. Third, it involves a constant inducement for industry to undergo structural change toward environment-friendly production. Fourth, if new (scientific) information about the climate problem and its impacts becomes available, the tax can be modified relatively easily.

However, there are also several disadvantages to an international carbon tax, which should not be ignored. As we have only a rough idea of the price elasticity of the supply and demand for fuel, particularly as concerns the great dimensions we would be dealing with in practice, there is considerable uncertainty as to how large a reduction in emissions would be (two examples are shown in Figure 10.1). Furthermore, it is widely held that the final incidence of a carbon tax is regressive. In addition, the real distribution effect of a tax solution is usually concealed, while that of a quantitative solution—as will be shown below—is transparent, at least in the initial stage.

2. The following examples of greenhouse-gas emissions refer to carbon dioxide (CO_2) emissions or the equivalent amount of carbon (C)—calculated at a ratio of 3.67:1. If other greenhouse gases such as methane (CH_4) and nitrous oxide (N_2O) are included in the discussion about climate policy, it is recommended that they be expressed as equivalents of carbon dioxide in order to introduce a common "currency unit" on the emission certificates market.

Figure 10.1 Emission Reduction Effect of a Carbon Tax on Fossil Fuels—Two Examples

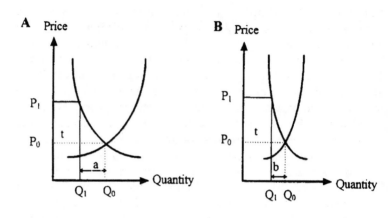

Probably the weightiest argument against the introduction of an international carbon tax is not concerned with economics but with organizational factors: the tax volume needed to initiate an appreciable global reduction in emissions would be so immense (the literature speaks in terms of several hundred billion dollars) that centralized administration would be unacceptable. Yet an acceptable decentralized redistribution would probably be very difficult to organize (but see Hoel 1991 and his comments on reimbursement parameters).

There is also, however, an important ecological argument that can be put forward against an international carbon tax. In situations with rapidly increasing marginal environmental damage, taxes symbolize a possible economic compromise which the ecological system itself does not (cannot) accept. In this case, quantitative (and immediate) restrictions are the only meaningful solution. Nor should one forget the problem of nonharmonized tax systems from country to country and region to region (particularly in the case of a mineral oil tax), which would be no less acute in the case of a carbon tax. And finally, of course, one should keep in mind the apparent reluctance of the OPEC countries (particularly

Saudi Arabia) to compromise on the subject of global climate policy, especially a tax solution.

It needs also to be mentioned that a tax on *carbon* (or carbon equivalents) would be necessary as a response strategy to the climate problem, not a tax on *energy* in general. This has to do with the fact that the main task lies in extensively replacing fossil fuels with renewable sources of energy. This substitution effect would not occur if solar energy, for example, were also to be taxed on a global scale.

While efficiency and equity are central criteria of the Framework Convention and the Berlin Mandate, it is surprising to see that in these documents no specific proposal is made for an international tax solution. This is different in the case of the two other policy instruments, which are referred to explicitly or implicitly, and will be dealt with in the following sections.

Joint Implementation

As concerns the choice and structure of the policy instruments of global climate policy, Article 3, section 3 of the Framework Convention is especially relevant. This provision calls on the parties to implement the measures agreed on in a cost-effective way: the desired reductions in emissions are to be achieved at minimum cost. In view of the ecological and economic context of a global climate policy, this efficiency clause is particularly significant. Ecologically speaking—i.e., as regards the effect of greenhouse gases on global climate—it is completely irrelevant where in the world action is taken to reduce emissions, but if the costs of those reductions are to be kept at a minimum, then account will have to be taken of the fact that the marginal costs of reducing emissions (marginal avoidance costs) vary largely across the globe. In other words, strong economic arguments enter the climate policy arena. It was with this in mind that the instrument of joint implementation found its way into the Framework Convention (especially Article 4, sections 2a and 2b). At the first Conference of the Parties in Berlin in 1995, it was decided to introduce a pilot phase in order to gain respective experience.

Basically, joint implementation is an offset version of a quantitative policy with tradable certificates: a country (a branch of industry, a company) can fulfill its reduction obligations through a combination of national (internal) reductions and international (external) offsets (offsets here means emission reduction credits which, once they have formally been certified, could be traded internationally). Until recently, this has usually been interpreted as meaning that an Annex I party to the Framework Convention on

Climate Change (i.e., an OECD country or a country with an economy in transition) can fulfill its emissions target not only by domestic reductions, but also by investing in avoidance activities in other Annex I countries. The 1995 Berlin Conference resolved that non-Annex I states can also be included, on a voluntary basis. Joint implementation has thus become a policy instrument in the North-South context, and this provision can be seen as a first step toward a global climate policy of quantitative control and a system of internationally tradable emission certificates.

A series of questions will have to be answered before it can be said how significant this policy instrument is or can become in the future (Jepma 1995). Those questions, which I feel to be most important, particularly from an ethical point of view, shall now be dealt with in some detail.

The Framework Convention on Climate Change does not contain any definite target for the reduction of global emissions. According to Article 3, section 1, the industrialized countries, because of their "historical debts" and their high emission levels, should "take the lead in combating climate change and the adverse effects thereof."

Along with their general commitments, i.e., developing inventories, promoting research etc., the industrialized countries assume certain additional obligations, particularly as regards the reduction of greenhouse-gas emissions and the financial and technological transfer to developing countries. Since March 1994, all industrialized countries, including Eastern European states and the Russian Federation, are obliged "[to] adopt national policies and take corresponding measures on the mitigation of climate change, by *limiting* [their] anthropogenic emissions of greenhouse gases and *protecting* and *enhancing* [their] greenhouse gas sinks and reservoirs" (Article 4, section 2, italics added).

The exact legal scope of the term "limiting" is difficult to assess, since the Convention does not provide any exact definition, but only a range of different aspects to be taken into account, inter alia, the corresponding need to maintain strong and sustainable economic growth in the developing countries.

Despite the lack of any precise timetable, Article 4, section 2a, clearly stipulates that the national policies to be adopted by the parties have to be directed toward the "limitation" of emissions, which should, according to the ordinary meaning of the term in the light of its object and purpose, amount to a significant modification of present emission trends, but does not have to amount to the return to 1990 levels by the year 2000. The duty under that paragraph is therefore not merely a duty of conduct—as in paragraph 1, which applies to all parties—but a duty of *result*. However, since no definite time frame has been agreed upon, a certain increase in carbon dioxide emissions after 1994 may be considered as still falling under the scope of "limiting."

On the other hand, if the United States, for example, would entirely ignore their duty to *limit* their emissions for a long time, they would certainly act in breach of the Framework Convention. The agreed final aim as stipulated in the 1992 Convention is still "returning *individually* or *jointly* to their 1990 levels these anthropogenic emissions of carbon dioxide and other greenhouse gases not controlled by the Montreal Protocol" (Article 4, section 2b, italics added).

So far, then, there does not exist a *binding* global reduction target on absolute reductions below the (ecologically much too high) 1990 emission level nor any *country-specific* reduction target. Certain countries and groups of countries have, however, unilaterally committed themselves to definite reductions in emissions, including Germany, which, at the Berlin Conference, confirmed its assertion that by the year 2005, it would "reduce its emissions of carbon dioxide to a level 25 percent lower than that of 1990" (speech by the federal chancellor, 5 April 1995).

In this respect, joint implementation is for the time being only a policy instrument to make *unilateral* targets more flexible. However, in view of the fact that marginal avoidance costs for greenhouse gases vary from country to country and especially between North and South, a clear reduction in the cost of reducing emissions can be achieved. Or, to put it differently, an additional reduction in emissions can be achieved at no extra cost.

Joint implementation can also unlock positive economic effects via the transfer of low-emission technologies to developing countries. The otherwise tremendous increase in emissions that is to be expected, for example, when China and India become ever more motorized and industrialized, could be neutralized or even reduced. This positive effect of joint implementation is especially important, as no targets for the reduction of emissions have hitherto been set in these and (almost all) other developing countries.

One further important argument in favor of this policy instrument is that it can be applied without further delay, even if there were no global agreement on reduction obligations, or if no such agreement can be reached in the next few years.

Joint implementation, then, is a potentially powerful policy instrument, both for the ecologically necessary reduction of emissions and for the economically desirable transfer of efficient technology. However, its implementation is faced with potent obstacles, which can be summed up under the categories of *search costs, transaction costs*, and *control costs*. These obstacles have been analyzed in quite some detail (see, for example, the 1994 Annual Report of the German Advisory Council on Global Change (1995: 21ff.) and need not be repeated here.

The success of the joint implementation instrument will depend crucially on the institutional arrangements that are agreed upon. Several models are conceivable:

- simple bilateral systems of negotiation and information—the participating states report the reductions in emissions they have achieved to the other parties to the Convention;
- inclusion of an international institution (such as the Secretariat of the Framework Convention); this would act as a clearing house promoting the emergence of a joint implementation market;
- in addition to that, an international institution (the Secretariat) monitors and verifies the reductions in emissions achieved as a result of joint implementation.

One important component of these arrangements would consist in ascertaining the reduction in emissions effected by joint implementation in the form of "emission credits" for the investing country (branch, company). These credits are essential for two reasons. First, they provide the necessary incentive for investing capital abroad and, second, they must not run counter to the reduction of emissions at home (allegation of "modern sale of indulgences"). The Berlin Mandate, however, stipulates that "no credits shall accrue to any Party as a result of greenhouse gas emissions reduced or sequestered during the pilot phase from activities implemented jointly."

In order to avoid possible failure of the joint implementation policy instrument inherent in this restrictive condition, the following compromise can be suggested: emission credits should not be credited in full to the national emissions account, but only in part— 50 percent, for example (as suggested by France), or 75–80 percent (as suggested by the German Advisory Council on Global Change; WBGU 1995). In this case, if the reductions in emissions that have been achieved were used to strengthen national reduction targets (for the EU, OECD, or Annex I states), then joint implementation would indirectly lead to more stringent climate protection.

It must be recalled that participation in joint implementation projects should not lead to any reduction in the overall financial obligations resulting from the Framework Convention or, indeed, in the actual and otherwise pledged development aid payments (Norway has submitted a proposal to this effect).

Taken together, then, the debate about joint implementation ought to be seen as an opportunity to sound the trumpet that political possibilities exist for stabilizing the climate and for coupling them with proactive development policy. Nevertheless, the quantitative significance of joint implementation in the global context should not to be overestimated. Although this policy instrument would activate private money for a common purpose (the global climate), it will only allow the industrialized countries to fulfill the minor part of their obligations. Even so, in the developing countries a process can be undertaken that would only otherwise occur late (or even too late)—and in the end, this process could lead to a more comprehensive system of internationally tradable emission certificates.

Internationally Tradable Emission Certificates

Tradable emission certificates differ in various ways from joint implementation (or "external offsets"). Binding global obligations to reduce emissions will (must) result from the pending negotiations. The German Bundestag's Enquête Commission on Climate Policy, and also the Intergovernmental Panel on Climate Change (IPCC) assumes that a reduction of global carbon dioxide emissions by 50 percent compared to the 1987 levels (requiring an 80 percent reduction in the industrialized countries) must be reached by the year 2050 if the aim of stabilizing the climate system is to be achieved (see Table 10.1).

For the present, let us assume that an agreement of this kind (or similar) is reached in the "climate protocol," to be negotiated on and resolved at the Third or the Fourth Conference of the Parties in 1997 or 1998. What could this mean for the form and structure of a system of internationally tradable emission certificates? As part of the system of agreed quantified permissible global emissions, tradable certificates would be handed out—for the whole duration of the agreement or, better still, for certain time periods—to the participating parties on the basis of an allocation procedure that would also have to be agreed on (both would probably be negotiated in

Table 10.1 CO_2 Emission Plan, Enquête Commission on Climate Policy (Benchmark 1987, in %)

Year	Industrialized Countries	Developing Countries	Whole World
1990	+5	+11	+6
1995	+6	+24	+10
2000	-4	+37	+4
2005	-20	+50	-5
2020	-40	+60	-20
2050	-80	+70	-50

Source: Enquête Commission (1990).

parallel). When the agreement came into force, the participants would receive certificates corresponding to the emission quantities they had been allocated. If this initial allocation were insufficient for a participant (a country, a branch, a company), the participant would have to acquire additional certificates via trade. For those participating in the system, therefore, an incentive to reduce emissions would be established, be it to minimize payments for the purchase of additional certificates *or* to maximize earnings from the sale or lease of surplus certificates. If the initial allocation to developing countries led to substantial quantities of surplus certificates there, a potent mechanism for the transfer of resources would be created: developing countries could sell or lease their surplus certificates to industrialized countries for money, technologies, or patents.

So, there are certain similarities between an international emission charge (*price solution*) and tradable emission certificates (*quantity solution*). The issue of the initial allocation of certificates is similar to the issue of allocating the revenue from a charge. However, there are also several differences. The most important of these is that emission certificates exactly meet the emission reduction target in terms of quantity; the concurrent financial expenditure would be the result of the costs connected with achieving this target. This contrasts with an emission charge, which regulates financial expenditure but does not directly regulate the volume of the emissions. A further difference is that a charge generally means monetary transfers, while certificates could easily be traded for gratuities other than money (such as technologies or patents). A system of tradable emission certificates, therefore, increases the scope of the negotiations between North and South—and might therefore be met with broad (possibly sufficient) political approval for precisely that reason.

Unlike joint implementation projects, monitoring a system of tradable emission certificates would be concerned with the (relatively simple) measurement of total emissions from a contracting state rather than the (more difficult) measurement of emission reductions of specific projects. The question of responsibility for adhering to the rules of procedure (i.e., compliance) is also easier, as one is not dealing with direct investments but with the sale or lease of a tradable good (i.e., certificates).

There are other theoretical and practical issues connected with a system of emission certificates—the issues connected with implementation will be dealt with in the following section. Let me end the present section with a quotation from the 1996 IPCC report, which in its chapter on response strategies (Chapter 11) states the following:

> The consequences of climate change policy will be determined by the choice of policy instruments.... For a global treaty, a tradable quota system is the *only* potentially cost-effective arrangement where an agreed level of emissions is attained with certainty (subject to enforcement).... A choice of tradable quotas at the international level would (at the same time) provide maximum flexibility for instrument choice at the domestic level. (Italics added)

Emissions Trading: From Theory to Practice

We started by saying that a practicable agreement on policy instruments to limit or reduce greenhouse-gas emissions has to satisfy several criteria, in particular those of *efficiency, equity,* and decision making under *uncertainty*. The weight given to the individual criterion will determine which of the possible policy instruments or combinations of instruments is recommended. If, unlike on the national level, the criteria of equity and uncertainty (particularly because of irreversible ecological processes) play a special role on the international level, then there is much to be said in favor of tradable emission certificates. Yet, their practical organization entails many potential snares which can be decisive for their acceptance. The following section will look in some detail at the questions of market organization, rules of procedure, and the initial allocation of emission certificates. Other issues, which I feel are less problematic, will not be addressed here (see Epstein and Gupta 1990).

Market Organization

Creating a market for internationally tradable emission certificates is no easy undertaking, to put it mildly. Monitoring, certification, market access, and market extension require careful management —what is more, they take place in a highly complex area of policy. A debate about these implementation issues has at least begun, and thus one may expect the system to become established in the not too distant future. A United Nations Conference on Trade and Development (UNCTAD) study done in 1992 has already looked into the institutional issues of market organization.

One such issue is the number of actors on this market. A "mixed" trading system in which both governments *and* companies participate could be optimal. Governments would remain subject to their international obligations, particularly to ensure that the certificates tally with actual emissions. Trade at the company level would enlarge the technical options of emission reduction. Yet, this could also mean that the volume of trade becomes too large. However, the major worry in the literature is that cartels could be formed. Whether or not this threat can be conquered will in the first place depend on the number of market participants, which speaks in favor of a more substantial number. If one were, for example, to start with the producers and importers of raw materials containing carbon, then, according to Maier-Rigaud, there would be about five hundred actors in an EU certificates market.

There are several ways of avoiding cartellization on the emerging certificates market. Regular rounds to reallocate or replace certificates could ensure a liquid and flexible market, and rules against hoarding and price rigging could be agreed on. The final, drastic sanction against improper conduct could be "exit," although this would have an adverse effect on all the market participants.

Rules of Procedure

One question is whether emission certificates should be valid endlessly. Although any such "perpetual certificate" would not necessarily prevent the revision (and especially the tightening) of the global emission reduction target—a part of them could be withdrawn from the market or devalued regularly—much speaks in favor of certificates with only limited validity. For one thing, not all parties to the Framework Convention will participate in the system from the start and, for another, this would counter existing fears of certificates being *bought up* by industrialized countries or multinational corporations. The other extreme version, whereby certificates would be *leased but never sold*, would only lead to more flexibility if a (more) frequent new issue was agreed on. One must say that the question of an *optimum* term for emission certificates is still an open one. In the literature, the ideas range from two to twenty years.

In this context, Bertram (1992) has proposed an *overlapping procedure*, under which ten-year certificates would be issued and 10 percent withdrawn from the market every year. This proposal could be summed up by the following formula: "If certificates are valid for *L* years and a certain proportion *P/L* is withdrawn from the market every year, then a new tranche of certificates valid for *L* years can be issued." At any given time, therefore, the market would consist of a mix of certificates, some long-term, some short-term; countries (branches, companies) could accordingly maintain a mixed portfolio and a futures market (comparable with existing other "futures markets") could emerge.

The benefit of such system flexibility is obvious. It would be possible, on the basis of the most recent *natural* science evidence about pollution and the adaptability of the ecosystem, as well as on the basis of *social* science evidence regarding the economic system's limits of adaptability, to hold subsequent negotiations on permissible emission limits. It would also be possible to include new sources and sinks of greenhouse-gas emissions, and to allow additional countries to participate.

Whatever happens, this benefit should not turn into a disadvantage as a result of excessive complexity or bureaucracy. Grubb and Sebenius (1992) have shown that, in an overlapping system, revision periods of two to four years might be the best possible solution. Given the probable institutional details of the future global climate regime (such as annual conferences of the parties, two-thirds majorities, gradual tightening of the targets set), this may well be a realistic assumption.

Allocation of Certificates

The crucial factor for the political acceptance of tradable emission certificates will probably be that their design be ethically based, and that their initial allocation be perceived as fair. Indeed, for many authors (myself included), the system hinges on the "equity factor." While the initial allocation of certificates does not predetermine the final distribution effect (i.e., real incidence), which ultimately is the result of market decisions (certificate price and quantity), it does predetermine the direction and possible volume of transnational resource transfer the system will involve. A certain distribution effect will, of course, result from all conceivable instruments of climate policy, especially where the dimensions are globally significant, but also in national solutions, be they price or quantity solutions.

There are different ways of effecting the initial allocation of emission certificates. One distinction is between *burden-based* and *responsibility-based criteria*: the former emphasizes the burden of adjustment involved in the desired reduction in emissions, while the latter stresses the polluter-pays principle, either in terms of the current emissions or in terms of historical and accumulated emissions. To a certain extent, the search for an ethically acceptable allocation formula in global climate policy reflects the old debate between "realists" and "idealists" in development policy.

- "Realists" would argue that certificates (and the rights to pollute that they entail) must be allocated on the basis of either the *current emissions* or the gross domestic product (GDP), since any other formula would be unacceptable (see, for example, Pearce 1991). Ethically, this position is extremely weak and completely fails to satisfy any criterion of equity. In no way can either current emissions or historical and accumulated emissions be defined as "fair." Furthermore, this position ignores one, if not *the*, crucial advantage of an international system of certificates, which is that an *additional* transfer of resources can be set in motion. The "realistic" position is also unrealistic in that it almost completely ignores the developing countries, which are beginning to take an interest in global climate policy precisely because ecological necessity may turn out to be to their economic blessing.
- On the opposite side we have the "idealists," who insist, explicitly or implicitly, on the inclusion of historical and accumulated emissions (as a sign of "ecological guilt" or "historical debt"—indeed, some of them even argue that developing countries, for the time being, should not be integrated into the global climate regime [see, for example, Hayes and Smith 1993]).

Various allocation proposals have been put forward, with *globally uniform per capita allocation* presenting the strongest ethical claim. In this case, the initial allocation of emission certificates would be directly proportional to national population (in the current year or, as a softer version, in a base year, like 1992, for instance). It can be said that the practical consequences of this proposal would be considerable, if not revolutionary. Any industrialized country with above-average per capita emissions would have to purchase certificates from developing countries, not only in respect of fossil fuel consumption but also in respect of all other sources and sinks of greenhouse gases, possibly with the exception of deforestation (slash-and-burn, clear-felling). Even using moderate projections of the certificates prices that would ensue, there would then be a complete reversal of the presently existing net South-North transfers. (Grubb and Sebenius assume that it would be at least as much as current official development assistance [ODA], which is in the order of $60 billion per annum.)

Of course, the alternative to any extreme position is to find a *mixed formula*—a formula which will at least guarantee that there is a net transfer from the industrialized to the developing countries (and not *vice versa*) in implementing a global climate policy. Personally, I find the formula developed by William R. Cline (1992) extremely appealing:

$$Q_i = Q_g \left[w_h \Phi_{0,i}^h + w_y \Phi_{0,i}^y + w_p \Phi_{0,i}^p \right]$$

where Q_i is the emission target of country i; Q_g is the global emission target; w, the weight of the criterion in question (sum of $w = 1$); h is historical emissions, y is GDP at purchasing power parity, p is population; Φ is the share of country i in the global total; and 0 is the base year.

This allocation formula includes the most important alternative criteria under discussion and weights them, a practice that has also been applied by the IMF (definition of country quotas), the United Nations Committee for Development Planning (definition of least less developed countries; LLDCs), and other institutions (Levi 1991). The formula could be described as the necessary mixture of efficiency, equity, *and* realism.

Cline provides an illustrative example of this formula in action. The US currently (1992) accounts for 25.7 percent of global GDP, 17.5 percent of global greenhouse-gas emissions (including deforestation), and 4.8 percent of the world's total population. The simple average of these three figures comes to 16 percent. Were a global emissions target of 4 billion tons of carbon to be agreed on by the Conference of the Parties to the Framework Convention, the US's initial share would amount to 640 million tons. Current emissions, however, total 1.2 billion tons. Accordingly, the US would either have to reduce its emissions by 50 percent, or purchase an additional 100 percent of its initial share of allocated certificates.

By contrast, India's share would come to 8 percent of global emissions or 320 million tons of carbon, which would correspond to a surplus of some 50 million tons (or 17 percent above current emissions), which India could then sell or lease on the international emission certificates market.

As befits the logic of a mixed formula, the weighting of the *three* components could be *modified* in the course of time. For example, the weighting of the first criterion (historical, accumulated emissions) could be reduced from one-third down to zero over a period of, let us say, twenty years ("phasing out") and that of the second criterion (GDP) from one-third down to zero over a period of forty or fifty years. The final result then would be an ethically strong position, namely globally uniform per capita emission rights (i.e., the population criterion).

A less formal, more "political" solution of the allocation problem might lie in a compromise that could be described as follows: "The allocation of emission certificates changes over time, from a position based (more or less) on *current emissions* to a position of (more or less) *equal per capita emissions.*"

A strategic compromise of this nature might be acceptable both for the industrialized countries and the developing countries, since it offers a strong incentive for a fair (or fairer) future emissions situation for the whole world in general, and for the linking of environmental protection with economic development in particular—even though this perspective was not explicitly aimed for at either the 1992 Rio de Janeiro Conference on Environment and Development or at the 1995 Berlin and 1997 Kyoto Climate Conferences.

Conclusion

Efficiency, equity, and uncertainty, it was said, are the three major topics in formulating a global climate policy. As regards policy implementation, we tried to answer the question of how the instruments should be tailored to facilitate global environmental protection *and* economic development simultaneously, and to meet *both* the efficiency and the equity criterion in international relations. As far as *national environmental policy* is concerned, and in view of the high degree of institutionalization and the specific historical and cultural background of policy formulation and implementation in the industrialized countries, the author is very much in favor of a *balanced instrumental mix*, which includes market-oriented and regulatory, price-based and quantity-based policy instruments.

As regards the structure of the international system and the emerging contours of global environmental management in general, and international climate policy in particular, I do favor market-oriented quantity solutions, especially *joint implementation* in the regime's initial phase and *tradable emission certificates* in its final phase. If a system of certificates were prepared with the necessary care, equity would gain importance and Peter Bohm's succinct judgment would then seem justified: "Making emission quotas tradable among countries implies not only that a globally efficient limit to total emissions is attained with *certainty*,... but also that the initial emission quota distribution of the treaty is shifted in favor of *the poorer countries*" (Bohm, 1992, p. 112, italics added).

This first best solution, of course, does not exclude regulation or taxation as a second best solution. When confronted with global environmental problems threatening human survival, new and additional efforts may have to be undertaken. In particular, if the institutionalization of the Global Environment Facility (GEF) is to be enhanced, then it will have to be financed by taxes, as conventional multilateral development assistance would otherwise be affected negatively. In this case, other forms of taxes and bases of assessment again appear feasible, which had been proposed on strong ethical grounds, namely a tax on arms trade (see Brandt Report 1983), on long-distance tourism (see Mishan 1970), or on international financial transactions (see Brundtland Report 1987, and Qureshi and von Weizsäcker Report 1995).

Whatever decision is being taken, equity issues have become part and parcel of international relations, this time in the arena of global climate policy. And what is more, the experiences with climate policy will be of value to additional environmental treaties in the future, such as global agreements on marine protection, biodiversity, soil and water conservation, and desertification. When these global issues finally come onto the agenda, similar financial and procedural provisions may be stipulated, and here, again, it is experience that counts.

References

Baumol, W., and W. E. Oates. 1975. *The Theory of Environmental Policy.* Englewood Cliffs.

Bertram, G. 1992. Tradable Emission Permits and the Control of Greenhouse Gases. *Journal of Development Studies* 28 (3):423–446.

Bohm, P. 1992. Distributional Implications of Allowing International Trade in Carbon Dioxide Emission Quotas. *World Economy* 15 (1):107–114.

Cline, W. R. 1992. *The Economics of Global Warming.* Washington, D.C.

Commission on Global Governance. 1995. *Our Global Neighborhood.* Oxford.

Enquête Commission. Protecting the Earth's Atmosphere: Report of the Study Commission of the Eleventh German Bundestag, ed. 1989. *Preventive Measures to Protect the Earth's Atmosphere.* Bonn.

Epstein, J. M. and R. Gupta. 1990. *Controlling the Greenhouse Effect: Five Global Regimes Compared.* Washington, D.C.

German Advisory Council on Global Change (WBGU). 1995. *World in Transition: The Threat to Soils.* 1994 Annual Report. Bonn.

———. 1996. *World in Transition: Ways Towards Global Environmental Solutions.* 1995 Annual Report. Berlin.

Grubb, M., and J. Sebenius. 1990. Participation, Allocation and Adaptability in International Tradable Emission Permit Systems for Greenhouse Gas Control. In *Tradable Permits for Abating Greenhouse Gases. Practical Options,* ed. OECD. Paris.

Hayes, P., and K. Smith, eds. 1993. *The Global Greenhouse Regime. Who Pays?* Tokyo, New York, Paris.

Heister, J., and P. Michaelis. 1991. Handelbare Emissionsrechte für Kohlendioxid. *Zeitschrift für angewandte Umweltforschung* 4 (1):68–80.

Hoel, M. 1991. Efficient International Agreements for Carbon Dioxide-Control. *The Energy Journal* 12 (2):93–107.

Howe, Ch. W. 1994. Taxes *versus* Tradable Discharge Permits: A Review in the Light of the U.S. and European Experience. *Environmental & Resource Economics* 4 (2):151–169.

Independent Commission on International Development Issues: Common Crisis, North-South. 1983. *Cooperation for World Recovery* (= Brandt Report). London.

Independent Working Group on the Future of the United Nations. 1995. *The United Nations in Its Second Half-Century* (= Qureshi and von Weizsäcker Report). New York.

Intergovernmental Panel on Climate Change (IPCC). 1991. *Climate Change: The IPCC Scientific Assessment.* Cambridge.

———. 1996. *Climate Change 1995: Economic and Social Dimensions of Climate Change.* Cambridge.

————. 1996. *Climate Change 1995: Impacts, Adaptations and Mitigation of Climate Change: Scientific-Technical Analyses*. Cambridge.

————. 1996. *Climate Change 1995: The Science of Climate Change*. Cambridge.

Jepma, C. P., ed. 1995. *The Feasibility of Joint Implementation*. Dordrecht, Boston, London.

Levi, M. D. 1991. Bretton Woods: Blueprint for a Greenhouse Gas Agreement. *Ecological Economics* 2 (4):253–267.

Maier-Rigaud, G. 1994. *Umweltpolitik mit Mengen und Märkten. Lizenzen als konstituierendes Element einer ökologischen Marktwirtschaft*. Marburg.

Mishan, E. J. 1970. *Technology and Growth: The Price We Pay*. New York, Washington, D.C.

OECD. 1992. *Climate Change. Designing a Practical Tax System*. Paris.

————. 1992. *Climate Change. Designing a Tradable Permit System*. Paris.

————. 1995. *Global Warning. Economic Dimensions and Policy Responses*. Paris.

————. 1997. *Environmental Taxes and Green Tax Reform*. Paris.

Pearce, D. 1991. The Role of Carbon Taxes in Adjusting to Global Warming. *The Economic Journal* 101:938–948.

Simonis, U. E. 1994. Toward a "Houston Protocol." How to Allocate Carbon Dioxode Emission Reductions Between North and South. In *Ethics and Environmental Policy: Theory Meets Practice*, ed. F. Ferré and P. Hartel. Athens, London, pp. 106–124.

Sterner, Th., ed. 1994. *Economic Policies for Sustainable Development*. Dordrecht, Boston, London.

Tietenberg, Th. 1994. Implementation Issues for Globally Tradable Carbon Entitlements. In *International Environmental Economics*, ed. E. C. van Ierland. Amsterdam, pp. 119–149.

Tisdell, C. A. 1988. Sustainable Development: Differing Perspectives of Ecologists and Economists, and Relevance to LCDs. *World Development* 16 (3):373–384.

UNCTAD. 1992. *Combating Global Warming: Study on a Global System of Tradable Carbon Emission Entitlements*. New York.

Victor, D. G. 1991. Limits to Market-Based Strategies for Slowing Global Warming: The Case of Tradable Permits. *Policy Sciences* 24 (2):199–222.

World Commission on Environment and Development. 1987. *Our Common Future* (= Brundtland Report). Oxford, New York.

11. Sustainability: A Challenge and an Opportunity

Marion Caspers-Merk

The Principle of Sustainability

Sustainable development offers us the opportunity to make our economy fit for the future. The essence of this approach is that instead of plundering global stocks of raw materials and thus eroding our natural resource capital, we live off the "interest" we have accrued in this area. To do so we need to develop new sustainable products as well as new consumption patterns and lifestyles. Whether or not these far-reaching requirements are satisfied will depend on the extent to which they can be reconciled with humankind's desire for economic and social progress.

At the Earth Summit in Rio de Janeiro in 1992, a unique process of global consensus took place during which the vast majority of the world's nations agreed upon the essential principles of sustainable development. Now that the excitement that accompanied the Rio conference is over and our attention is once again on everyday life, we need to consider the current situation with regard to sustainable development.

The feelings of optimism and enthusiasm prompted by the Earth Summit have undoubtedly evaporated. Although major events such as the special session of the UN General Assembly to mark five years after Rio and the Climate Summit in Kyoto ensure that the arguments in favor of sustainable development receive widespread publicity, this is effective at best only in the short term. Those who resist change and defend the status quo are still in the majority. They consider sustainable development too risky, although they know that to continue as before is not realistic in the long term. The role of the Social Democratic Party (SPD) in promoting sustainable development is particularly significant, given its reputation as a progressive party. It falls to the SPD to develop a new blueprint for society and win majority support for it.

People everywhere are calling for change, for the renewal of institutional structures as well as for environmentally sound production and consumption patterns. Although efforts have been made to realize these demands, they have tended to focus solely on individual environmental problems or on specific industrial sectors. Moreover, the supporters of sustainable development advocate different approaches to achieve their aims. Some are convinced that sustainable development should be implemented at international levels; they call for a reorganization of the United Nations, for internationally tradable permits, and for the establishment of new bodies linked to the WTO, the World Bank, and the IMF. Others endorse a "bottom-up" approach and contend that consumers and local authorities who have taken various steps to implement Agenda 21 at a local level are at the forefront of these efforts.

In the meantime, the wheel of technological change spins ever faster. Economic activity has been affected by globalization, in particular by the progress of information technology, which has led to a greater division of labor and to a greater availability of information than ever before. Nevertheless, one has the impression that the left hand does not know what the right hand is doing. As long as the relationships between technological, economic, and social change are ignored, there is no chance that sustainable development will succeed.

Steps toward Sustainable Development

To coordinate social, economic, and environmental objectives in realizing sustainable development, the following steps must be taken.

- Natural resources, including energy, must be used more efficiently. To achieve this, it is particularly important that innovation be tailored to demand and that economic conditions be created to facilitate widespread use of environmentally friendly products and services. In doing so, consideration must be given both to the global trend toward the information society and to the social and cultural diversity of the world.

- A system of taxation and levies is required that takes account of environmental considerations and facilitates an appropriate distribution of gainful employment. Financial and technological incentives must therefore be provided to countries in the South, and pledges concerning the financing of the Global Environmental Facility must be upheld.
- Public awareness of environmental matters must be raised and information must be made available on new and sustainable consumer patterns and on life styles that do not depend on exploiting and damaging the environment. This information must be transformed into clear indicators that can be internationally coordinated and that accurately reflect global environmental and social problems.

There is obviously no ideal way in which these prime objectives can be achieved. Specific strategies must be developed at each political level so that these objectives can be realized at international, national, and local levels. Some politicians in Germany typically respond by arguing in favor of global action—claiming, for example, that otherwise Germany's location for industry will be undermined. However, they resort to this argument all too often in an attempt to evade the issue. There are a huge variety of optional measures to be taken. Only those who take the initiative and act before anyone else will reap the benefits. No progress has ever been achieved by standing still and doing nothing.

Information Must Take Priority

The promotion of sustainable development requires that both the public and experts be supplied with relevant information. Such information is currently unavailable, a reason being that the global effect of various emissions on industrial countries has only recently become a focus. We now know that substances generally regarded as harmless can threaten our existence by virtue of their sheer quantity. This can occur, for example, when too much carbon dioxide accumulates in the earth's atmosphere due to human activity or when harmless substances such as sand and limestone are used as building materials and are spread across wide areas of land. According to estimates by Germany's Federal Office of Statistics, if these substances continue to be used extensively on building sites, all of Germany will be contaminated within the next eighty years. (As

Paracelsus once said, the toxicity of a substance depends on the dose in which it is consumed.)

The consumption of renewable and nonrenewable resources in industrialized nations is far too high. This is the conclusion reached in a recently published report entitled "Resource Flows: The Material Basis of Industrial Economies," drawn up by the World Resources Institute, the Dutch Ministry for Building, Regional Planning, and the Environment, the Japanese National Institute for Environmental Studies, and the Wuppertal Institute for Climate, Environment, and Energy (in cooperation with the German Federal Office of Statistics). The report has established that the demand for natural resources in the participating states can add up to eighty-five tons per person per year. This far exceeds the supply of natural resources that the earth can produce; it also far outweighs the demand for raw materials by the rest of the globe, whose population is almost four times higher than that of the industrialized world.

Given the level of natural resources available and the capacity of ecosystems to absorb waste products and materials, the notion that global equality means every household in China and India, for instance, will eventually own a car, a refrigerator, and a personal computer is unrealistic. It is important that efforts are made soon, both in technology transfer and in the context of international agreements, to take account of the demands placed on threshold countries. If these countries are not involved in the process of sustainable development, there is a danger that environmentally harmful industries will continue to relocate to these countries in large numbers.

In view of the rapidity with which raw materials and products are now flowing into industrial countries, the dangers facing our natural resource base cannot be ignored. If sustainable products and services are to be given a real chance for success, it is essential that a life-cycle analysis be carried out on every bulk product. This involves examining the entire substance chain, beginning with the extraction of resources from the natural environment, moving to various aspects of product manufacture and consumption, and ending with the recycling of residual substances such as emissions and waste. Initial experience with life-cycle analyses has shown it to be particularly important to develop a step-by-step procedure so that accurate estimates can be made. Considering that the environmental effects of even the simplest of products can be extremely complex, a thorough examination of all aspects involved is often too costly.

Progress through the Appropriate Use of Technology

If we want to determine roughly which products and services are ecologically sound, we should reduce global substance flows to half their present volume. To achieve this we should first adopt a strategy to promote the use of environmentally efficient technology and thus establish the need for a particular service. The products required for the provision of the service should then be manufactured in a way that minimizes the depletion of natural resources as much as possible.

If the industrialized nations adopt such an approach they will not, by any means, suffer an economic decline. On the contrary, if labor productivity continues to rise as heretofore without due consideration being given to natural and human resources, then economic progress will come to a halt. Time and energy that could have otherwise been used more usefully will be wasted on the production of unnecessary goods. This is why every potential technological innovation should first be examined with consideration given to its necessity and whether it will increase the productivity of resources.

Some observers of the information technology sector have made the optimistic prediction that, thanks to new information and communication technologies (ICTs), the adverse effects of our excessive consumption of natural resources will soon become a thing of the past. But is this true? At first glance, new technologies in this field appear to offer an answer to many environmental problems:

- Serious environmental problems such as the depletion of the ozone layer and the greenhouse effect would not have been discovered without information and communication technologies;
- Effective emission controls and effective environmental monitoring would be impossible without digital monitoring and telecommunications systems;
- Information and communication technologies can help optimize traffic flows, eliminate congestion, and make public transport more competitive;
- Simulation techniques, such as virtual reality and computer-aided design, and greater production efficiency through computer-aided manufacturing and miniaturization help conserve materials and energy;
- The new technologies do not produce unpleasant odor and are extremely quiet, for example, when compared to the

punch-card system and the dot-matrix printer of less than twenty years ago.

There is, however, a flip side to this scenario. Although traveling on the data highway does not produce air pollution, it appears that information and communication technology—a sector experiencing rapid advances—consume vast quantities of materials and energy. According to initial estimates, a single personal computer (PC) requires a massive twenty tons of raw materials during its lifetime—for its manufacture, during the course of its average life span (three to four years), and for its disposal. This corresponds to two-thirds of the raw materials that a small car (minus electronics) requires during its life cycle. However, the materials contained in the body of the product itself—just over twenty kilograms for a PC without a screen and around one ton for a small car—are not significant in this regard. The bulk of the materials consumed are fossil raw materials such as coal or oil, which are used as energy sources in the production and running of the product. Everyone now realizes that the dream of the "paperless office" said to be hailed by the PC has not been realized. On the contrary, draft and botched copies produced by PCs have increased the output of waste paper considerably.

This development has even greater implications for the consumption of raw materials in other industrial sectors. While individual sectors have reduced their consumption somewhat by increasing their production efficiency, thereby lessening their impact on the environment, the situation across the industrial sector as a whole is rather different. Increased production and increased pollution in other sectors outweigh the progress made in some sectors, for example, through the use of monitoring and filtering techniques to cut emissions. As long as companies continue to exploit the "strengths" of information and communication technologies—such as globalization, rationalization, and timely production—as a means of boosting their output, environmental pollution will continue to rise.

According to the laws of economies of scale and of increasing efficiency by automation and the division of labor, a company can reduce its unit costs and thereby sell its goods more cheaply than its competitors. This stimulates demand and, in theory, the company can then control a greater share of the market. This is only realistic in theory, however, because the company's competitors will gradually catch up and possibly even overtake it. With everyone wanting a bigger slice of pie, the pie must be bigger. It therefore becomes a matter of not only satisfying consumer demand but of creating new demand so that every company can benefit from the advantages associated with increased efficiency. With the help of information and communication technologies, the system develops a momentum of its own, which boosts consumption.

In keeping with the spirit of the modern age, more and more answers are given to questions that one would never have thought of asking; in more economic terms, more and more products are available that one might never have thought of purchasing. Global PC, telephone, and television networks have acted as catalysts in this development. Products unknown yesterday can be easily found today with the help of global networks. Tomorrow they will be the latest acquisition for large numbers of individuals; the day after tomorrow they will already be ancient history.

The same development can be seen in the PC sector itself. As a result of the multitude of add-on devices available for the present generation of computers and the rapid onward march of digital technology in the field of telecommunications, more and more modules are added to the computer, and old modules are exchanged for new versions that offer more comprehensive or more efficient functions. Equipped with a CD-ROM drive, loudspeakers, a video card, a video camera, a modem, and the relevant software, a PC can in principle replace a large number of other finished products. In reality, however, consumers tend to purchase one product after another.

It can be generally maintained that a technology is appropriate as long as its effects, both good and bad, are understood or promote understanding of environmental concerns, and as long as the technology is the focus of public discussion. When one applies this theory to information and communication technologies, one sees that no guarantee can be given for the information that is communicated via a network, even if it is more important for sustainable development than the network technology itself. In the end it can only be hoped that the dialogue and free exchange of information generated by international networks will encourage people to take at least as much interest in sustainable development as they do in sex and crime.

Raising Public Awareness

In seeking ways to promote sustainable development it might be useful to consider not only relevant technological developments but also the issue's social aspects. The promotion of individual responsibility is another important element in this regard. For example, we do not yet have a consumer magazine in Germany that, by using modern database technology to amass all the existing data on product tests and combine this data with environmental information, provides the consumer with information on the environmental compatibility of various products and offers comparisons of product prices at a local level. A magazine of this kind could be partially financed through advertising. The same method could be used as a source of funding for campaigns to promote awareness of sustainable development or for the establishment of an accreditation agency for organizations planning to market environmental labels. The huge volume of information produced by advertising and the increasingly trivial nature of most advertisements requires urgent action. Such advertising typically encourages consumers to indulge in indiscriminate consumption; it does not help them to make intelligent choices and select inexpensive alternative products that are environmentally friendly.

Also key to raising awareness is the negative way in which environmental issues are often presented to the public and the tendency of many environmental organizations to focus on individual environmental problems. Who wants to be subjected daily to accusations or to be reminded of the responsibility one bears without being told clearly how one can fulfill this responsibility and how one can benefit from it? When environmental organizations focus their publicity on one individual pollutant or on one environmental target and change the target from one week to the next, not only does it distract attention from other environmental issues, but it also confuses the public because they are bombarded with conflicting opinions from different experts. Many advocates of sustainable development even go so far as to place the responsibility for entire future generations on our shoulders. Of course we all want our children's lives to be as good as, or better than, our own, but can we really only achieve this by suffering the discomfort of public transport or by forgoing our hard-earned holidays abroad?

The same applies to people in the so-called developing and threshold countries. For instance, when Southeast Asian timber traders want to fell trees in the rain forests of Papua New Guinea, they adopt the following "win-win" strategy. Rather than going through official channels and approaching the government, they talk with the people responsible on the ground, namely the tribal chiefs. In their world a little bit of tropical forest does not matter. As far as they are concerned, the rain forest stretches as far as the eye can see. What they do not have, however, are shiny jeeps and other status symbols, so they are willing to swap.

When faced with a situation like this, it does little good to appeal to the global conscience or to pass laws, which will only fail because they are not sufficiently understood. An appropriate use of technology would be to try to promote dialogue with the people directly affected by taking a few members of the tribe, who may have never before gone beyond their world of seemingly endless rain forest, on a helicopter flight over the island so that they could see the extent of the tree felling from an appropriate perspective.

With regard to what must be done in the industrial nations and specifically in Germany, in the long run it will not be enough for individual companies to develop a niche market in environmental products. Production and services must, from the very start, be demand-oriented and focused on environmental compatibility. This will strengthen domestic markets from which the bulk of substance flows will originate. It is not enough for the government to make pompous pronouncements about pollution-control targets, which are then never met. Germany's experience so far with carbon dioxide emissions has been a painful reminder of just how futile lengthy negotiations and discussions can be. And if the industrial nations in the West are themselves unable to fulfill the commitments they have undertaken, the rest of the world will continue to believe that we in the West put our own economic growth before climate protection and sustainable development.

In our efforts to implement environmental objectives we should therefore give priority to fostering dialogue and promoting mutual understanding. We need to do more than simply demand action from other countries. It is imperative that we develop new methods of cooperation and new alliances that change lifestyles and alter consumption patterns. This cannot be achieved by Greenpeace or by the government alone, but requires the participation of society as a whole. Besides, it would be too easy for us to simply pin the blame on individual countries for failing to make progress with regard to sustainable development. The fact that progress is slow is primarily due to the changes that have taken place in the global economy and that, as already discussed, have occurred as a result of the information age. Unfortunately, the intensification of global competition and the progressive development of global economic networks have not led to the emergence of the oft-mentioned global village but have created a global metropolis with all its inherent disadvantages in terms of sustainable development.

It is certainly more tempting for us to focus on more immediate concerns such as finding work, securing a decent income, and maintaining our standard of living, and to put remote issues to the back of our mind. In other words, it is easier to attach greater importance to economic imperatives than to environmental ones. However, if we proceed down this path, there is a real danger that the progress we have made in cutting pollution and restoring environmental and social equilibrium across the globe will be undone and that, in our struggle to overcome present problems, we will fail to take the necessary precautions for the future. Indeed, there is a real danger that in today's globalized economy, environmental policy will become an illusion.

Developments in Germany in this regard are symptomatic of what is taking place in most other industrialized countries. The German government appears increasingly incapable of taking action when it comes to restructuring society in the interest of sustainable development—and society as a whole needs to be reorganized along these lines. Yet even key nongovernmental bodies, such as trade unions and environmental and industrial organizations, have maneuvered themselves into a situation where none of them are able to realize the goals they espouse: the trade unions are unable to achieve a fair distribution of wealth; the environmental organizations cannot achieve further improvements for the environment; and the industrial organizations are unable to achieve further deregulation.

The SPD therefore prides itself on taking a forward-looking approach to sustainable development. Social Democrats do not advocate separate laws for separate environmental problems, nor do they claim to possess the expertise needed to solve all of society's ills. Instead, Social Democrats wish to create the conditions necessary to allow all those involved to work together and achieve results that are target-oriented, effective in the long term, and therefore "sustainable." It is only logical that environmental policy should be structured in this way. We have, after all, only just come to the uncomfortable realization that in a world where there are over 100,000 chemical substances and several million consumer goods, any attempt to reduce environmental pollution in a sustainable way by legislating for specific problems is doomed to failure. Environmental exploitation in all its forms—from the extraction of raw materials to the pollution caused by waste material and greenhouse gases—is increasing. Although the technologies used for filtering waste and gas emissions are becoming increasingly sophisticated, a solution to the problem is not in sight. If we want our economic fortunes to improve, popular wisdom dictates that we should produce and export more. However, if we do so, we will further deplete the natural resources on which we depend and saw off the branch on which we are sitting.

Promoting Social Innovation

Anyone who seeks to force the pace of technological change or who lets themselves be driven by it without first considering the effects it will have on social harmony runs the risk of causing social fragmentation. It is therefore crucial that at least as much importance be attached to social renewal as to technological innovation.

The relevance of institutional structures in this regard has become a regular subject of debate among social scientists. At the heart of the debate is the question whether established institutions are capable of meeting present-day requirements and, if not, whether they can be reorganized or whether new institutions should be set up. Although these issues need to be urgently discussed, discussion in itself is not enough, as the roots of the problem are more profound. Society today is clearly experiencing a crisis of overproduction. The economy is growing at the expense of the environment, and the gap between rich and poor is steadily widening.

Sociologists such as Ulrich Beck and Anthony Giddens argue that the industrial nations can no longer afford to put gainful employment at the top of their social agenda. They say that we are moving from a society based on gainful employment to one based simply on work, where the growing automation of production processes will lead to the emergence of new forms of employment, such as community-oriented work. When properly financed, this kind of work will replace normal working arrangements for many people.

At a time when structural change is making job security a thing of the past and when the gulf between the desire for gainful employment and available jobs is growing ever wider, it is essential that new and appropriate forms of employment be created. Sustainable development does not stand in the way of this. In fact, the opposite is the case. It is perfectly reasonable to argue that we will actually benefit if capital and technology are channeled in new directions. Although the defenders of the status quo constantly remind us that this will undermine our country's status as a location for industry, it is the only practical and socially viable solution to our problems if we do not want to forgo the comforts we have acquired.

Women have a particularly important role to play in sustainable development. On the one hand, they have traditionally done the bulk of unpaid work both inside and outside the home; on the other, the nature of the work they do makes them more attuned and committed to environmental and social causes than the average person. The potential represented by women must be utilized. They should have a special role to play—not just for the sake of equality—in the efforts to change social values and encourage greater environmental awareness among current and future generations.

Particular attention should also be paid to promoting small and medium-sized businesses. It is in this sector that innovation takes place and that three-quarters of all new jobs are created. In Germany, as in other countries, there is no shortage of innovative companies or innovative ideas. What we lack is appropriate legislation in this area, the absence of which is jeopardizing the success of many such innovative projects.

Germany continues to be regarded as a market leader in the field of innovative environmental technology. The government, however, is undermining Germany's position in this respect by failing to provide enough support for relevant innovations. This is clearly reflected by the size of budget appropriations for this sector. One example of an innovation that has failed through lack of political support is the so-called "green television" developed by the company Loewe Opta. Between 1995 and 1997, the company designed a television that satisfied certain environmental criteria. A limited number of materials were used in its manufacture, and the product was designed to be easily dismantled so that it could be recycled more effectively. Particular attention was also paid to making it as durable as possible and as easy as possible to repair. If appropriate legislation had been in place and funding had been available so that the product could have been marketed on a large scale, then it might have been a success and helped considerably to reduce the number of televisions thrown away. However, things remained unchanged: due to existing legislation, the company was unable to maintain its prices at a competitive level and had to abandon the project. Those who argue that the project failed because of global competition and cheaper wages in Southeast Asia have not given due consideration to the issues involved.

Another way in which the government could foster commercial innovation is by passing legislation establishing clear and reliable minimum standards on environmental compatibility. The environmental legislation currently in place is not precise enough. At present, Germany has a massive 6,000 separate laws and ordinances on the environment. They have now become much too complex and unwieldy to be practical and must be reorganized and simplified so as to become more manageable and effective. Moreover, particular attention must also be given to legal instruments such as environmental norms, environmental labeling, and voluntary environmental auditing.

Finally, efforts should be made to encourage companies to undertake voluntary commitments with regard to the environment. This is an important tool that should be utilized. If companies fail to meet their commitments, they should be liable to penalty, and they should also be obliged to reveal information on their activities. Of course, regulatory legislation alone will not solve all the problems mentioned. Ineffectual voluntary commitments negotiated by industrial associations obliged to make allowances for those members that have made the least progress will certainly not go far enough.

Another important issue that must be addressed is the promotion of economic development. Governments have frequently gone so far as to sustain economic activities that are inefficient and clearly harmful to the environment by subsidizing them. Serious errors have been made in the agricultural sector, for instance. The government should review its policy of providing subsidies on the basis of environmental criteria. It should, in addition, grant more subsidies to the many environmentally compatible innovations. Moreover, environmental compatibility should be one of the elements of the long-overdue reform of the tax system.

Many economists continue to claim that global environmental standards have the same effect as nontariff barriers. This is an argument that is difficult to ignore. The technology currently used on a wide scale to reduce emissions is expensive, as are the efficient and largely automated environment-protection methods used during the production process. Close cooperation between the industrialized nations and the developing countries is essential if the developing countries are to avoid repeating the mistakes of their industrialized counterparts. For developing countries to assert their right to do so would be extremely foolish.

Viewed from this perspective, sustainable development appears in a new light. Environmental protection no longer appears as an additional problem competing with the many other economic and social problems that are often considered more urgent. The logical response to the social fragmentation caused by the increasing trend toward automation and the increasing urge to boost prosperity—evident not only in the Third World but increasingly also in the First—is to reform taxation policy with an eye to protecting the environment and encouraging the responsible use of raw materials.

Strategies

The following strategies must be adopted to overcome the obstacles to sustainable development.

Modern structures for sustainability Sustainable development must become the top priority of government and of international organizations. Cross-ministerial structures must be established. Environmental objectives must form part of a sustainable economy that is able to escape the vicious circle of rising growth and production combined with falling employment and prosperity. In order to launch a compulsory process of sustainable development, each national parliament must adopt a national strategy that details the objectives and the means by which they are to be realized. Such a strategy must give equal weight to both technological and social innovation.

A new culture of dialogue at local, national, and international levels The many different initiatives that have already been launched must be strengthened, and closer networks must be established between the various consensus groups involved. In particular, support must be given to the efforts undertaken by many town councils and local authorities to implement a version of Agenda 21 at the local level. At the national level we need to agree on a strategy for sustainable development that states the goals and the steps to be taken to implement them. Support must be given to the individual efforts made to establish national and international networks providing information from experts and giving practical examples of appropriate technologies, such as the efforts undertaken by the Working Group on Sustainable Product Design of the United Nations Environment Program (UNEP) in the Netherlands.

Lean environmental law A reform of German environmental law is long overdue. Not only should efforts be made to organize and simplify the 6,000 individual laws and ordinances in this area that have become much too complex and unwieldy, particular attention must also be give to instruments such as environmental standards, environmental labeling, and voluntary environmental auditing.

Efforts should be made to encourage companies to undertake voluntary commitments with regard to the environment. This is an important tool that should be exploited. If companies fail to meet their commitments, it should be possible for penalties to be imposed on them; they should also be obliged to make information available on their activities. Regulatory legislation alone will not be sufficient to solve all the problems mentioned. Ineffectual voluntary commitments negotiated by industrial associations, which are obliged to make allowances for those members who have made the least progress, will certainly not go far enough.

Taxation The long-overdue reform of the taxation system should take environmental compatibility into account. Many states have already taken the first step in this direction by increasing energy prices and cutting nonwage labor costs—a strategy that has proven successful. In other EU countries, such as Denmark and Sweden, renewable energy sources have already become a growth market, which has improved the employment situation there. Studies have shown that such measures would also be effective in Germany.

Indicators to measure success Internationally applicable indicators must be developed and become the basis of decision making. One example is the GNP, which until now has not taken the consumption of natural resources into account. Environmental information must be comprehensible and relevant to economic and social factors. Information of this kind must not only relate to that part of the product life cycle between manufacture and consumption. Global substance flows that occur because of the need to satisfy mass requirements need to be the subject of a comprehensive analysis dealing with the entire life cycle of individual substances.

A debate on the limits of growth is certainly not an exercise in sentimentality and doom mongering but an attempt to develop positive arguments in response to those who put profit and technological progress before the preservation of natural resources. Progress and profit, environmental protection, and social justice do not need to conflict with each other. In the end everything depends on how society defines its economic system. Systematic efforts must be made to introduce a change in values and structural and social innovation, alongside technological innovation. We need to consider whether the three-liter car will really reduce environmental pollution as hoped, or whether the reduction in consumption it represents will lead to greater overall consumption of raw materials. We must consider whether, for example, consumers would wish to acquire a second or third car; whether the three-liter car itself would include electronics which are expensive to produce; and whether other factors might arise which we have not yet considered. We need not only a three-liter car but also a three-liter driver and a three-liter town. The new high-tech vehicles will only be sustainable if they are used in an intelligent way—for example as part of a car-sharing scheme—in conjunction with public transport or as part of a coordinated and integrated transport system. At the same time, the possibilities and limits of teleworking must be discussed in regard to the productivity of resources. Optimum logistical strategies should be discussed in a similar way; this has particular implications for regional structures.

If industrialized countries were to reduce substantially their consumption of (renewable) resources and target their use more effectively, it would considerably increase the chance that urgently sought-after new markets would be developed. Moreover it would allow those countries that have not yet become industrialized to control their economic recovery in a manner that is sustainable and responsible without making themselves unduly dependent on the technological prescripts of others. Only those who are able to satisfy their basic needs in a logical and independent manner can be free to consider calmly what else the world has to offer—and they can be confident that others will be interested in what they can offer in abundance.

Part VI

TECHNOLOGY AS A DRIVING FORCE FOR GLOBALIZATION

12. The Digital Economy As an Engine for Globalization

Siegmar Mosdorf

Windows 21

While the French Revolution of the eighteenth century was sustained by the bourgeoisie, the revolutions of the nineteenth and twentieth centuries were a product of the labor movement and created a new balance between freedom and justice. The revolution of the twenty-first century, however, will be triggered by global economic and technological changes. By way of electronics, they will accelerate our move from the mechanical age to the information age; give a new shape to the international division of labor; release new productive potential; and, in the process, drive out old forms of labor while creating new ones. They will redistribute the balance of the world economy.

The world is undergoing fundamental change. Three factors play an especially important role in this. First is the dissolution of the systemic conflict between East and West and the collapse of centrally administered economic systems. The second factor is the emergence of former so-called developing countries, above all in Asia, which is creating a new competitive arena in the international economy. This arena of competitors in the world economy is being rapidly expanded, not only by Asia's small tigers but also by the big ones—China, India, Brazil, and Indonesia. Nor will the current financial crisis in Asia, which came about because the economic foundation was inadequate for the dynamic rate of growth, change the long-term secular trend of catch-up. The third change regards

---

References for this chapter are on page 217.

the new, dynamically accelerating information and communication (I & C) technologies, the ongoing process of globalization, and the worldwide division of labor.

The most powerful motor in this dynamic development triad is the lightning-fast development in the field of I & C technologies. Looking through a window into the twenty-first century, we can detect some of the indicators for the economy of an information society in transition from a classical industrial society to one based on information. Many people are still not aware of how I & C technologies are going to change our lives. We are dealing with an economic, technological, and cultural quantum leap, which historically can only be compared to the invention of printing about five hundred years ago and the telephone one hundred twenty-five years ago.

The Importance of Digital Technology

The development of computer technology is often described in terms of "Moore's Law." In 1965 Moore, the cofounder of Intel, stated that the number of transistors per chip would double every twelve months; in 1975 he revised the figure to every eighteen months—a prediction that has been continuously confirmed since that time. The computer industry has been developing for fully forty years in a series of quantum leaps. Just in the fifteen years between 1979 and 1994 the cost of computer capacity (in millions of instructions per second) was reduced by a factor of 10,000, while at the same time the turnover in the semiconductor branch grew by a factor of ten. Today many ordinary consumer commodities such as automobiles and household appliances have more than two hundred chips built into them. The computer is penetrating more and more industries.

Similar quantum leaps are taking place in the area of communications technology. The quantity of information (band width) that can be transmitted by the fiber optic cables at the heart of the Internet and other communications infrastructures quadruples every two years (the so-called "Metcalfe's Law"). For example, forty years ago, fifty-six telephone conversations could be carried on an underwater copper cable that had been laid in 1956 between Scotland and Newfoundland. On the FLAG-System (Fiberoptic Link Around the Globe) that is now being installed, each fine thread of glass fiber can transmit 150,000 conversations. Since the introduction of transatlantic telephone conversations between London and New York in 1927, the cost has declined by a factor of 1,000, from £500 to less than fifty pence for three minutes (in constant prices). Hence, Frances Cairncross of *The Economist* writes of the "death of distance," which will result in the cost of communication soon being independent of geography.

Since Arthur C. Clark had his vision of satellites at the end of the 1940s, they have come to exercise a strong influence on our everyday life. No one finds it particularly astonishing nowadays to see reports transmitted by satellite from Jerusalem or Peking or entertainment from Hollywood. Along with the Global Positioning System (GPS) and the information from surveillance satellites that is increasingly open to the public, more precise information gives us the information to use our scarce resources better, for the benefit of agriculture, city planning, and global environmental protection. Thus work is now in progress in Germany on an intelligent automobile that, with the help of GPS and geographic information systems, will save time for its user. In the next few years the global mobile telephone will become available, and as a result there will be no place on the surface of the earth closed to the communications revolution. Work is also proceeding on an Internet in the sky. The structure of work is changing already as a result of the options opened up by mobile data transfer.

The number of Internet users doubled every year between 1985 and 1995. Many observers expect that in the next few years the number of users will exceed the number of telephone connections in the world. The Internet is, at the present time, the most important platform for the convergence of various communications technologies and industries. It is thus important to retain the Internet as an open platform on which innovative business people, founders, and operators of small and medium-sized firms, can present their achievements worldwide. With Internet telephoning, "narrowcasting" (individualized radio), and electronic commerce, the Internet is in the process of transforming the traditional telecommunications, media, and financial markets.

Effects on the World Economy

The I & C technologies are presently the ones with the farthest-reaching effects on international financial markets. From the very beginning they were among the most important users of the new communications technologies. Even today more is being invested in these nonpublic networks, such as SWIFT, than in the Internet, which is much more in the limelight. In this regard, Saskia Sassen points out that the international financial networks, in contrast to the decentralized Internet, have led to a concentration of power in the hands of speculators and investors. At present there are more than DM2.25 trillion in capital transactions on the financial markets every day, and by the year 2000 they will equal the value of the annual GDP of the United States, the world's largest economy. By contrast, the daily value of transactions in world trade in goods and services is fifty times less. This figure lies at about DM45 billion, and the gap is widening. As a result, there has been a shift in the power relationship between national governments and the financial markets that has already manifested itself in the pound sterling's fall from the European Monetary System and the current crisis in East Asia. In the process, a form of power not under anyone's control has come into being—for example, the effects of the credit-rating analyses of Moody or Standard and Poor. It has become more difficult for nation-states to influence economies. These developments could be further accelerated by the development of electronic money.

I & C technologies have also changed the world of industry and the service society. Because geography has become less of a factor in communication and because the growing efficiency and declining costs of transportation (through the development of aviation and standardized containers for harbors and trucks), industries can make use of completely new forms of production. With improved logistics, delivery systems, and inventory management, industry and trade can react more quickly to the market and abandon old forms of mass production. Here, too, the Internet (and Intranets) will open up new possibilities.

The information society will bring change particularly in the service sector. In the information society of the twenty-first century, even very sophisticated services will be capable of delivery anywhere in the world. The globalized world economy with its twenty-first century industries, technologies, and infrastructures will be able to buy services at any time, all over the world, and integrate them into the chain of value creation or offer them locally. There are already examples of this: Swissair and Lufthansa have their air-ticket accounting done in India; legal questions are researched for French firms on the Ivory Coast; the New York Life Insurance Company has its damage claims handled in India; in

Bangalore (India) highly qualified software engineers work for American and European computer firms for one-tenth of the salary customary in the OECD countries; and automobile companies put their research programs on-line and send them around the earth on a three-shift basis.

Such trends will become even stronger through the development of telework and the use of video-telephone and other technologies. This can be a positive development for the industrial countries as well. In the United States, rural areas with good educational standards such as North and South Dakota, which in the past were considered geographically remote, have used call centers to create jobs and to keep young, well-trained workers from leaving. There have been similar experiences in Europe. In the British Isles—for example, in Scotland, England, and Wales—telecottages have been established in which freelance and independent teleworkers or employees of various firms can share working space and a communications infrastructure, as needed, right where they live. This was made possible especially by British Telecom, which agreed to give every teleworker who became independent a rebate on his or her telephone bill. These communications infrastructures produce changes in the relationship between the city and the surrounding country and create new opportunities, especially for structurally weak areas.

In the information society, the megastructures of industrial society—gigantic factories that provide the entire world market with goods and services from a central location—no longer exist. Rather, there is central guidance, but production is handled in a decentralized way in quasi-transnational firms located in the sales markets. All of this can be done on-line by new I & C technologies. There will be linked systems of research and production across all the time zones. For large infrastructure projects, virtual firms will be set up in temporary consortia. Large firms acting worldwide will turn into networks. Sony Chief Morita once called this "global localization."

In the future the struggle for markets will become more and more a struggle for locations. "We are living through a transformation that in the next century will give rise to new forms of politics and economic activity. There will be no national products and technologies any more, no national firms, no national industries. There will be no national economies" (Reich 1992). "The world economy is involved in a break-neck globalization process and is moving toward a quasi-borderless world economy" (Ohmae 1991).

New Technologies and the Study of the National Economy

In the economy of the information society, information will be at once the number one production factor and a commodity. The worldwide spread of new I & C technologies has further accelerated globalization. As a result of these technologies, the speed of innovation increases in development, production, and distribution. Economist Paul Romer of the University of California at Berkeley emphasizes in his work the importance of information and technology for growth and for the further development of industrial societies. Along with the classic factors of capital, labor, and resources, which are subject to natural limits and to which the law of "diminishing returns" applies, Romer emphasizes how the creative power of human beings can actually boost the efficiency of these factors so that it is possible, in the final analysis, to have "increasing returns." Thus the skepticism of Ricardo and Keynes, who believed that capitalism would lose its capacity for growth, has been broken.

Although this new view of economics is quite optimistic, Romer and Brian Arthur of Stanford University also mention new problems that economic policy must face. Our laws governing competition are still based on ideas relating to industry and stem from the world of "diminishing returns." But in the new computer industry, where standards play an outstanding role and there are very clear "increasing returns," these old ideas and the legal instruments do not take hold. The following are just two examples: (1) Beta was not able to win against VHS, even though it was technically superior, and (2) the Alpha Chip has a market share of only 1 percent, even though it is twice as fast as Pentium. Also in communications technology, standards like HTML, TCP/IP, and Ethernet tend to be adapted to faster systems rather than accepting new standards like ATM. Moreover, consider the antitrust action under way against Microsoft, which through its control of the DOS standard has made Bill Gates the richest man in America.

The "Microsoft case" is nothing unusual in the history of industry, however. In every phase of industrial society's development there has been a kind of "biography" of specific branches. At the beginning are the pioneers who give a boost to technological development with their innovative product ideas. This attracts the gold diggers, who want to market the ideas and make big profits. Their profit fantasies bring in investors, who invest directly in the product or in stocks, thus expanding the undertaking. But as a result of increased competition and the extremely high investments required for further development, a phase of sectoral reorganization begins. This is when the hour of the monopolists strikes. Many of the competitors have passed their zenith, and the firms that have established the standards can begin to take monopolistic positions. This does not mean at all that the reorganization phase is over because the technological development goes on, and completely new competitors and new arenas for competition appear, as shown by the Internet and by the success of Netscape. Owing to global linkages, however, and the increasingly important role of standards in the information-technology area, we shall have to create the infrastructure for an effective international antitrust and competition law and coordinate it.

Another structural phenomenon can be observed that takes account of both the winds of competition and the convergence of various branches. Thus the main competitors in the United States in the media, telecommunications, and information branches are reorganizing themselves. It is apparent in the case of the five largest US media conglomerates (Time Warner, Disney/ABC, GE/NBC, TCI, News Corporation) and of Microsoft in the software branch that there is a very high level of willingness to enter into strategic alliances. With regard to the markets of the future in Internet-, cable- and satellite-TV, the media conglomerates are forming new kinds of alliances. This has to do with economies of scale, on the one hand, since huge investments are needed in these new markets; on the other hand, the partners profit from each other's know-how in an increasingly convergent sector. This kind of linkage between American firms, going beyond individual branches, has been described in *The New Yorker* (referring to the highly linked Japanese economy) as "American Keiretsu." Our German media houses will have to prepare themselves for competition with these new conglomerates.

Borrowing from population ecology and the developing field of complexity research, Arthur and researchers at the Santa Fe Institute have determined that a new technology must be two to three times as efficient in order to displace an established one. Still, as a rule it is not possible to predict which technology will carry the day in a new market, although Intel has demonstrated that the effects of a standard can be further intensified by clever marketing.

For the economy as a whole, this means moving away from the old mechanistic image of national economy in which there was always balance in the marketplace and the mechanics of bookkeeping dominated because classical competition has been supplemented by other kinds of cooperation. Economic consultant James Moore in Cambridge, Massachusetts, sums this new paradigm up with the phrase "death of competition," which means that the American media have by this time achieved a structure in which the most important players compete with one another in some areas while in others they work directly together.

For economic policy this means that more must be done, through expenditures for research and education and with the help of venture capital, to help German firms succeed in new branches such as cryptography and electronic commerce. Moreover, there must be an international effort to ensure that firms like Microsoft do not abuse their market power and that more attention is paid to the early and decisive phase of technological development.

There are tendencies in the service society similar to those in the computer world. In movies, television, and other branches, the "stars" earn many times what their competitors get—something described as the "winner-takes-all society." These tendencies are further intensified by the I & C technologies, which make new applications and consulting services accessible everywhere. Robert Reich, among others, points to the growing earning power of the "symbolic analysts," which leads to an increasingly uneven distribution of income.

Politics in a Global Information Society

The global linkage provided by worldwide communications structures is a challenge particularly for countries with high production costs. Easy worldwide transmission of any and all information makes it easier to farm out industrial functions of all kinds. Outsourcing and global sourcing are increasingly taken for granted. Following the transfer of industrial jobs, I & C technologies are threatening to transfer increasing numbers of highly qualified service jobs as well. Labor, which until now has been regarded as a largely immobile production factor, is becoming more mobile. Well-trained and talented workers can sell their competence anywhere in the world, regardless of where they live. Under these circumstances, the competition for sales markets is increasingly developing into competition for locations, jobs, and also social systems. Moreover, the starting points are far apart. There is the risk of a deep split in world society between the "users," those who make use of the new technological possibilities, and the "losers," those who have not mastered them. It becomes all the more important to stress training, equality of opportunity, basic services for all, and information. We are competing with countries in which the living conditions of early capitalism have entered an alliance with the high technology of the late twentieth century, which confronts economic policy with new challenges.

Germany's problems as a place for doing business must first be attacked at home. Nevertheless, globalization has inevitable effects on national policy. Policies pursued only from the vantage point of the nation-state are bound to fail. We have to recognize that while the German economy has not worsened, others have improved. German firms are at the present time successful in the field of mid-level technology—say, in making automobiles, in electrotechnology, and in machine building. But in the high-tech markets, which are expanding much more rapidly, German firms are less well represented. At a time when markets are being globalized, this is a dangerous development. Because simple and routine activities are being transferred abroad as a result of outsourcing, the German economy must, in this competition between business locations, put more emphasis on technology, innovation, and human capital. But these new information technologies will also open up opportunities to create many new jobs in Germany (or secure existing ones) as a result of new markets and new applications. Whether prospects for the labor market are ultimately positive or negative in Germany will depend on the economy's success in maintaining a leading position in technology. For that reason, Germany must invest more in I & C technologies so as to avoid falling further behind the United States.

There is some catching up to do in the biotechnology sector as well. We need more creativity and innovation and, above all, much more openness to technology in Germany so that our people can secure the prosperity they have attained.

Our economy, too, is going to change in fundamental ways. By the year 2000 the 300,000 telework jobs in Germany will have become 800,000, which will affect the structures of our society and where we live. The flow of commuters in and out of the urban centers will be substantially reduced. This could work to the benefit of the environment. The strict separation between residential and business areas in our cities and communities will, in this way, gradually be erased. A new kind of worker will come into being, one looking for more personal responsibility, flexibility, and mastery over his or her own time when at work. We might be able to adjust the relationship between job and family in a better way. This opens up opportunities for the best-qualified generation of women in history. We are, moreover, on the eve of a rebirth of independence. It is precisely around the new media that small firms spring up to provide new services for new markets.

Owing to the growing pace of innovation, in the future businesses will only be able to assert their market position over the long run by engaging in a continuous learning process. This new kind of business, the "learning business," will have to assign a particularly high priority to continuous on-site training. Individual workers will have to seize the initiative as well and invest in their own human capital. Not least in view of demographic developments, we cannot afford to have whole age groups disconnected from the technical and, hence, social course of development. In this area telelearning offers new opportunities for all. As Lester Thurow has put it, the heads of the workers are becoming, for the firms themselves, the most important factors of production. For that reason businesses will invest in the training and continuing education of these factors, especially in the media skills of the workers.

One idea that might be conceivable and desirable, for example, is what Dieter Klumpp of the Alcatel Foundation suggested in his initiative "Qualification for the Net"—that firms give their employees a PC, a modem, and appropriate software. The worker would work at home with this equipment, acquire appropriate skills, and bring the new ideas (that he might have got from his experience with the Internet) back into the firm. Thus the worker would continue training at home, and the initial investment would pay off for the firm. The path into the information society will call for such novel creative ideas.

Shaping Change on a Global Scale

The problems in influencing global developments are growing. National means for controlling the process more and more frequently fall short; indeed, the very concept of an "economy" is no longer appropriate for the dimensions of international linkage. As globalization of the world economy grows, so does the need for more international cooperation. The instruments that were developed in the post–World War II period are today no longer adequate for the job. The rules governing international economic relationships are in need of reform. A cooperative policy on the part of nation-states is needed. This policy must start with the World Trade Organization (WTO), but it will not be effective until there is a multilateral consensus. Following Bretton Woods, we need a new world economic order by which unemployment can be overcome and the prosperity of peoples both secured and more fairly distributed. The social and ecological market economy can serve as a model for this.

Let me name a few fields in which there is a need for action as a result of globalization and the development of I &C technologies driving it.

- The international financial markets, which did not exist in their present form until the new technologies created them, must be subjected to a regime of international regulation—as demanded by George Soros—to avoid crises such as the one in Mexico or in Asia.
- The idea developed in the last GATT round to have the WTO develop rules to prevent predatory exploitation of natural resources or evasion of minimum social standards should be implemented. But we must be careful that the call for minimum ecological and social standards does not become an excuse for new protectionism on the part of the industrial countries. The concerted introduction of ecological taxes in the OECD countries along with the transfer of environmental know-how to the Third World could lead to a new burst of innovation while at the same time helping to rescue the world from the danger of environmental catastrophes. Such joint efforts could work against environmental problems and lay the foundation for new forms of international solidarity and cooperation in dealing with the environment. We must help countries like India, China, and Indonesia find a durable development model that does not repeat our mistakes on a much grander scale.
- An international antitrust law should be developed under the aegis of the WTO so that we will be better able to deal with the power of firms like Microsoft that cuts across national economies.
- Inadequate bilateral investment agreements must give way to a multilateral agreement that, if possible, would encompass all economies. The OECD has been working on such a multilateral cooperation agreement (MAI) for two years and plans to present a first draft at a ministerial conference in 1998.

- The protection of intellectual property and copyrights must be made effective worldwide so that there are no unjustified advantages due to "unfair play." A revision of the International Copyright Agreement under the aegis of the World Intellectual Property Organization (WIPO) is urgently needed. But the cultural and social interests of the users and of research must be taken account of with "fair use" rules.
- Parallel with liberalization, we must take care that distinctive European characteristics, especially regarding cultural, social security, and social partnership, are maintained. The OECD and the UN should agree on worldwide standards and rules for the media as part of an international media convention. Internationally valid and uniform rules governing the control of media concentration (mergers) are indispensable for securing democracy.

Outlook

Inventing the future is actually the task of social elites. But politics have lost their momentum and for that reason are not in the running for this particular inventive task. Political reactions tend to be too structurally conservative when creative modernization is really needed. Anyone who does not recognize the changes going on in the information age, who does not use his or her opportunities and limit his or her risks, must expect to be punished not only by the markets but by a loss of prosperity. Our chance to be a winner in the globalization sweepstakes lies in the triad of excellence, fairness, and international cooperation. We must be very good once again; we must work for fairness and justice at home and abroad; and we must intensify international cooperation—in that order.

The job of politics is to be the loom on which creativity and competence, craft and efficiency are woven into a social fabric, thus helping to create a new model for the "economy of the information society." The matter is too important to be left in the hands of the culture pessimists or of the technology fanatics. The "world domestic economy" that now exists must be supplemented by what Carl Friedrich von Weizsäcker in the 1960s called "world domestic politics," a politics capable of dealing with global dangers such as the nuclear arms race of the Cold War and the economic, social, and ecological dislocations of today.

References

Ohmae, Kenichi. 1991. *The Borderless World.* New York: Harperbusiness.
Reich, Robert. 1992. *The Work of Nations: Preparing Ourselves for 21st Century Capitalism.* New York: Vintage Books.

13. The Impact of Globalization on Vocational Training and Continuing Education

Hermann Schmidt

What Is Globalization?

Globalization of Markets

Globalization designates the way that important spheres of life are becoming oriented toward worldwide developments, predominantly in the economy. The motor driving these developments may be found above all in information and communication technologies, television, and in the expansion, streamlining, and cost cutting experienced by international air travel.

Globalization means worldwide communication that is quick and easy to carry out by telephone, fax, and the Internet, both analog and digital. In order to take part, the very minimal requirement is mastery of English, the Internet's lingua franca. Foreign-language learning (not just of English) is therefore an important precondition for participating in globalization.

It is in the free, worldwide movement of finance, services, goods, and persons that globalization manifests itself. Freedom and freedom of movement are therefore the preconditions for globalization. As long as the world's states were divided into two blocs and a bloc-free group, there was a growing internationalization of trade and business, but no globalization. The barriers between the states of the different blocs were too impervious. Globalization had a starting date: the collapse of the Soviet Union in 1990, which coincided in Germany with the unification of the two German states.

Since then, the distances between the economic regions of the world have shrunk. The expansion of financial markets has been the quickest and most obvious sign of this. Financial activities wander across the globe from one time zone to the next. Of all markets, it is the financial markets that exhibit the tightest networking. Companies are becoming "global players." What is decisive here is that multinational corporations are not the only carriers of globalization. To a significant extent, small and medium-sized businesses are caught up in globalization and required to meet its challenges. When, for example, a German small business with forty employees, which supplies plastic parts to the automobile industry, purchases several components for its products in Singapore or Malaysia, it is moving in the global marketplace. These kinds of activities that transcend national borders sharpen our focus on developments in the world economy and demand new attitudes and skills from management and qualified personnel.

Globalization of Education and Prosperity

The globalization of the general conditions under which a market economy operates—of conditions like freedom of movement for goods and persons, cooperation between business partners, and competition between companies—cannot take place in an economic context alone, isolated from other aspects of life. It also raises the question of civil liberties. Here we already begin to see major contradictions in the globalization of the economy. There are numerous states participating in the global market where only a few civil liberties are guaranteed and where opposition, freedom of opinion, and the right to dissent are brutally suppressed. Globalization, however, must also promote enlightenment and information by means of competing ideas. Education and training are therefore necessary preconditions for successful globalization. One of the prosperous countries' most important tasks must be to help reduce the discrepancy in affluence and education between the different countries participating in the global market.

Globalization of the economy also means globalization of the social and ecological questions, of "sustainable development," of the division of wealth in this one world, which cannot any longer be comfortably divided into a First, Second, and Third World, each with different rights and responsibilities. Globalization cannot be reduced to its economic dimension, to a radical capitalism. Rather, it requires an ethical-legal framework, capable of countering the threat to the securing of ecological gains and the dissolution of democratic structures and norms. Justice and prosperity have to be the simultaneous goals of economic globalization.

More clearly than ever before, globalization elucidates the connection between the social responsibility and the market activities of business. The worldwide media are constantly showing us, for example, how the success of any peace process (be it in Northern Ireland, Israel/Palestine, Bosnia/Herzegovina, Cambodia, or Mexico) depends on a balance of economic interests and, by extension, on education and training. A globalization that is not going to deepen inequalities in the world has to give consideration to worldwide balance and to free access for all people to vocational training and continuing education.

The Impact of Globalization on Traditional Vocational Training and Continuing Education

The Ability to Learn and Independence

The rapid development of information and communications (I & C) technologies is the technical precondition for globalization, in the same way that the dissolution of the two world blocs liberated globalization politically. As early as the 1980s, I & C technologies have been influencing training goals according to their impact on work organization and markets. They led to a de-Taylorization of work, contributed to the disappearance of repetitive and routine activities in many fields, led to "lean" concepts in management and organization, eliminated hierarchies, and (finally) led to raising skills and responsibility among qualified personnel via job enrichment and the incorporation of these skilled personnel into teamwork.

As a result, for example, "independent planning, implementation, and control" of personal job tasks became the new goal guiding all regulations in the German training system. This went hand in hand with a more thoroughgoing housecleaning effort to rid curricula of antiquated knowledge. The following essential training goals were formulated: (1) the ability to learn and to take up continuing education independently, and (2) the ability to manage professional tasks independently

In the shift from the 1980s to the 1990s, generalism increasingly replaced specialism as the goal of vocational training. The call for "independent capability of action" moved into the center of the public discussion on education and training. This shift clearly assigned the task of specialization to continuing education. Continuing education received an enormous boost, since every innovation in the manufacturing and service sector, and especially in the application of I & C technologies, initially gets taken up by a work force via continuing education before it enters into the vocational training curricula of schools and colleges. At the beginning of the 1990s, for the first time in Germany, expenditures by firms on continuing vocational education (at DM36 billion) exceeded expenditures for (basic) vocational training of qualified personnel (DM30 billion).

New Vocational Standards Are in Demand

Rapid changes in the economy's structure of qualifications—elicited by a new organization of work, by the I & C technologies, and (in their wake) by globalization—had an enormous impact on the training system. Content and methods also changed along with these goals. The usual time lag, which keeps the educational field limping behind economic, technical, and societal developments, started to signal a danger that the educational and employment systems might become completely detached from each other. Understandably, these problems are even vastly greater in the transforming economies of Central and Eastern Europe and the Asian successor states to the Soviet Union than they are in Western industrial countries.

In Germany, whose training system was always closely tied to business corporations, a reform of the dual-education system has taken place over the last few years. The procedures for modernizing curricula in firms and schools have been enormously accelerated and reduced from an average of two and a half years to a single year. From 1995 to 1997, over one hundred vocational regulations were modernized and brought up to date, while twenty completely new vocations were created, including four professions in information and communications technologies.

For several years now in the European Union, a great deal of thought has been given to creating "European core qualifications." In the United States, work on "national skill standards" has been significantly advanced in connection with the development of numerous cooperative training systems following the School to Work Opportunities Act of 1994. The work of the National Center on Education and the Economy in Washington, D.C. (here one should single out the report of the Commission on the Skills of the American

Workforce, which laid the foundation for the rethinking that led to the School to Work Opportunities Act) and other institutions in this field have won worldwide recognition. The development of national standards for vocations in the United States (but also in many other nation-states) is a new experience having an impact on the entire educational system that should not be underestimated.

European Vocational Education As a Preliminary Step toward a Global Vocational Education?

Vocational Education in the European Union: Diversity in Unity

The vocational training systems of the European Union's member states remain as fundamentally different as they ever were. At first sight, it would be hard to recognize that the Community's forty years of common vocational education policy had achieved any standardization among national training systems, especially since joint activities of any scope worth mentioning have only taken place within the last fifteen years. Thus, for example, the largest member states (Great Britain, Germany, and France) really represent opposing models of vocational training for youth: a largely market-oriented vocational education system in Great Britain stands opposite a mixed system involving firms and schools in Germany and a school-based vocational education system in France.

In Great Britain, the state promotes training in firms but does not prescribe training goals and content for these firms. In Germany, the state stipulates general regulations for national training standards, whose basic values are then negotiated by business and labor. State planning predominantly directs the school-based training system in France. While the National Vocational Qualifications (NQV) in England are partial qualifications closely tied to specific activities, in Germany training takes place according to the occupational vocation principle (*Berufsprinzip*) with the goal of a broad vocational basic training combined with professional competence. In France the *diplome* degrees granted by the state tend to designate the acquisition of rather general vocational and occupationally theoretical knowledge; professional competence is only achieved after the *diplome* graduate has completed training and been broken in by the firm (and, occasionally, gone on to receive continuing education). In Great Britain, it has only been within the last few years that test standards, long used in Germany and France, have been introduced. In

France—as in the Netherlands and Denmark—school-based vocational training was partly dualized when longer terms for training were made obligatory in firms.

In analyzing the various national reform measures, it is hard to determine to what extent we are (or are not) witnessing the emergence of a common (Europe-wide) vocational education policy. In any event, it is evident that the pattern of past reforms was to implement the "best practice" without any recognizable tendency to standardize vocational training systems throughout the Community. In the future, however, there will be a much stronger inclination for the different national vocational training systems to approximate one another. One force pushing in the direction of convergence is the increasingly similar character of challenges to vocational training in all the EU member states. The challenges include such special problems as mastering a profound economic adjustment process, high youth unemployment, and a growing preference among young people for continuing education that combines work with learning. The Community provides a framework for the common search for adequate solutions to these problems. Via the exchange of experiences in European vocational training policy and by means of cooperation in transnational projects of European vocational training programs, examples of "best practice" can be systematically determined and disseminated and new joint approaches developed.

Not "Harmonization," but Growing Together

Adjustment pressures also emanate from the formation of a common currency, economic, social, and skills zone within the EU, something that presents national vocational training systems with a new set of general conditions. National vocational training policies need to become increasingly "Europeanized" and lend a "European dimension" to each national vocational training system. The practice of training will have to open itself up to Europe so that European qualifications, which (at least, in some occupations) are acquiring ever greater importance, can be transmitted. These skills include, above all, the mastery of foreign languages and more intensive knowledge of European economic and cultural regions. One compelling consequence of this is that training residencies abroad have to become a matter of course.

In the meantime, at the national level there have been countless initiatives and pilot projects (with or without support from the EU) to develop concepts for vocational training that transcend borders and increase the stock of commonalties. These initiatives and projects are especially found in border regions at the level of individual economic branches. Here are some examples:

- A pilot project promoted by LEONARDO, the European vocational education program, is developing a joint core curriculum for motor vehicle mechanics as the possible base for a European standard.
- In cooperation with their counterparts in the Netherlands and Ireland, German chambers of industry and commerce and chambers of handicrafts are implementing binational examinations for skilled workers.
- Certain principles of the German dual-training system in the firm and the school—such as the link between working and learning, common planning by business and the state, and the occupational vocation principle—have entered into the development of other training systems. This demonstrates how the singularity of one training system should not—and will not—lead to its isolation within the community of European member states so long as that system remains open to receiving innovative elements from other systems.
- The vocational training policy of the Community has to create the appropriate framework for exchanging experiences and transnational cooperation and to stipulate common goals. The drawing together of vocational training throughout Europe will arise out of substantive necessities. A forced harmonization, however, not only violates the basic European principle of subsidiarity laid down by the European Commission for educational policy; it also promises little chance of success in light of the diversity of different educational systems.

It is certainly conceivable that European forms of internationalizing vocational training systems, as they are increasingly being practiced in the countries of Central and Eastern Europe, could become a model for the globalization of vocational education. The cultural peculiarities of countries are especially expressed in their educational systems, which makes standardization of educational systems seem undesirable. However, if "best practice" examples are used, standardizing educational and training goals in terms of content, level, and examinations standard could be conducive to the globalization of skill qualifications.

The Construction of New Vocational Education Systems under the Sign of Globalization

Are Vocational Education Systems Exportable?

In all countries, global technical, economic, and societal developments have led to an evaluation not only of educational goals and content, but of entire educational systems. Since the 1980s, "educational benchmarks" and the search for "best systems" have increased enormously. In this context, the European vocational education systems have earned worldwide interest, not only because they exhibit low youth unemployment compared to other vocational education systems, but also because employers and trade unions frequently participate in planning for vocational education. In Germany, the dual system of vocational training has contributed enormously toward getting a good bit closer to the political goal of allowing all young people to complete a vocational training course during the transition from school to the world of work. Ninety-seven percent of all school graduates in Germany today start vocational training in school, at a firm, or in college, and 85 percent successfully conclude these courses. A major effort must be undertaken in order to give those young people who still do not have a vocational degree the opportunity to acquire skills later on.

There is only one answer to the question posed at the outset of this chapter: vocational education systems are not exportable. They are so intricately tied up with their countries' social systems as to make a transfer impossible. What is exportable, by contrast, are ideas, elements of systems, and individual solutions to problems that can be tested for their compatibility with the social system of the receiving country and built into the existing educational system.

Since the end of the 1970s, I have been asked—in a variety of ways, by foreign governments, academic institutions, and private offices—for advice about how to develop vocational education systems. Cooperation in matters of vocational training has tied me closely to the United States since the 1970s and to China since the mid-1980s. As chairperson of the "standards" working group set up by the European Training Foundation in Turin, which from 1994 to 1996 advised twenty Western and Eastern European countries on this vital topic for the development of systems, I have become acquainted with many different perspectives, all of which have their advantages when it comes to safeguarding national goals in the advising process.

Building a Best System: Best Practice in Maine/US

As an example of how globalization influences the development of vocational education systems, a project from the United States will be described—the development of a cooperative vocational education system in the state of Maine. At the beginning of 1992 I had an opportunity to consult intensively with the governor of Maine, John McKernan. On the basis of my own experiences, I answered his question about how to approach constructing such a system in the following way:

- The installation of the system has to be a top-down affair for business and the state: the construction of the system is an executive matter.
- At least ten years are required for the system's construction.
- The system requires a legal foundation.
- And, finally, the system requires an institution providing a platform between the state and the private sector—between the school and the business firm—capable of preparing data, developing strategies for implementation, and pursuing marketing for the system among the public, parents, and young people.

The governor of Maine created these prerequisites, and there is now a legislative foundation. The Center for Maine Career Advantage, anchored in Maine's technical-college system, serves as mediator. Three hundred businesses, along with all the state's high schools and technical colleges, participate in training. In 1997, four thousand young people received a training course or got practical training in this dual-training system. The German, Danish, and Austrian dual-training systems served as models. This is how the American version now operates:

1. The young people participating receive a training contract with a business, but they remain school students. Insurance costs are carried by the state.
2. The training firm pays a general reimbursement of $6,000 to the Maine technical college system, which pays out this sum in monthly installments to participating youths after deducting a small contribution for infrastructure costs. During the school year, $80 is available; the amount is $200 for the "summer internship" that takes place during school-free weeks spent at the firm.

3. After a transitional period from 1993 to 1996, the original three years of training was reduced to two years. As a rule, a young person enters vocational training after the eleventh grade, attends high school in the twelfth year, and goes to college for the thirteenth year while he or she is being trained in a company.

4. At the conclusion of training, the young men and women can take two tests, one with the goal of earning a skill mastery certificate, the other with the aim of earning college credits for an associate degree.

5. Time is about equally divided between school and the firm, with 880 hours of instruction or lessons (compared to 480 weeks of lessons in Germany) over forty-four weeks. In addition, six weeks for the summer internship with 240 hours of training at the firm are planned. Vacation amounts to two weeks (six weeks in Germany).

6. The name "Maine Youth Apprenticeship Program" was changed to "Main Career Advantage" because the apprenticeship name proved inappropriate in several respects and led to misunderstandings.

7. In 1996 and 1997, there began an exchange of trainees between businesses in Maine and Berlin, financed by the federal minister for education, science, research, and technology in Bonn and the state of Maine. Such an exchange program is supposed to be implemented also in other US states.

Lessons to Be Learned

As one can easily see, these American solutions are also of interest to the reform debate in other countries for many reasons. Over the last several years, as a member of the international advisory board that the governor of Maine nominated in order to follow the development of the system, I have often regretted how the company-based part of our vocational training system (its planning, implementation, and control) was all that interested the Americans about the German and the Danish model. This points to a problem in the German system. The vocational school, which in my opinion has taken a positive turn over the last thirty years similar to what has been happening with vocational training, is unfortunately given a bad rap—sometimes with, but often without, good reason. In interviews that the Bundesinstitut für Berufsausbildung (Federal Institute for Vocational Education) conducted last year with forty of the largest German companies on the future of the dual system, the vocational school was consistently given good grades. Why, then, does it not play a role in the "export discussion?" It may have something to do with the training of vocational teachers. This training lacks a clear set of goals and the sort of professionalization on its own terms that can meet the high demands placed on vocational teachers as well as meet new demands for skill qualifications.

On the way toward the European Union, and in the context of globalization, Europeans have good reason to be preoccupied with current developments worldwide, for it is pragmatic solutions that are called for. This is especially the case with respect to degrees whose mutual recognition at the skilled-worker level is rejected by the European Union's member states. Therefore, in order to promote globalization, employee mobility, and greater flexibility for vocational training system, two steps are urgent:

1. The implementation of the individual portfolio or vocational training pass (both of which have been discussed for years), including elements of a training degree, continuing-education degrees, and vocational experience
2. The development of European or international qualifications standards at the skilled-worker level, which can provide states with an orientation, though not with binding standards for degrees. Germany disposes over professional knowledge in this field, including how to rapidly adjust curricula to technical change.

Vocational education in Europe has disposal over a multifaceted practical and theoretical potential permitting it to absorb global developments of a technical, scientific, and societal nature and to use them for their own further development. Europe can also exercise a positive influence on vocational education systems on other continents via the application of fruitful ideas and well-tested innovations.

Dualizing the Educational System—Further Developing Vocational Education

Alongside the strategy once pursued in Germany of increasing permeability between the vocational track and the system of general education, we increasingly find emphasis placed on the concept of an independent dualized educational system that appears both plausible and suitable for employees in global competition because of its proximity to the practical world, its motivational components, and its economies of time and cost.

Reflections on "dualizing" the educational system revolve around the following theses.

The Duality of Learning and Working Is the Optimal Organizational Form for Vocational Training and Continuing Education

Experiences with the traditional training system and the transfer of its principle of learning to other educational systems make it clear that it is worth imitating the link between learning and working within an educational course. A "dualized educational system" restricts the state monopoly within the educational system in ways that favor the participation of societal groups. The chief beneficiaries of a qualitatively high-grade vocational training and continuing education, employers and employees, participate significantly in the planning, implementation, control, and certification of educational processes. The consensual principle practiced by the state in the planning and regulation of vocational education guarantees these societal groups a wide-ranging voice in vocational education's goals, content, duration, and graduating degrees. This principle simultaneously makes it possible to undertake a continuous joint adjustment of curricula to societal, technological, and economic changes. In this manner, to be sure, the usual quantitative and qualitative frictions that take place during the transition from vocational training to employment will not be eliminated, but in contrast to purely state-run educational systems they can be significantly minimized. An important component of dual-vocational training is constituted by the final examinations for a state-certified vocational occupation conducted before the chambers of business and commerce. From the standpoint of the individual, this professional degree has a status-forming importance. But—in light of collective bargaining and social insurance law, not to mention the national standardization of the skill qualifications transmitted—its significance also extends to securing a better future.

The general framework conditions for the dual system of vocational training can be transmitted to other parts of the educational system. Dualizing the entire educational system requires that the general conditions framing the dual-vocational training system (at school and in the firm) be transmitted to continuing education in the vocational field. Or, at the very least, there is a need to adjust the structures that characterize these subfields to fit those of dual-vocational training. This requires more precise knowledge about the decision making and cost structures of each individual place of learning, company, and training site. The oft-lamented paucity of information about the type and amount of expenses for different educational paths is not only attributable to different accounting systems (here an official fiscal outlook, there commercial book-keeping). It may also be attributed to an unwillingness to create transparency in cost structures and among the individual institutions financing education. Since costs of quite different amounts result from planning or implementing educational measures and examining or setting up infrastructure, significant synergistic and cost-cutting effects may be anticipated from dualizing these training courses. Dualizing the educational system, therefore, also needs to orient itself around the consensual principle, the joint approach taken by business and the state toward planning and regulating the educational system.

Dualizing Creates a Continuing Education System That Is Transparent and Professionally Distinguished

In many industrialized countries, the system of vocational continuing education is characterized by positive traits like diversity and plurality, but also by negative attributes like opaqueness and lack of profile. Up until today (in places like Germany), a paucity of concepts about the further development of vocational continuing education in a dualized form (e.g., after the model of England's "further education colleges" or the American "community colleges") continues to prevent systematic and substantive links between vocational training and continuing education and hinders postprofessional career planning in a number of fields. A dual system of vocational continuing education, in which (in addition to regional and sectoral continuing education degrees) national standards for generally accredited continuing education degrees are created, would lend transparency and a profile to vocational continuing education. It is also the prerequisite for developing a dual educational system extending to every stage.

Without Dual Courses of Study, the Dualized Educational System Remains a Torso

As a result of the continually developing link between working and learning, forward-looking models of a dualized educational system integrate action-oriented learning with reflection-oriented study in both a company and a college. In a dual study, where the firm is a steady component both as a site of learning and studying, the point is to develop concrete notions about content and goals, about the forms and the organization of this study, and to synchronize these with the college curriculum. An essential moment in shaping study within the firm is the increasing transfer of managerial powers and functions to the students. The colleges have to accredit previous occupational training, and achievements accomplished at the firm's study site must also be taken into consideration and integrated into a unified examination system.

The Dualization of the Education System Has a Positive Effect on Economies of Time and Cost within the Entire Educational System

Available experience and scholarly findings about the length of training and the costs of dualized courses of study in Germany prove that companies have different self-interested motives for assuming their share of the costs for dualizing educational courses (i.e., for simultaneous training in the firm and the school). At the same time, the motivation of the trainees/students and their individual career planning contributes significantly to shortening the courses of study. The general conditions for dualizing the educational system (e.g., consensual principle, selection of trainees/students by companies) lead one to suspect that the quantitative dimensions of the dual-training system (approximately 65 percent participation for the relevant age group in Germany) can hardly be achieved when that system is transferred to vocational continuing education and a dual study. But it may be assumed that even if only 10 percent of all students complete a course of professionally integrated occupational training, the reduction in the number of semesters spent studying and in state expenditures achieved thereby would have a considerable impact on the rest of student operations.

Conclusion

At the center of my observations we find:

- Globalization, which leads to the dissolution of existing structures and the formation of new structures. These structures (or, if one likes, new qualities within society) come into being with the aid of education and vocational training.

- Globalization also leads to new structures in training and continuing education. Generalism is increasingly in demand as a goal of training, while the early onset of continuing education leads to specialization.
- Basic international demands upon training systems are taking shape in which proficiency and knowledge form tight associations with key qualifications that span different occupations (such as systemic knowledge and abstract thinking) and with special kinds of behavior (such as communication and reliability).
- In this fashion, "new" national education systems come into being that are organized in different ways yet directed toward the same or similar goals.
- For Germany, the development of an independent dual-vocational education system (from training, through continuing education, to college study) indicates that cooperation between firms and schools and the link between working and learning are becoming generalized as proven fundamental principles.

It is becoming clear that globalization tendencies are not just restricted to the economic sector, but are being extended to all societal spheres. Here an important role is taken on by a kind of training and continuing education that, with a view toward global adjustment processes, strives not only for professional qualification, but is also aiming at the formation of social personality.

Conclusion: A Memorandum on Globalization

Ernst Ulrich von Weizsäcker and Wolfgang Thierse

Globalization: A Historical Process

Globalization has two faces. On the one hand, it is a multifaceted reality. Global trade barriers have largely fallen. It is possible to buy the same goods almost everywhere today. The loss of economic borders goes hand in hand with the various ways that large global competitors are reshaping traditional cultural habits and regional peculiarities. International financial currents and markets have taken on a magnitude of domineering proportions. Currency fluctuation and speculation, the explosive growths of stocks, shares, and other derivatives—these trends have led the international market to become dangerously decoupled from manufacturing. It is now possible to dismantle and relocate production and work processes as a result of new, technologically driven production methods and information that is instantaneously accessible across the globe. Nor do global ecological dangers stop spreading when they reach national borders.

On the other hand, globalization is a concept used for ideological combat—global competition as a thumbscrew. By referring to the "pressures of the world market," politics is reduced to the task of protecting or improving competitive conditions for "Germany as a Business Site" (*Standort Deutschland*) by cutting taxes and reducing costs. Whoever diminishes political responsibility in this fashion has already lost the global competitive race. We take a different approach. Against the background of global realities, we seek responses to globalization both as an opportunity and political challenge.

The internationalization of trade and competition, moving in the direction of a single world market, is a process as old as the seafarers of bygone centuries. But since the 1970s—both in the course of the "microelectronic revolution" and as a result of deregulation—internationalization has rapidly accelerated, especially after the collapse of Europe's borders between 1989 and 1991. The real center for this process, therefore, is located among the trilateral countries, where it appears as a restructuring of capitalism following the end of East-West system competition.

But the latest push toward real "globalization" also rattles at some of the foundations of democracy. More than ever before, economic processes overlie and even threaten democratically legitimated decisions. The apparent pressures of global competition are out-leveraging hard-won accomplishments. In Europe alone (still extremely rich by worldwide standards), 57 million poor are registered, with disposable income under 50 percent of their national averages. The trend toward growing mass unemployment in industry and services has not been stopped.

Germany is not in any position to withdraw from this historical process of economic globalization. This process also has major advantages. It promotes economic, and therefore cultural, exchange among the peoples of the world. People who trade with each other tend not to place their trade in jeopardy by going to war. Germany in particular, as a world leader in exports (*Exportweltmeister*), profits from a globalized economy. International agreements instead of national barriers, the stimulus of competition instead of bureaucratic restrictions—these things tend to increase economic efficiency and everyone's share in prosperity. Yet, in the long run markets can only work to the benefit of people when they are supported by forward-looking regulations and embedded in a reliable legal framework. It is also important for codetermination and democracy to remain effective mechanisms in the marketplace.

It is therefore a matter of political necessity that we actively shape the process of globalization. We seek to serve that goal here.

The Market Strengthens the Strong

The basic idea behind a "free market" is to foment free and creative human endeavor. It should help competition to unfold and efficiency to develop. Wherever competition is maintained (beyond the realm of "disempowered markets"), market relations make it possible to do business effectively, search for better solutions, and avoid faulty developments. Under competition, the stronger competitors prevail, but (basically) so do more attractive goods and services over less attractive ones. Choice lies fundamentally with the consumer, both domestic and foreign. But choice is also influenced and constricted by trade, advertisement, and the formation of cartels.

The market thus turns suppliers of more attractive products into strong competitors, while it makes all others into weak competitors, into losers. The free market thus has the effect of getting the strong to prevail over the weak, the quick against the slow. Competence and creativity is not just something that applies to entrepreneurs, but equally well to the people who work for them. Their health, skills, motivation, and company loyalty are highly relevant to the company's ability to compete. And they have to be included among the winners and losers, depending on the success of their market performance.

An essential part of competition is competing over cost. Competition therefore has a tendency to make market success depend on lower costs when it comes to procuring capital, paying workers, using infrastructure, and protecting the environment. Competition even rewards lower prices when they are achieved by government subsidies, cost-free infrastructure, inhumanely low wages, the suppression of women, child labor, the ruthless exploitation of nature, neglect of environmental protection, or immoral political influence peddling.

Cost advantages and the competitive advantages that result from them are, therefore, not always signs of creativity and competence. They can also be bought by the political abuse of power or by exploiting the weaker members of society. And they frequently are based on ruthlessly exploiting nature with irreparable damage. The exploitation of nature keeps getting "cheaper" because of subsidies and progress in exploitative technologies. Here ends the rosy picture of a market that is supposed to be creating more prosperity for everyone to share. Under certain circumstances, the market's destructive effects overlap and even outweigh its impact on effectiveness, adaptability, innovation, and product diversity.

Capital Concentration

Compared to earlier times, modern production is extremely dependent on capital. Cost competition and the reduced cost of exploiting nature have intensified this trend. Cost-saving technologies, and especially the rationalization of labor, are capital intensive as a rule. The costs for research and development, implementing new technologies, and marketing have risen enormously. They have triggered, or at least intensified, a powerful movement of concentration throughout industry and commerce. At the same time, the relative contribution of labor to net output has declined. The result has been increased marginalization of workers and especially of the unemployed. In many markets, the only ones still capable of keeping up are the major, so-called "global players." However they (again, on cost grounds) eagerly farm out subsidiary tasks to dependent suppliers. This produces a distorted picture of reality, in which it looks as though the majors are shrinking while the minor players appear to be thriving.

Under globalized conditions, those companies have the best advantages who have their pick of the best production sites based on information and technological know-how that is accessible worldwide. In this way, technological development and capital requirements have lead to a concentration of economic power in relatively few hands. Jointly, some 400 billionaires own more than the world's three billion poorest people taken together.

This economic power is tied to political power. Owing to an ever-present concern about jobs, political representatives from municipalities, regions, and even the nations of the world depend on the benevolence and cooperation of business leaders. Politics becomes chronically weakened.

Taking note of this dependence, the owners of capital can keep getting better terms for their business locations. The rapid increase in capital mobility that results does not necessarily lead to more prosperity (and most certainly not everywhere). Opportunities for exploiting "tax-and-write-off paradises" and for shifting production deprive the public purse of funds for a balanced economic and social policy. In many places, investments simply lie in ruins. Employee skills are squandered. Sometimes the only thing left behind is literally scorched earth.

With all due recognition of the reality of globalization, we must not overlook that it captures only a certain portion of social and even economic reality. Many commercial and even noncommercial activities remain largely preserved. Thus, for example, most of the work done by physicians, lawyers, teachers, and artisans is hardly affected by international capital flows. Furthermore, globalization triggered a kind of countermovement fairly early. In recognition of the dangers that globalization poses to diverse cultural identities, the cultural sense of belonging to regions, cities, villages, and neighborhoods throughout the world has been getting stronger again.

The Primacy of Democratic Politics

When Adam Smith devised the basic principles of free competition in the eighteenth century, capital accumulation and economic power in the hands of business leaders were still out of the question. As these tendencies began to show up early in the history of capitalism, a social countermovement arose that managed (with enormous effort and in the course of about one century) to achieve at least a certain degree of balance in economic and political power. The constitutional state, general elections, representative parliamentary democracy, social security (later on, the "social market economy"), and environmental protection are important accomplishments won in this power struggle. They all operated as correctives to the unadulterated competitive economy.

Limiting its power did not inflict damage on capital. On the contrary, it ultimately also led to a balance of social-welfare interests, to a broad tendency toward the maintenance of peace (for prosperity's sake), to a rapid utilization of technical progress on behalf of the broad masses, and to a stronger hearing for the environmental perspective. Without these attractive accomplishments of social democracy, both East and West, the worldwide victory of the market economy over "bureaucratic state socialism" would scarcely have been imaginable. Bureaucratic state socialism was not known for having brought about anything even remotely resembling that balance of different powers.

The Loss of Balance

The globalization of economic activity seems on the verge of ratcheting down in the balance of power between economics and politics. Since capital has virtually liberated itself completely from national commitments. it no longer really appears to require social consensus within a national framework. Intense competition for optimal returns to capital is leading the donors of capital to regard cost reduction as a higher priority than cultivating consensus. As a result, they increasingly call for reducing social welfare and environmental standards previously upheld and gained via the democratic process.

There have been attempts to implement ambitious social welfare and environmental standards internationally. The European Social Charter, first ratified by Great Britain in 1997, and numerous European environmental directives demonstrate that there is a certain leeway at the regional level. But it has been extremely tough to shape policy at the international level. This became evident at the December 1996 WTO Conference in Singapore, where the majority of developing countries sensed mere protectionism in corresponding demands by industrialized countries.

When it comes to complaints about the worldwide discrepancy in social-welfare and environmental standards, however, we should recall that the consumption standard of the highly developed industrial countries could not (on ecological grounds alone) be extended to six billion people—at least, so long as current technologies that waste material and energy continue to prevail. To the extent that globalization also demands an adjustment of living conditions in different parts of the world, it will be necessary for us to lower our expectations (as it will be possible to communicate this imperative) here at home. But the "spread" of incomes demanded by capital (in shorthand: the rich must get richer, the poor even poorer) would lead to (even more) marginalization and exclusion, and to heightened social tension. This demand is also economically counterproductive because its lasting impact is to weaken the importance of mass incomes as an economic factor.

What seems especially threatening is the way a hard-won democracy is being undermined. Especially for those who undertook the enormous effort to liberate themselves from the yoke of "authoritarian state socialism" for the sake of democracy, it has been more than just a serious disappointment to witness the power shift that subsequently happened in favor of capital markets not democratically controlled. The danger that people will inwardly start turning away from the market-oriented democracy approaches a worldwide scale.

The regulation of international financial markets has so far been completely inadequate as a counterweight to globalized economic players at home and abroad. It needs to be significantly strengthened for the sake of democracy's credibility. Political regulation as a necessary counterweight to the unadulterated interests of capital investment is no longer something that can be sufficiently organized at the level of the nation-state. Opportunities for political intervention need to match the scope of international conglomerates. Therefore, European integration with a common currency is an indispensable and fundamental precondition for the future of effective politics.

Social Democratic Responses

Social Democratic policy cannot remain complacent about the erosion both of social democracy and of the balance of interests resting on it. But it also cannot remain stuck in inconsequential protest and the invocation of a beautiful past. But what is to be done? It is a matter of regaining the offensive on an active policy-making will as well as of strengthening national and international capabilities for political action. To this end, we elaborate seven guidelines for action:

1. Global democratic policy making
2. Internationalization of social-welfare and environmental policy, especially within the framework of European institutions
3. Regulating international financial markets
4. Improving national competitiveness
5. Protecting spheres of life independent of the world market
6. Reducing damaging subsidies and market distortions
7. Public education and encouragement

All seven fields of action challenge Social Democrats at every level where they are called upon to shape public opinion and popular will.

Global Democratic Policy Making

During his lifetime, Willy Brandt had already called for a system of global policy making. This means, in the first instance, strengthening and reforming the United Nations. The great UN conference resolutions of the 1990s, the result of exhaustive negotiations, must finally be concretized and implemented.

Regional organizations, most notably the European Union, also deserve additional strengthening, with simultaneous improvement of democratic participation. The strengthening of the European Parliament vis-à-vis the EU member states and European Commission is overdue. By contrast, there are fewer decent prospects for the attempt to establish parliamentary structures in an even larger arena (or, conceivably, worldwide).

Compared to this, the internationalization of democratic behaviors and codetermination rights via the nongovernmental sector is largely *terra nova*. Here it is a matter of such things as codetermination at the level of the firm (only now worldwide). Under current new conditions, countervailing power for those in the middle of the labor process needs to be strengthened internationally: minimum wages, social security, prohibition of child labor, and worker safety need to be implemented worldwide—if need be, with backing from the industrialized countries. This is a lengthy process, which will be made more difficult, though by no means hopeless, by global unemployment and the resulting vulnerability to extortion.

When it comes to globalizing democracy, a brand new political phenomenon has special importance: the worldwide networks of voluntarily organized nongovernmental organizations in civil society. New groups have shown up to demonstrate what can be done, even against big international corporations, to change behavior using spectacular actions and publicity. In many instances, human rights organizations like Amnesty International, environmental organizations like Greenpeace and the World Wildlife Fund (WWF), but also churches, scientific associations, and international clubs have already become the bearers of an international conscience and guardians against locally exercised injustices. Because of the latent threat posed by consumer boycotts, company management takes these groups very seriously. Actively establishing and cultivating international contacts among like-minded activists has been made much easier because of the Internet and other media. The new groups have created publicity, sharpened consciousness, and prevented grave errors from being decided—and this is worthy of support. But the rubber dinghies of Greenpeace are not, and cannot replace, real politics.

Internationalization of Social-Welfare and Environmental Policy

Since 1972, there have been enormous efforts in the European Union to move in the direction of a binding common environmental policy, which has found expression in over two hundred guidelines, decrees, and decisions. In spite of considerable deficiencies in implementation, especially among the Mediterranean member states, but also in Germany (numerous complaints lodged against the federal government for nonenforcement of EC guidelines), this has also created a legal framework shielding the German economy to a considerable extent from the price disadvantages of environmental protection measures.

Since the victory of the Labor Party in Great Britain and the Socialists in France, European social-welfare policy has moved into action again. In addition, within the framework of "coherence policy," an adjustment of living standards within the European Union space has been pursued (albeit chiefly in favor of "disadvantaged regions"). For the German economy, this has led to major relief in the form of regional promotion for the new East German states.

Attempts to take up something like a worldwide initiative for social-welfare standards (at the 1995 World Social-Welfare Summit in Copenhagen, the 1995 World Women's Conference in Peking, or the 1996 WTO Conference in Singapore) have proved to be very exhausting. At most, rapid progress is achievable on behalf of restricting child labor, unhealthy working conditions, and other practices affecting human rights. However, here too, it would be hard to count on any victories if political pressure is not simultaneously created at the nongovernmental level mentioned above.

"Sustainability," the guiding aim of the 1992 Rio de Janeiro Conference, presents an opportunity for intensive international cooperation, since it creates a common system of coordinates for all countries. Within the framework of global ecological diplomacy, some additional progress may be discerned. We may hope to see a Kyoto protocol specifying concrete goals for the climate protection convention, so that this might go into effect by 1999. However, it is initially likely to make manufacturing more expensive in the more climate-damaged industrial countries before it starts to affect their competitors from the South.

Regulating International Financial Markets

The notion that capital may be allowed to transcend borders unhindered and without cost is an ideology as new as it is contestable. But, above all, it is a new reality. David Ricardo, who founded the international trade theory of comparative advantage (that different states possess and use to their mutual advantage with the help of trade), proceeded from the firm assumption that capital was tied to place and that only goods would cross borders.

Should there remain no regulatory limits on capital mobility, the decoupling of international financial markets from commodity markets, and the game of currency fluctuations and exchange-rate parities, then government efforts on behalf of policies for more employment will remain condemned to ineffectiveness. The attractive pull that speculative profits exert on financial markets weakens the power of investment in the productive sector and leads to a lasting burden on labor markets.

The first goal must be a return to a policy of international monetary cooperation with the prospect of achieving stable exchange rates, such as via securely negotiated target zones. This, too, is a direct way of securing jobs. Exchange-rate turmoil contributes to fair competition.

A convincing concept for inhibiting currency speculation and abuse of power has been put forward by Nobel Prize-winning economist James Tobin. He suggests subjecting all international capital transfers with a (minuscule) tax. Germany and the European Union should become advocates for the international implementation of this proposal. Even if only a tenth of currency transactions were captured by this tax, it would bring returns of 720 billion dollars to state budgets. The "Tobin tax" does, however, have one snag in that it can only reach its goal if all the world's major financial centers subject themselves to such an instrument.

Therefore, it is necessary for all those regions that are already broadly integrated economically and politically to harmonize their tax policies (by introducing such measures as a clamp down on tax oases, minimum rates for corporate taxation, and minimum regulations for tax assessment) and arrive at an international law for fair competition and nondiscriminatory border equalization charges. The European Union offers an appropriate framework for this kind of coordinated policy.

The euro will create a third world currency, next to the dollar and the yen, within what is already the world's largest market. This will make Europe more independent of both the dollar's fluctuations and the speculative effects of financial markets. Therefore, introducing the European Monetary Union on time is not something that can be allowed to fail. A unified Europe with a unified currency can and must exercise greater influence on progress in the international organization of finance. In this manner it can have other and broader possibilities for promoting the international implementation and observance of social-welfare and environmental standards.

Improving National Competitiveness

No country can withdraw from the dynamic of the world market. The doorway exiting into protectionism is blocked and, in any case, not desirable. Maintaining competitiveness is an important pre-condition for securing and creating jobs. Inevitably, for this very reason, the high cost of labor is on trial. Reasonable, well-thought-out proposals for reducing wage and fringe benefit costs that are too high by international standards are on the negotiating table. Trade unions are always ready to pursue a responsible wage policy when employers make corresponding concessions to reduce over-time, show flexibility in shortening weekly and career-long work times, and securing the maintenance or creation of jobs. This pathway needs to be traveled further.

Another, more attractive strategy consists of strengthening com-petitiveness through innovation. A systematic increase in the effi-ciency with which energy and resources are used seems to be a strategy of innovation with special promise for Germany as a busi-ness site. Today it is technically possible to multiply the efficiency with which energy and raw materials are used. A factor of four seems technically feasible for many household appliances, gro-ceries, everyday items, and production procedures. For exports to rapidly growing economics regions such as Asia, with their oppres-sive resource scarcity, developing this efficiency potential could be of overwhelming importance. A stronger shift of the innovation emphasis away from labor saving and toward resource saving can simultaneously slow down the decline in jobs.

A stronger emphasis on the opportunities in the service sector also cannot hurt Germany as a business site. Especially rich in opportunity are service packages that use domestically produced high value-added products to offer a high degree of security for the firm and a high degree of quality in service maintenance; such products, with their high levels of consumer satisfaction, are espe-cially conspicuous when competing with cheaper foreign products (which lack service guarantees).

The ecological tax reform long promoted by the SPD as well as the implementation of the "least-cost-planning" principle in the energy business are among the political steps that can precipitate an innovation avalanche.

Protecting Spheres of Life Independent of the World Market

In spite of the German economy's unavoidable—and desirable—ties to the world market, it is also necessary to promote, rediscover, and protect spheres of life independent of the world market. Goods and services produced locally create a nonextortionate bargaining climate. In most developing countries, economic forms that are independent of the world market (inasmuch as they are not romantically idealized or turned into political ideology) are the most important mainstays of survival for the majority of families. Even in industrial countries, nothing speaks against rediscovering and promoting this second level of the economy, characterized by in-house production and the neighborly exchange of goods in kind.

Above all, preserving a basic structure of foodstuff provisions in times of crisis is a legitimate concern against vulnerability to extortion. In Switzerland, this concern even has constitutional status.

Tax legislation should reward the preservation of artisanal and small handicraft skills. This way we can significantly reduce the expenditure undertaken in pursuit of illegal "moonlighting."

Reducing Damaging Subsidies and Market Distortions

Early industrialization gave us countless regulations in which government promoted or gave tax breaks for the use of energy and raw materials as well as for a broad network of transport infrastructure. Subsidies amounting to at least 700 billion dollars annually go toward environmentally damaging activities. The price is paid not only by the taxpayer, but also by those who inevitably lose out in the resulting competition for existing subsidies. An international initiative to dismantle the kinds of subsidies damaging to the economy and environment must become a Social Democratic policy goal.

For example, the tax break for fuel in international air traffic, something that has become completely untimely, needs to be quickly replaced by an international agreement. The SPD has proposed such an initiative in the Bundestag. Whenever energy, transport, and export subsidies are drawn back, regional economic systems are simultaneously made more livable, and better use is made of regional capacities.

Public Education and Encouragement

The pursuit of social justice is in the Social Democratic tradition. It is in accordance with this tradition when we make an effort to help those whom globalization has weakened by developing the necessary countervailing powers. The first precondition for this is public education and encouragement of reform.

Educating the public means honesty about what the superiority of the liberal market society over bureaucratic state socialism means. In a liberal society, the "disempowering" tendency of the market is tamed by democratic control. In brief, the free market sees to it that the strong prevail over the weak, while democracy protects the weak from the strong. To the extent that democratic feedback becomes nothing but a farce in the effort to provide a counterweight against capital mobility in the international economy, one of the strongest arguments for a liberal society and market economy becomes inoperative. To the degree that economic globalization undermines the democratic mechanism, it deprives itself of much of its legitimacy.

At the same time, Social Democratic policy must offer encouragement to all politically thinking persons. It must encourage the chance both to take hearty advantage of the special opportunities lying in store for a technologically advanced country like Germany, as well as the chance to oppose the dangers of heightened inequalities bound up with globalization. We cannot just put up with the tendency inherent in globalization toward an extremely unjust distribution of goods and privileges at home and abroad. The free market economy is not, of its own accord, capable of organizing justice and prosperity for all. It repeatedly requires continuous development in the direction of a social market economy and of democratic control, as described by the Social Democrats in their Berlin Program of Fundamental Principles. To this extent, for those of us who are Social Democrats, globalization is not an argument against an active state. Now as before, there is a need for a policy that can resist the "free" market by aiming at social cohesion and balance. Only the yardstick for measuring these goals has changed; it has just become a global standard.

Everyone is called upon to make a constructive contribution toward mastering this new dimension of democratic politics: the various branches of the SPD, its members (especially if they can exercise influence on the direction in which society is developing), as well as all those other groups and people who are committed to the ideals of democracy and justice.

Notes on Contributors

Marion Caspers-Merk is currently Parliamentary Whip of the Social Democratic Party's Parliamentary Group in the Bundestag, and also served as Chairwoman of the Enquête Commission on the "Protection of Humanity and the Environment" of the German Bundestag. She has been a member of Parliament since 1990. Ms. Caspers-Merk studied political science, German, and joined the Social Democratic Party in 1972. She is a member of the German Federation for the Environment and Conservation of Nature and has published widely on issues concerning the protection of the environment and communal affairs.

Dieter Dettke has been the executive director of the Washington Office of the Friedrich Ebert Foundation since 1985. He studied political science at the Universities of Bonn, Berlin, and Strasbourg (France). Prior to his tenure in Washington, Dr. Dettke served as political counselor to the SPD Parliamentary Group of the German Bundestag from 1974 to 1984, and as staff director at the Office of the State Minister of the German Foreign Ministry in 1982. He is the author of *Allianz im Wandel* and has published numerous articles and papers on security issues, East-West relations, and US foreign and domestic policy.

Rudolf Dreßler is Deputy Chairman of the SPD Parliamentary Group of the German Bundestag, and is also a member of the National Executive Committee of the SPD. Educated as a typesetter, Mr. Dreßler has been a member of the National Executive Committee of the Printer Trade Union for nine years and is now the chairman of the Social Democratic Working Group of Employees (AfA) within the SPD.

Heiner Flassbeck is the State Secretary of the Minister of Finance of the Federal Republic of Germany and was the director of the Department of Macroeconomics at the German Institute for Economic Research (DIW) from 1990 to 1998. He studied economics at the Free University of Berlin and served as a professional staff member of the Council of Economic Advisors of the Federal Republic of Germany. Dr. Flassbeck has written numerous articles, papers, and books about economic trends and economic policy.

Jürgen Hoffmann is professor of political sociology at the School of Economics and Politics in Hamburg. He studied at the Free University of Berlin, earning his diploma and doctoral degree in political science. Prof. Hoffmann's research interests and publications focus on the political economy of Germany, German trade unions, and national economic policy. He has authored publications on German history and several articles on globalization and European trade unions.

Reiner Hoffmann has been director of the European Trade Union Institute (ETUI) in Brussels since 1994. He is the former head of the department of Research Promotion at the Hans-Böckler-Stiftung, where he was employed from 1984 to 1994. Mr. Hoffmann studied economics at the University of Wuppertal. He is the author of numerous books and articles, concentrating in particular on the future of trade unions in a globalized world.

Oskar Lafontaine is currently Minister of Finance of the Federal Republic of Germany and has been chairman of the SPD since 1995. He studied physics at the Universities of Bonn and Saarbrücken and joined the Social Democratic Party of Germany in 1966. He served as lord mayor of the city of Saarbrücken and as prime minister of the state of Saarland from 1985 until 1998. He is the author of several books on social, economic, and political issues, including globalization.

Siegmar Mosdorf is currently Parliamentary State Secretary of the Ministry of Economics of the Federal Republic of Germany. A member of the German Bundestag from Baden Württemberg since 1990, he also served as chairman of the SPD Parliamentary Group's study commission on "The Future of the Media in the Economy and Society—Germany's Road into the Information Society." He served as a member of the Advisory Council to the Federal Ministry of Economics on Foreign Trade and Payments and as Chairman of the Carlo Schmidt Foundation in Germany. Mr. Mosdorf studied economics, social sciences, and administrative science at the University of Constance.

Reinhard Pfender is an economist by profession and training. He served as a US country specialist in the Federal Ministry of Economics in Bonn before joining the SPD Parliamentary Group as an economic advisor. His international economic experience includes an affiliation with the OECD in Paris. His more recent work focuses on globalization, macroeconomics, and international trade issues.

Fritz W. Scharpf has been director of the Max Planck Institute for the Study of Society (Max-Planck-Institut für Gesellschaftsforschung) in Cologne since 1986 and is also the former director of the International Institute of Management at the Science Center (Wissenschaftszentrum) in Berlin (1973–1984). He studied law and political science at the Universities of Tübingen, Freiburg, and Yale (US). In June 1987, Dr. Scharpf was a fellow at the Center for Advanced Study in Behavioral Sciences at Stanford University (US). His research interests include organization and decision processes in the ministerial bureaucracy, joint federal-state decision-making, implementation research, comparative political economy, federalism and European integration, and the empirical application of game theory.

Rudolf Scharping is currently Minister of Defense of the Federal Republic of Germany. He served as chairman of the SPD Parliamentary Group in the German Bundestag and as president of the Party of European Socialists (PES) since 1995. Mr. Scharping studied political science, law, and sociology at the University of Bonn and joined the Social Democratic Party of Germany in 1966. From 1991 to 1994 he served as prime minister of the state of Rhineland-Palatinate and from 1993 to 1995, he also served as chairman of the Social Democratic Party.

Hermann Schmidt served for twenty years as the president of the Federal Institute for Vocational Training in Berlin and Bonn (1977–1997). He is currently a member of several committees, including at the Advisory Board of the European Training Foundation and the Board of Directors of the Center for Research on Innovation and Society in Santa Barbara (US). Dr. Schmidt studied economics, social science, and pedagogy at the University of Cologne and today works as a consultant in human resource development, education training policy, and international skill standards.

Ulla Schmidt is currently deputy chairwoman of the SPD Parliamentary Group in the German Bundestag. She served as chairwoman of the SPD Parliamentary Group's commission on the "Equality of Women and Men" from 1991 to 1998 and has been a spokesperson for the project group "Policy for Families in the Twenty-First Century." She has been a member of the German Bundestag since 1990. A former government official from the city of Aachen, Ms. Schmidt earned her degree in special education (for disabled children) from the University of Hagen.

Gerhard Schröder is Chancellor of the Federal Republic of Germany. From 1990 to 1998 he held the position of prime minister for the state of Lower Saxony. Educated as a lawyer at the University of Göttingen, he joined the Social Democratic Party of Germany in 1963. He is a former national chairman of the Young Socialists within the SPD and has been a member of the National Executive Committee of the Social Democratic Party since 1989.

Ernst Schwanhold is deputy chairman of the SPD Parliamentary Group. He has been the speaker for Economic Affairs of the SPD Parliamentary Group in the German Bundestag since 1995. Prior to this position, he was the chairman of the German Bundestag Committee on Economic Affairs and chairman of the Enquête Commission of the German Bundestag on the "Protection of Humanity and the Environment." He studied chemical process engineering at the University of East Westphalia in Paderborn and joined the Social Democratic Party of Germany in 1972.

Udo Ernst Simonis has been a distinguished research professor for environmental policy at the Science Center (Wissenschaftszentrum) in Berlin since 1988. He studied economics at the Universities of Mainz, Freiburg, Vienna, and Kiel and was a research fellow at the University of Tokyo from 1973 to 1988. A former member of the German Council on Global Change, he is currently chairman of the German Society of Scientists (VDW). Dr. Simonis is editor of the *Jahrbuch Ökologie* (Ecology Yearbook) and the author, coauthor, or editor of fifty books and over five hundred contributions to books and journals.

Wolfgang Streeck has been director of the Max Planck Institute for the Study of Society (Max-Planck-Institut für Gesellschaftsforschung) in Cologne since 1995 and an honorary professor at the Humboldt University in Berlin (1996). Educated at the University of Frankfurt and Columbia University, Dr. Streeck taught sociology and industrial relations at the University of Wisconsin at Madison from 1988 until 1995. He is the author of numerous publications on government and economics including "The Political Economy of Modern Capitalism: Mapping Convergence and Diversity," published in 1997.

Wolfgang Thierse is President of the Bundestag. He became a member of the German Bundestag in 1990 and served simultaneously as deputy chairman of the Social Democratic Party and as deputy chairman of the SPD Parliamentary Group. Following employment as a typesetter, he studied at Humboldt University in Berlin. From 1975 to 1977, Mr. Thierse was employed at the Ministry of Cultural Affairs of the GDR and in 1977 became a research assistant at the Academy of Sciences of the GDR. Today he is a member of the SPD National Executive Committee, chairman of the SPD Commission on Basic Values, and chairman of the Social Democratic Cultural Forum.

Ernst Ulrich von Weizsäcker is a member of the German Bundestag since 1998 and president of the Wuppertal Institute for Climate, Environment, and Energy. A member of the Club of Rome, he studied chemistry, physics, and biology at the University of Hamburg and earned his Ph.D. from the University of Freiburg in 1969. Dr. von Weizsäcker has held various positions at the Universities of Heidelberg, Essen, and Kassel and served as director of the Institute for European Environmental Policy in Bonn from 1984 to 1991. He received the Italian Premio De Natura in 1989 and the WWF Conservation Medal in 1996. Dr. Weizsäcker is the author of over 350 papers published in scientific journals, conference proceedings, and books, including most recently "Factor Four: Doubling Wealth—Halving Resource Use: A Report to the Club of Rome."

Christoph Zöpel, the former minister for Urban Development and Transportation in the state of North Rhine-Westphalia, is now a member of the German Bundestag for the Social Democratic Party and a member of the Committee for Foreign Affairs of the German Bundestag. He studied economics, philosophy, and public law at the Free University of Berlin and the University of Bochum. Dr. Zöpel is also a member of the Parliamentary Assembly of the OSCE and served as a member of the National Executive Committee of the Social Democratic Party (1986–1995).

About the Friedrich Ebert Foundation

The Friedrich-Ebert-Stiftung (FES) is a political nonprofit, public-interest institution committed to the principles and basic values of social democracy and the labor movement. Named after the first democratically elected president of the Weimar Republic, the Friedrich-Ebert-Stiftung was founded in 1925, the year Ebert died while in office. To honor his legacy, the Friedrich-Ebert-Stiftung supports education, research, and international cooperation in the spirit of democracy.

Headquartered in Bonn, the foundation maintains six educational centers and twelve regional offices in Germany. With eighty-nine offices in Europe, Africa, Asia, Latin America, and North America, the Friedrich Ebert Foundation is a major contributor to international cooperation, particularly in the fields of economic and social development, research and education, as well as political, economic and trade union cooperation. Two hundred fifty projects in over one hundred countries worldwide receive support from the Friedrich Ebert Foundation.

The Mission of the Washington Office of the Friedrich Ebert Foundation

The mission of the Washington Office of the Friedrich Ebert Foundation is to contribute to a comprehensive transatlantic dialogue by offering public programs (such as seminars, workshops, and conferences) as well as publications on the following issues:

- Overall political developments in Germany and Europe, including domestic policy issues and attitudes, as well as public opinion studies
- General social topics, including migration, minorities, multiculturalism, education, and gender issues
- Economic developments in Germany, Europe, and the United States, including labor-market and trade-union issues, as well as problems of economic and political transformation in Eastern Europe
- Foreign policy and security issues such as NATO and European Union enlargement, ethnic conflict, as well as arms control and disarmament
- Political and economic consequences of German unification
- Historical and cultural issues

Programs of the Washington Office of the Friedrich Ebert Foundation are based on partnership and cooperation with American institutions, such as trade unions, universities, research institutes and think tanks, as well as the media. The Washington Office also offers visitor programs in Germany and the United States for high-level representatives and experts.

Index